Abstracts of Philadelphia County Pennsylvania Wills

1682-1726

F. Edward Wright

HERITAGE BOOKS
2007

HERITAGE BOOKS
AN IMPRINT OF HERITAGE BOOKS, INC.

Books, CDs, and more—Worldwide

For our listing of thousands of titles see our website
at
www.HeritageBooks.com

Published 2007 by
HERITAGE BOOKS, INC.
Publishing Division
65 East Main Street
Westminster, Maryland 21157-5026

Originally published 1995 F. Edward Wright

International Standard Book Number: 978-1-58549-302-9

INTRODUCTION

These wills were abstracted under the auspices of the Historical Society of Pennsylvania in the early 1900s. Copies of these abstracts were made available to various libraries in Pennsylvania and microfilm copies made by the Genealogical Society of Utah (LDS). Recently bound photostat copies of the abstracts were offered for sale by the Genealogical Society of Pennsylvania.

We extend our appreciation to the staffs of the Historical Society of Pennsylvania (1300 Locust Street, Philadelphia, PA 19107) and encourage use and support of its facilities and to the Genealogical Society of Pennsylvania whose collections are housed in the Historical Society Library. We also encourage membership in the Genealogical Society of Pennsylvania (address same as HSP).

F. Edward Wright
Westminster, Maryland
1995

WILLS OF PHILADELPHIA COUNTY
1682 - 1726

FREAM, THOMAS. Avon, County of Gloster.
September 5, 1682. 8/10/1682. A. 1.
Estate to his friend Ann Knight who is sole executrix. Legacies to Giles Knight and his brother Thomas Knight. James Crafts, a debtor, is named.
Witnesses: John Somers, Thomas Madox, Thomas William, William Humsre (?).

MARTIN, ISAACK. Philadelphia County. Felt maker.
November 20, 1682. 5/18/1683. A. 2.
Estate to wife Katherine who is executrix. Daughter Elizabeth.
Witnesses: John Goodsonn, Samuel Jones.

HERIOTT, THOMAS. Late of Hurstprepoynt, Sussex Co., England. Yeoman.
September 19, 1682. 5/2/1683. A. 4.
Nuncupative will. Estate to his brother-in-law, Dennis Rothford. Legacy to his sister Anne Strate. Declared on board the ship Welcome, Robert Greenaway, commander, thus bound by permission of God for Pennsilvania.
Witnesses: George Thompson, grocer; Thomas Wynne, chirurgeon; David Ogdin, weaver; Joshua Morris, tynnplate worker.

CLARKE, WILLIAM.
May 12, 1681. 6/10/1683. A. 5.
Whole estate up Neshampanesse Creek to wife Anne. No children named.
Witnesses: Edmond Draughton, Robert Draughton.

CLARKE, ANNE. Bucks Co. Widow.
December 1, 1682. ---. A. 6.
Estate to friends Richard Noble and Judith, his wife. Legacies to two children whose names are not given.
Witnesses: John Sagner, Ailce Heiton, Grace Heiton. [The original will is missing.]

CLIFT (CLIFTE), SAMUEL. Bucks Co. Husbandman.
November 23, 1682. 6/2/1683. A. 7.
Wife's name is not given. Estate to son Jonathan who is sole executor. Legacy to son-in-law Joseph English.
Overseers: Christopher Taylor, Richard Noble.
Witnesses: Robert Heiton, William Unicorne, Stephen Noble, Judith Noble, Richard Dungworth.

TAYLOR, WILLIAM.
March 6, 1683. 6/23/1683. A. 9.
Wife Margaret, lately deceased, near Chester alias Upland Estate to son Joseph and other children whose names are not given.
Executors: John Simcock of Ridley Creek, Thomas Minchall.
Witnesses: Peter Taylor, Mary Stevenson, Allen Robinett.

BARBER, JOHN. Shipley, County Sussex. Yeoman.
7/20/1682. ---. A. 10.
Whole estate to wife Elizabeth, eldest daughter of John Songhurst who is sole executrix. Reference is made to her being pregnant. Legacies to his mother whose name is not given, brother Edward and sisters Mary, Sarah and Hannah Barber. He held an estate in England. Signed on board the Welcome going to Pennsylvania.
Witnesses: George Thompson, Joseph Woodroofe, Thomas Gillett.

INGRAM, ISAAC. Late of Gaston and Surrey. Yeoman.
7/26/1682. ---. A. 11.
Estate to Adam, Miriam and Anne Short, children of his deceased sister Miriam Short, and to the poor of the Quakers. Legacies to Jane Batchelor, Thomas Fitzwater, David Ogden, John Songhurst, Thomas Wynne, friend Ambrose Rigge of Galton, Surry Co. Signed with his mark on board the Welcome, Robert Greenaway, master, bound for Pennsylvania.
Executors: John Songhurst and Thomas Wynne.
Witnesses: Richard Ingels, Zechariah Whitpaine, George Thompson.

WADE, WILLIAM. Late of parish of Hankton, Sussex Co. Yeoman.
September 20, 1682. 6/6/1684. A. 12.
Legacies to brothers Edmond and Thomas, Edmond and Thomas Wade sons of his brother Edmond. Samuel Webb, Moses French and

Maskcoll Picknoll are trustees of a fund for poor Friends. Philip Ford of London, merchant, is executor for the English portion of estate.
Executors: John Songhurst, Benjamin Chambers.
Witnesses: George Thompson, Richard Ingels, William Lushington.

ANDERSON, ANDREW.
September 26, 1683. 8/22/1683. A. 15.
Mention is made by him of sea wages which indicates he may have been a mariner. Whole estate to Andrew Love who is sole executor. Friend Ris Wiese.
Witnesses: Joseph Houldin, James Bisiks (Basiks).

BLINSTORE, ISAAC. Parish of Eling, Southton Co. Malster.
May 15, 1684. 7/25/1684. A. 16.
Estate to wife Mary and daughter Mary, who are with his friends Matthew Paine and John Swift, Executors. Legacies to daughter-in-law Frances Kirkes, cousins Ann, Robert and Elizabeth Coleman.
Witnesses: Katherine Carter, Thomas Gaudy, John White.

FLOWER, ENOCH.
6/21/1684. 7/25/1684(?) A. 17.
Legacies to John Flower, son of his brother Seth Flower, and to mother Susanna Flower. Memorandum 7/2 - Legacy to Margery Dobby. Executors: Brother Seth Flower and his son Henry.
Witnesses: Mary Vuet, S. Hersent.

BEZER, JOHN. Chichester alias Markers Hook, County of Chester.
7/13/1684. 7/25/1684. A. 18.
Whole estate to wife Susannah who is sole executrix. Two sons and two daughters whose names are not given. John Hall of London as adviser in old England.
Overseers: Brother Edward and friends William Chanton and Thomas Usher.
Witnesses: Richard Farr, Edward Kinnison, James Widers.

BAKER, JOHN. Late of Edgmond in Shropshire in old England. Husbandman.
1/12/1684. 6/31/1685. A. 19.
Wife's name is not given. Estate to children Rebecka, Mary, Dorothy and Sarah.

Executors: Dennis Rothford, his brother Joseph Baker and Evan Oliver.
Witnesses: Joseph Brow, William Roules, Dennes Rothford.

LUFFE, JOHN.
7/27/1684. 12/17/1685. A. 20.
Estate to wife Jane, who is sole executrix and to son John.
Overseers: Father Edward Luffe and William Clayton.
Witnesses: Thomas Bradford, John Goodsonn.

CLARKE, JOHN. Province of PA
5/16/1685. 7/24/1685. A. 21.
Estate to servants Barnard Littlejohn, Mary Chapman and Christian Chapman. Legacy to William Beale, a servant.
Executor: Barnard Littlejohn.
Witnesses: John Goodsonn, John Claypole.

LINCOLNE, ELLISH.
November 13, 1685. 9/16/1685. A. 22.
Kinswoman Mrs. Mary Cantwell. Signed "on board."
Witnesses: Hellen Mayow, Michaell Booth.

BUTTERE, RICHARD. Pemmepecca Creek, Phila. Co. Yeoman.
September 16, 1685. 9/17/1685. A. 23.
Legacy to George Eaton who is Executor. John Randall of Pascataway in the Province of East Jersey, John Eaton brother of the aforesaid George, John Watts.
Witnesses: Allen Foster.

FARMER, MAJOR JASPAR.
September 25, 1685. 11/2/1685. A. 25.
Estate to wife Mary and son Edward who are the Executors.
Legacies to children Sarah, John, Katherine, Robert and Charles, to sister Alice Scull, and to children Richard, Samuel, Jasper and daughter Webber all in Ireland.
Overseers: Capt. Thomas Holmes of Phila. and Mr. Turner, late of Dublin but now of Phila., draper.
Witnesses: Samuel Hunt, Edward Farmer.

LEE, CHARLES. Late of Phila. Husbandman.
6/28/1685. 7/1/1685. A. 27.
Nuncupative will. Estate to wife Anne and daughter Anne Lee. [See Admus. Book A]
Witnesses: Edward Luffe, Anne Lee, Margaret Fisher.

LUFFE, JOHN.
This is a duplicate of will No. 16, page 20, Book A.

CALVERT, THOMAS.
1/15/1685. 12/17/1685. A. 30.
Nuncupative will. Wife's name is not given. Estate to daughters Elizabeth and Margaret. It is mentioned in the probate that he was of Chester Co., PA, and a husbandman.
Witnesses: Joshua Hastings, Randall Vernon, Peter Taylor, George Read.

JONES, WILLIAM. Meriwithshire, Wales. Husbandman.
---. 1/1/1685. Sealed and proved. A. 34.
Nuncupative will. Wife Ann Reynald deceased. Estate to children John Williams, Alice, Katherine and Given Williams. [The original will is missing.]
Trustees: Hugh Roberts of Merion, Phila. Co. and John Roberts of the same plantation.

JOHNSON, JOHN. Markers Creek, Chester Co.
March 16, 1685. 2/17/1686. A. 35.
Estate to wife Elener and his children whose names are not given. Wife and children are the Executors.
Witnesses: Moton Knuson, Henry Reynolds, Sydrack Whitworth.

TAYLOR, CHRISTOPHER.
10/28,1685. 1/1/1688. A. 37.
Wife's name is not given. Estate to children Joseph and Mary Taylor. Legacies to son Israel Taylor and housekeeper Margaret Thompson. [The original will is missing.]
Executors: William Penn, Proprietary and Governor of Pennsilvania, and Ralph Fretwel of Barbadoes.
Witnesses: Joseph Vaughan, Thomas Hooton.

AP EDWARD, JOHN. A. 37.
The copy of the last will and testament of John ap Edward the original lying in the Executors hands, being omitted to be registered in the new book parchment covers in folio 247, John Moore being Register General.

EDWARD, JOHN AP.
8/16/1683. 2/8/1683/4.
Children Evan, Edward and Elizabeth who as Elizabeth Jones received her portion and her share of her deceased brother Evan's portion in 1699. Nephew John Evan, brothers Evan and William ap Edward. Servant Mary Hughes. [Recorded Book B, pg. 270.]
Executors: Friends Hugh Roberts, David Darries, John Roberts and Hugh John Thomas.
Witnesses: Gabril Jones and William Morgan.

HENNET, JOHN.
August 3, 1686. 6/5/1686. A. 38.
Lately arrived in Pennsilvania in the ship called the Amity, Richard Diamond, commander, from Allrestford in Hampshire in old England, and departed this life the last of July 1686 at the house of Zechariah Whitepaine, merchant. Nuncupative will. Estate to Edward James his servant, and also his time of servitude.
Witnesses: Robert Peacey, William Freeman, John Dorsey.

HICKMAN, FRANCIS.
November 27, 1685. ---. A. 39.
Estate to wife Elizabeth and sons Joseph and Benjamin. Legacies to daughters Mary and Hanah Hickman. Robert Adams of Phila. of whom land was bought is mentioned. [The original will is missing. See Admin Book A, pg. 23.]
Overseers: John Barns commonly distinguished by Bristoll Barns there being one more of the same name, and Thomas Durket.
Witnesses: Robert Jeffes, Richard Dungworth, Mary Jeffes, Jonathan Jeffes.

DE LA NOE, CHARLES. Minister.
September 11, 1686. ---. A. 41.
Estate to Jacob Pellison of Phila. Co. who is Executor. [The original will is missing.]

Witnesses: William Salway, John Goodson, S. Hersent, Pat. Robinson.

FRAMPTON, WILLIAM. Phila. Merchant.
7/9/1686. 9/8/1686. A. 41.
Nuncupative will. Estate to wife Elizabeth who is sole Executrix and to children whose names are not given.
Overseers: Samuell Jenings of West Jersey, Samuel Carpenter of Phila. and brother-in-law Philip Richards of New York.
Witnesses: Samuell Spicer, Samuell Bulkley.

This is a probate of will No. 30, Book A, page 41. Recorded page 42.

FARMER, MARY. Widow of Maj. Jaspar Farmer of Ireland.
October 31, 1686. July 1, 1687. A. 45.
Son Edward sole Executor. Legacies to son Edward Badsforth, daughter Sarah Farmer, daughter-in-law Katherine Farmer, maid-servant Elizabeth Mayo. Thomas Webes, Robert Jefs(?) of "Frankfoud," and a plantation called "Farmer Towne" are mentioned.
Witnesses: John Farmer, Jacob Chapman, John Vaus.

HICKMAN, FRANCIS.
This is a duplicate of Will No. 28, page 39, Book A. Recorded page 64.

CLAYPOOLE, JAMES. Phila. Merchant.
12/5/1686. 8/12/1687. A. 67.
Estate to wife Helena, who is sole executrix and to his children, John the eldest and Mary, his wife; Mary eldest daughter, Helena second daughter, Priscilla youngest daughter, sons James, Nathaniel, George and Joseph the youngest. Legacy "of ten bushels of Indian corn for the poor of this towne to be disposed of by the overseers of the poore." Plantation in Lewis Creeke in Sussex Co. benefit of his brother Norton Claypoole.
Overseers: William Penn, our Governor, Thomas Lloyd, Keeper of the broad seal.
Witnesses: Da: Lloyd, Alexander Beardsly, Edward Lord.

MOSS, JOSEPH. Willspring, Phila. Co.
7/23/1687. 9/9/1687. A. 71.

Estate to wife Ellinor who is Executrix.
Witnesses: Michaell Holme, Thomas Holme.

JONES, HENRY.
October 8, 1683. 9/17/1687. A. 71.
Estate to wife Gundelo who is Executrix. Legacy to son Philip Jones living in Wales.
Witnesses: Peter Rambo, Ebenezer Taylor.

LEHNMANN, PHILLIP TH.
10/26/1687. December 31, 1687. A. 72.
Estate to Charles Pickering who is Executor. Legacies to Silas Crispin; Ellinor Moss; Captain Thomas Holmes who receives the plantation called Green Spring in Sussex Co., PA; Susanah James, wife of John James; William Penn, Proprietary and Governor, plantation at Broad Creek, Sussex Co., PA; Charles Pickering land in Kent Co., PA; Samuel Bulkley; James Nevill of West New Jersey; cousin Th: Kolbans; John Southworth; John Hill and his wife, Elizabeth; William Dyer and his wife, whose name is not given; his maid servants Elizabeth Tucker and Ann Heckles. Mention is made of James Bradshaw, John Fenwick late of West New Jersey and John Barker, all debtors.
Witnesses: Wm. Salway, William Bethil, Elizabeth Frampton.

TAYLOR, CHRISTOPHER. A. 74.
This is a duplicate of Will No. 26, page 37, Book A.

HIGGENS (HIGGINS), WILLIAM. Phila. Co. Brickmaker.
May 11, 1688. 3/16/1688. A. 75.
Nuncupative will. Estate to Jarirse Bywater and Joseph Browne, the last-named he used to call father. Declared at the house of Joseph Browne, brickmaker.
Witnesses: Richard Shea, Thomas Cotton, Kathrine Robinson.

TURNER, EDWARD.
7/30/1687. 3/10/1688. A. 76.
Estate to wife Kathrine who is Executrix. No children are mentioned.
Overseers: William Forist, Richard Hilliard.
Witnesses: William Forrest, Jeremiah Powell, Richard Hellyard.

THOMAS, JOHN. Llaethgwn, Commott Penllun, Meriweth Co. Gentleman.
February 9, 1682. 3/10/1688. A. 77.
Estate to wife Kathrine who is sole Executrix and to children Thomas Jones, Robert John, Evan John, Cadwalader John, Kathrine John, Mary John, Sudney John and eldest daughter Elizabeth, wife of Rees Evan of the township of Penmaen, Meringth Co.; nephew John the younger son of his brother Cadwalader Thomas late of Kiltalgarth, deceased; nieces Jane and Kathrine daughters of his brother Cadwalader Thomas and nephew Thomas Cadwalader.
Overseers: John ap John of the parish of Phueabou, Denlrgh Co.; Thomas Ellis of Cyfanedd, Mesioneth Co.; Thomas Wynne late of Brouvadog near Caerwys in the County of Flint; Robert David of Gwerneul, Merionyth Co.; Hugh Roberts of Kiltalgarth in the said County; Edward Jones late of Bala, Chirurgeon of the same County; Robert Vaughan of Gwernevel, Merionyth Co.; Edward Moris of Havodgynfawr, Denbigh Co.; Robert Owen late of Frongoch and son-in-law Rees Evans of Penmaen both near Bala, Merionyth Co.
Witnesses: Robert Vaughan, Rowland Owen, Thomas Vaughan.

PARKER, HENRY. Phila.
6/15/1688. 7/18/1688. A. 82.
Estate to son Thomas. Wife's name is not given. Legacy to Isaac Pearson of the above said town, blacksmith.
Executors: Thomas Budd of Phila., merchant; John Hart living near Walter Frist's mill.
Witnesses: John Townsend, Isaac Pearson, Charles Pickering.

JONES, HENRY. Phila. Co.
6/19/1688. 8/16/1688. A. 83.
Estate to wife Rachell who seems to have been his second wife, for he directed his body to be laid aside his first wife, whose name is not given, in his own ground in Moyemensing, and to his children Joseph, John, Samuel, Henry, Daniell, Richard, Elizabeth, Kathrin and Mercy Jones, and daughter Sarah, wife of Phillip Alford; daughter Marie and William Long her husband. Friend John Weales. He held an estate in Barbados.
Executors: John Swinsted; John Jennings; Lt. Col. Humphrey Waterman the elder; John Weales, Senior and Junior; Maj. Robert Harrison, all of Barbados, and John Jones of PA

Witnesses: John Moore, John Dousey, Robert Logan, Henry Flower, Pat. Robinson.

HARDING, JOHN. Chichester, PA
1/23/1687/8. 9/3/1688. A. 88.
Wife Amy sole Executrix. Kinswoman Amy James.
Witnesses: Thomas Usher, Hester Chadsey.

HAMOND, ELIZABETH. Late of Phila. Widow of Michael.
6/5/1688. 9/6/1688. A. 89.
Nuncupative will.
Executors: Nathaniel Watson, Edward Doughty, Thomas Smith, Sarah Griscom, Hester Wood, William Hudson.

SALTER, JOHN. Son of Henry and Anna.
9/7/1688. 9/17/1688. A. 90.
Nuncupative will. He died 9/7/1688. Estate to mother Anna Salter. Legacies to John Salter and William Wait. He held an estate in Salem.
Witnesses: Richard Whitfield, William Waite, Mary Kitchin, Ann Kitchin.

SALTER, ANNA. Taconia, Phila. Co. (a)
9/7/1688. 9/17/1688. A. 91.
Estate to the Yearly Meeting of Quakers of Phila. Co. for the benefit of the poor of said County. Legacies to John Hart, William Stockdale, Robert Stacy, Daniell Wills, Thomas Fairman, John Walker, joiner. Christian Thomas and Richard Dungworth are named as debtors.
Executors: Richard Whitfield, Thomas Fairman, Robert Stacey, John Hart, Charles Pickering, Patrick Robinson.
Witnesses: George Walker, John Meredith, William Waite.

SALTER, ANNA. (b)
9/8/1688. 9/17/[1688]. A. 93.
A codicil devising to Thomas Fairman all debts due her in England, Jamaica and Carolina in the hands of William Jacobs, Timothy Waymouth and Thomas Jacob. Also land in Salem.
Executor: Thomas Fairman.
Witnesses: Daniell Wills, William Waite, Jo: Hart.

LUFF, EDWARD. Living in Vine Street. Cordwainer.
6/1/1688. 7/1/1688. A. 94.
Nuncupative will. Estate to wife Elizabeth who is sole Executrix. Legacies to son, daughter-in-law and grandson whose names are not given. John Moore is mentioned.
Witnesses: John Moore, Da: Lloyd.

WATSON, NATHANIEL.
9/4/1688. 9/29/1688. A. 95.
Legacies to kinsman Router of Burlington, James Marshall, James Claypoole, Robert Eyres and Ann his wife, Samuel Bulkley, Doctor Hutson, John Sanby, Hannah Decowe.
Executors: Charles Pickering, Patrick Robinson.
Witnesses: [Daniel] Hodgson, Med[ieus] Ann Eyre, Samuel Bulkley.

ELLETT, PETER. Marcus Hooke, Phila. Co. Tailor.
September 9, 1687. 10/4/1688. A. 96.
Estate to his three sons only one of whom is named. Legacies to wife Lucie, daughters Anne and Joan and son John.
Executors: Wife and son John.
Witnesses: Will: Gregory, Joseph Wood.

SHILLSON, JOHN. Plimouth, Phila. Co.
9/22/1688. 11/6/1688. A. 97.
Neither wife's name nor the names of his children are given. Estate to son-in-law James Shaddok who is sole Executor. Legacies to Joan Wall and her husband whose name is not given, Martha Moon, widow and Elizabeth Luff. He held an estate in England.
Witnesses: Saml. Richardson, Da: Lloyd.

TIBBY, JOHN.
---. 9/10/1687(?). A. 98.
Nuncupative will. Estate to wife and children whose names are not given. [The original will is missing.]
Witnesses: John Shillson, Archeball Mickell.

COLLYER, EDWARD.
6/20/1688. 7/22/1688. A. 98.
Estate to sister Rebeccah Hatbark of London, England. Legacies to wife Sarah; kinsman Andrew More and his brother John More of Chester Co.; John and Elis Nicholls; Christopher Sibthorp of Phila.;

John Goodson and Humphrie Murrie and to the poor of the people called Quakers in Phila.
Executor: Christopher Sibthorp, braysier.
Overseers: John Goodson and Humphry Murry.
Witnesses: William Hard, Young Morgan, Richard Hellyard.

* Declaring the decease of Thomas Ellis and the appointment of Patrick Robinson as Register. A. 120.

JENNINGS, JOHN. Late of Barbados, now of Phila.
10/12/1688. 11/28/1688/9. A. 121.
Estate to John Jones his brother who is sole Executor. Legacies to wife Sarah; his brother Nathaniell Jones and his son Nathaniell; sister Susanna Fulliero; Samuel and Daniell Jones, sons of Henry Jones, deceased; to the poor of the Quakers in Barbados and in Phila. and to the finishing of the Center Crick Meeting House. William Holder, planter, a debtor; John Lewgars of Spinestown, Barbados, and Fustics Gullie in Barbados are mentioned. He held estates in Barbados and in England. Witnesses: Tho: Lloyd, John Simcocke, Saml: Richardson; Pat. Robinson.
Codicil: January 8, 1688.
Revoking a portion of legacy to his wife and giving it to John Jones his heir and sole Executor.
Witnesses: John Farmer, James Cooper, Pat. Robinson.

This is the probate of Will No. 54, page 121. Book A. A. 124.

COCK, PETER. Kipha, Phila. Co.
June 25, 1687. 1/4/1688/9. A. 126.
Estate to wife Margaret. Legacy to son Gabriell wherein is mentioned an island known by the name of the Skuillkill Island. There are nine more children mentioned whose names are not given.
Executors: Sons Lawrence and Erick.
Witnesses: Lasse Cock, Erick Cock, Mounce Cock, John Cock, Peter Cock, Gabriell Cock, Gunner Rambo, Robert Longshore.

KENT, ROBERT. Phila. Cordwayner.
12/13/1688/9. 1/25/1689. A. 129.
Estate to wife Margaret who is sole Executrix.
Overseers: John Fuller, Walter Fossatt of Chester Co.

Witnesses: John Fuller, John McComb, Pat. Robinson.

STANLEY, WILLIAM.
2/14/1689. 2/27/1689. A. 132.
Estate to wife Rebecca who is sole Executrix. Legacies to sister Dorothy Taylor and her children whose names are not given; sister Elizabeth Hooton and her son Thomas; Abigail Perkins.
Witnesses: Stephen Bodkin, John Moorey, James Budd, John Budd, Junr.

FEW, RICHARD.
6/12/1686. 1/26/1689. A. 134.
Estate to wife Julian and son Isaac who are the Executors. Legacies to sons Walter and Daniell and daughter Joan, and granddaughter Susanna Few, and to the monthly meeting at Chester for poor friends. [No witnesses are given and the will is unsigned.]
Trustees: Thomas Brassee, Caleb Pussey.

HOOTON, THOMAS, SENR. Phila. Cordwayner.
11/7/1688. 3/1/1689. A. 138.
Estate to Thomas Hooton the younger. Legacies to wife Elizabeth; nephew Thomas son of Wm. Hooton, brothergerman; grandchild Thomas Hooton the youngest, and the wife of Thomas Hooton the younger whose name is not given. Anthony Morris and Samuel Carpenter, both of Phila. are mentioned. He held an estate in Burlington, New Jersey.
Executors: Wife Elizabeth and son Thomas Hooton the younger.
Witnesses: John Otter, John Greenwood and Pat: Robinson.

MARSH, ROBERT. South Hampton, Bucks Co., PA
1/18/1689. 3/17/1689. A. 142.
Estate to wife Sarah and children Hugh and Robert. Legacy to daughter Allice.
Executors: Wife and son Hugh.
Witnesses: Henry Poynter, Joseph Holden, Benjamin Johns, Jos: Growdon and Nicholas Waller, Justice of the Peace of Bucks Co.

LARSON, NELES. Upland.
December 20, 1686. 4/12/1689. A. 145.

Estate to his wife Ann Friend who is sole Executrix. (Letters testamentary granted to Ann Friend "relict and executrix of forenamed.") Fustaff Anderson and Cristina Creek are mentioned.
Advisers: Lassey Cock, John Cock, Wholle Dabbo.
Witnesses: John Hodgskins, Charles Springer.

MEDFORD, JOHN. Newtowne.
May 12, 1689. 9/1/1689. A. 147.
Estate to brother Joseph Wood who is sole Executor. Legacies to "intended wife" Martha Coburne, sister Mary Silence.
Witnesses: John Word, Joseph Wood.
Codicil revoking a portion of legacy to Martha Coburne, May 13, 1689.
Witnesses: John Wood, Joseph Wood.

ANDERSON, LAWRENCE. Myamencen, now resident in house of Michell Nielson, Shakamanson, Phila. Co. Husbandman.
5/17/1689. 9/1/1689(?). A. 150.
Estate to Michell Nielson, Senr., Andrew Wheeler and John Matson. Legacies to grandchild Utro Lum; Breta Lum widow of his son Swan, deceased; Cathrina Hiclase; Elonor Matson; Morton Garrat; Garrat Garratson.
Executors: Michell Nelson, Androus Wheeler.
Witnesses: Thomas Fairman, Guner Rambo, Barence Jerris.

THOMAS, WILLIAM. Radnor. Planter.
7/18/1689. 9/4/1689. A. 152.
Estate to wife Anne who is sole Executrix, with remainder to William Thomas, eldest son of my brother John Thomas, if he will come to this country. Otherwise, the property is to be sold and the proceeds equally divided between the children of my brother and of my sister whose name is not given. Legacies to cozen Rees Petter, Ellis Ellis, Humphrey Ellis, David Lawrence, Kathrine Morgan, Ellis Pugh, Evan Harry, Hugh Harry and Daniell Harry. "I give to Owen Morgan one sow and his son to be released after my departure and, if my wife shall depart before the time of his daughter be over, she also may be then released." My brother-in-law David Davies and sister-in-law Kathrine Davies.
Overseers: David Lawrence, Rees Petter, David Evan, John Humphrey.

Witnesses: Philip Evan, John Humphrey.

SONGHURST, JOHN.
7/26/1687. November 6, 1689. A. 155.
Estate to son John who is sole Executor. Wife's name is not given. Legacies to daughters Elizabeth and Sarah; servants James Portis and William Gaskin; Joseph Tuggwell; Thomas Clark and to each overseer.
Overseers: Thomas Budd, John Goodson, Benjamin Chambers.
Witnesses: John Goodson, Benjamin Chambers.

RIGGS, ANN. Late of Phila. Widow.
12/16/1689. 2/16/1690. A. 170.
Estate to Joseph Cooper of West New Jersey who is Executor. Legacy to brother William Thomas.
Witnesses: Margarett Cooper, Mary Denaviss, Will: Roydon.

SHAW, JOSEPH. Brandywine Creeke, County of New Castle, PA
March 14, 1689/90. April 19, 1690. A. 172.
Wife's name is not given. Two thirds of estate to his only daughter Mary Nichols, and should she die without issue to his brother Andrew Shaw. The remaining third to Jeremiah Collett who is Executor. Legacies to John Bennett, William Collett, George Strode, and servants John Chambers and Elisabeth Harrold. "I give unto those four who shall bear me to my grave each of them a pair of gloves."
Witnesses: Isaac Warner, Samuell Adams.

THROCKMORTON, JOSEPH. Mariner.
December 2, 1689. 4/16/1690. A. 174.
Estate to Joseph Throckmorton, son of his brother John Throckmorton of East Jersey who is Executor and guardian for the said Joseph.
Witnesses: Pat: Robinson, Willm. Biles, Edward Smoutt.

MORGAN, JANE JOHN, alias JANE ROBERTS. Haverford.
7/25/1688. ---. A. 177.
Nuncupative will. Whole estate to friend John Roberts of Marrion, Phila. Co., who is sole Executor. [The original will is missing.]
Witnesses: William Howell, Blanch Sharpus.

BURDEN, NICHOLAS. Barbados.
January 8, 1689/90. ---. A. 178.
Now being bound forth on a voyage to sea unto Virginia in the good ... or vessel called the Adventure, Master ---. Whole estate to wife Elizabeth, formerly called Elizabeth Eston, whom he lately married in Barbados, and now goeth with him to Virginia in the aforesaid vessel, and who is sole Executrix. [The original will is missing.]
Witnesses: David Garven, Wm. Roberts, Robert Barkley.

LEWIS, HENRY. Maencock, Haverford township.
6/14/1688. 8/8/1690. A. 180.
Wife Margaret who is sole Executrix. Eldest son Henry, youngest son Samuel and daughter Elizabeth. Lewis Davids of Landeroi, late of Pembroke Co.
Overseers: Ellis Ellis, Humphrey Ellis, Samuel Rees, John Bevan, John Lewis, William Howell, Lewis Daviss, Thomas Ellis, Daniel Humphry.
Witnesses: Lewis David, Griffith Owen, Thomas Elliss.

BRASSIC, THOMAS. Chester, PA
7/11/1690. 9/18/1690. A. 182.
Estate to daughters Rebecca and Mary. Wife's name is not given.
Executors: John Simcocke, Randall Vernon, John Bristow.
Witnesses: Caleb Pusey, Walter Fauset.

FULLER, JOHN. Phila. Merchant.
3/25/1690. 10/5/1692. A. 188.
Being about to depart this Province in the ship Tryall to go to England - Estate to Robert Turner, Elder of Phila., merchant, who is sole Executor. Legacies to mother Elizabeth Cuppage of Lemsvone (?), Ireland; Uncle Abraham Fuller, Anthony Sharp; Robert Turner the Younger and Mary Turner, daughter of Robert Turner, Senr.; friends George Keith of Phila., Benjn. Acton of Salem in West New Jersey; Samuel Carpenter; John McCombe; Patrick Robinson of Phila.; and to the poor of the people called Quakers in Phila.
Overseers: Samll. Carpenter, Patrick Robinson.
Witnesses: Andrew Robeson, John Test, Samuel Buckley.

SMITH, THOMAS. Phila. Co.
11/13/1690. 2/20/1692. A. 191.

Estate to wife Prissilla who is sole Executrix and to children Thomas Smith eldest son and daughters Mary and Ann.
Overseers: Saml. Jenings, Saml. Carpenter, Daniell Pegg.
Witnesses: Griffith Owen, John White, Pat: Robinson.

NORWAY, WILLIAM. Phila. Co. Labouring Man.
March 5, 1691. 3/22/1692. A. 194.
Estate to Peter Rambo, who is Executor.
Witnesses: Peter Bor, Edward Lane.

MORRISS, RICHARD.
August 20, 1690. 1/21/1692. A. 196.
Being about to depart the Province of Pennsilvania to England - Estate to wife Grizell who is Executrix, and at her death to Andrew Griscombe of Phila., carpenter and his son Tobias Griscom. The executors in the event of his wife's death, Jno. Goodson and Philip Richards.
Witnesses: John Densey, Patrick Robinson.

FORREST, WALTER. Byburg, PA
1/18/1692. 2/5/1692. A. 198.
Estate to wife Anne; William Alberson the Younger; Abraham and Rebecca Alberson; John and Samuel Denniss, sons of Thomas Denniss of Phila., shoemaker; Rebecca, Mary and Hanna Denniss, daughters of Thomas Denniss; brothers John and Francis. He held an estate in Salem Township by "unknown creek" in West New Jersey.
Executor: William Alberson, Senr. of West New Jersey by Newton Creek.
Witnesses: John Gilbert, Lasy Poore, Elizabeth Chappell.

WYNNE, THOMAS. Phila. Practitioner of Physick.
1/15/1691. 2/20/1692. A. 200.
Estate to wife Elizabeth who is Executrix and to children Jonathan, Mary, Rebecca, Sidney and Hannah all living in America, and daughter Tabitha living in England. At the death of his wife, son Jonathan is to be Executor. Brother-in-law Saml. Buttall. He held an estate near Lewistowne and Cedar Creeke, both in Sussex Co.
Overseers: Thomas Lloyd, Dept. Govr. of this Province, and Griffith Owen.

Witnesses: Arthur Cooke, Phinehas Pemberton, Richard Thomas, Theo. Roberts, Mary Holme.

BOCKENOGEN, JAN WILLIMSE. Cooper
5/24/1688. 4/7/1692. A. 203.
Wife Dina Hubers. Children Stephanus and Sytic. [The original will is missing.]
Executors: Jan Goodson, Jan Duplovys.
Witnesses: Angenite Boon, Jan Duplovys.

NEELSON, ONLY. Phila. Co. Yeoman.
April 6, 1692. 4/17/1692. A. 205.
Estate to wife Siscillia, sons Neels and Erick and two daughters whose names are not given.
Executor: Son Erick.
Witnesses: Peter Rambo, Neels Neelson, Erick Neelson.

HOOTON, OLIVER.
9/9/1690. 4/17/1692. A. 208.
Executors, uncle Lambert and John Snowden, who also receive legacies. Legacies to cousins Elizabeth, Thomas, John, James and Mary Lambert, and to cousin John Snowden's two children whose names are not given. Residuary legatee his father in England whose name is not given, and at his death to his two cousins in England, Thomas Sharp of Lincoln and Elizabeth Smith of Barnby, Nottinghamshire. Signed at the falls of Delaware River in West Jersie.
Witnesses: Samuell Bunting, John Bunting.

BENNETT, EDMOND. Phila. Yeoman.
September 5, 1692. September 24, 1692. A. 210.
Estate to wife Elizabeth who is sole Executrix. Legacy to nephew Jno. Barblett now in England.
Overseers: John Kinsey, John Jones, John Otter.
Witnesses: Thomas Roberts, Jane Austin, Theodore Roberts.

ECKLEY, SARAH. Phila. Widow.
6/17/1692. September 25, 1692. A. 213.
Sole Executrix of John Eckley, late of the same place whose will was dated July 17, 1686. Estate to children William and Mary Barge and

Sarah Eckley. Legacies to Friends Meeting in Phila. and her late husband's son, John Eckley. Friend Hanah Delavall.
Executors: Thomas Lloyd, Samuell Carpenter, John Delavall in PA and elsewhere in America, and James Lewis, Perigrine Musgrave and Richard Stafford, Junr., all of South Wales, in those parts.
Witnesses: John Goodson, Alexander Beardsley, James Fox, Abraham Hardiman, Dod. Lloyd.

WILLCOX, SARAH. Schoolkill, Phila. Co.
4/20/1692. 9/30/1692. A. 216.
Being the sole Administratrix of my deceased husband, Barnabas Willcox - estate to children George and Joseph, who are the Executors, daughter Rachell the youngest child, Hester, Hanah and Abigall. Willm. Clayton is mentioned in connection with a mill property.
Overseers: John Bristoe of Chester, Paul Sanders of Schoolkill.
Witnesses: Paul Sanders, John Roades, James Fapell.

ALLEN, NATHANIELL.
August 21, 1692. 11/25/1692/3. A. 219.
Estate to wife Ellinor and children Nehemiah, Lyddia and Joyce Brewer his daughter. Legacies to George Emlen and grandsons Nathaniell and Nehemiah, sons of Nehemiah Allen. James and Jno. Goodson and Nath: Lampbough are mentioned in connection with land purchases. He held a plantation called Alenbury near Neshaminy Creek, also land in Warminster Township.
Executors: Son Nehemiah, Thos. Bradford and Thoms. Paschall.
Witnesses: John Shippey, Joanna Paschall, John White.

HUMPHRY, RICHARD. Township of Radnor, Welsh Teach, Province of PA Planter.
12/12/1691. 12/18/1692/3. A. 221.
Estate to John Humphry, brother-in-law, who is sole Executor. Legacies to brothers John and Owen Humphry; sister Katherine or her children whose names are not given; cousin John Owen; Lyddia Ellis; Rebecca, Ann, Daniell, Benjamin and Joseph Humphry; also to the Friends Monthly Meeting for "the service of truth."
Witnesses: Tydyer Robert, Benjamin Humphrys, Rowland Elliss.

ELLISS, ELLIEN. Township of Haverford, PA Widow of Thomas.

1/27/1692. 12/18/1692/3. A. 223.
Estate to daughter Rachell Elliss, and in the event of her death to the six children, whose names are not given, of her (Ellien Elliss) sisters Lowry and Gwen.
Executor: Nephew Daniell Humphrey.
Trustees: Griffith Owens, William Stowell, Edward Jones, John Roberts, Robt. Owen and John Humphrey.
Witnesses: David Lewillen, Benj. Humphrys, Theodore Robert, John Humphrys.

LIVEZEY, THOMAS. Dublin Township, Phila. Co.
6/12/1691. 4/22/1692. A. 226.
Estate to son Jonathan and his son Thomas. Legacies to daughter Ann Littlemore and her three eldest children whose names are not given; daughter Margarett Lorensen and her eldest children whose names are not given; daughter-in-law Rachell Livezey; grand-daughter Mary Livezey, Richard Dungworth and William Preston.
Executors: Son Jonathan Livezey and William Preston.
Witnesses: Joseph Paull, Willm. Preston.

DELOVALL, JOHN. Phila. Merchant.
6/10/1693. September 20, 1693. A. 235.
Estate to wife Hannah who is Executrix and to son John. Sisters, Rebecca and Margaret.
Trustees: Father-in-law Thomas Lloyd, Samuel Carpenter, Alexander Beardsley and James Fox.
Witnesses: Arthur Cooke, Samuel Jennings, Saml. Richardson, Dad. Lloyd.

HOOTON, THOMAS. Phila.
7/29/1693. 8/5/1693. A. 237.
Estate to wife Elizabeth who is sole Executrix and to children Thomas and Mary. Legacies to mother Elizabeth Hooton; friend George Keith; Mary Bradshaw, widow; servants Jacob Usher and Ann Newington and to each trustee. He held an estate in West Jersey.
Trustees: Thomas Holme, Andrew Robeson, Thomas Budd and Joseph Willcox.
Witnesses: John Duplounys, Bulah Jaques, John Wilkinson.

HILLERD, RICHARD.

7/23/1692. October 5, 1693. A. 241.
Whole estate to wife Mary who is sole Executrix. Legacies to children, Richard, Phillip, Joseph and Mary.
Witnesses: Thomas Curtis, Willm. Trotter, Martha Shattick, Elent.(?) Roberts.

DUBUC, PETER. Phila.
October 14, 1693. October 20, 1693. A. 243.
Residuary legatee Samuell Peres who is sole Executor. Legacies to the Hon. Wm. Markham, Lieut. Gov. of the Province; Caesar Guiselin of Phila., goldsmith; Bernard Vige; --- Doe [The given name is omitted in the original will.] living at the Schoolkill; to the poor of this town and county, and Father Smyth now or late of Talbott Co., Md.
Witnesses: John Holme, John Amery, P. Bourdet, Theor. Roberts.

NELSON, JONAS. Kingsessin, Phila. Co.
January 14, 1691. October 23, 1693. A. 245.
Asks to be buried at the burying place of Wiccacoe. Estate to wife Gertrue and children Jonathan, Jonas, son Mountze, Neels and Andrees. Legacies to children John, Peter, daughters Guley, Gunla and Bridgett and Christian. James Hunt, Peter Gocumb are mentioned in connection with land purchases.
Executors: Wife, Robt. Longshore and Eusta Eustason.
Witnesses: Thomas Paschall, James Hunt, Robert Longshore.

LEWIS, CADWALLADER. Phila. Co.
September 4, 1693. October 28, 1693. A. 248.
Nuncupative will. Estate to his natural sister Mary Thomas. Legacies to the wife (name not given) of Owen Foulke; the poor children (names not given) that live at Griffith Jones' house, and to Robert Ellis. [The original will is missing.]
Witnesses: Robert Owen, Robert Jones, Thomas Andrew (?).

FEARNE, JOSHUA. Darby, Chester Co., PA Yeoman.
4/6/1693. December 2, 1693. A. 249.
Wife's name is not given. Estate to children Joshua and Mary.
Executors: His mother Elizabeth Fearne, Michaell Blinstone and Jno. Wood. Thomas Worth, Samuell Bradshaw, Anthonie Morgan and Robert Naylor are mentioned.
Overseers: Samuell Levis and John Blinstone.

Witnesses: George Wood, John Smith, Edmund Cartlidge, Benjamin Cliffe.

CROOKSHANKS, ALEXANDER. Parsion, Phila. Co.
8/3/1693. December 11, 1693. A. 251.
Estate to wife Elizabeth who is Executrix and to children, only one of whome is named, a daughter Hester who also receives a legacy of a "niger girle" called Hanah.
Trustees: David Lloyd and Henry Badcock.
Witnesses: Henry Badcocke, Nehemiah Allen, James Forman, Robert Willkins.

WHITE, JOHN. Phila.
7/26/1693. January 15, 1693. A. 253.
Estate to wife Mary who is Executrix and to children James, Mary and Grace. James Thomas is mentioned.
Overseer: Samuel Jennings.
Witnesses: John Lynam, Tho. Makin, Edward Farmar.

MILLER, THOMAS. Kent Co., PA
November 10, 1693. March 24, 1693/4. A. 255.
Estate to wife Sarah who is sole Executrix and to children Thomas, Rebecca, Sarah and Easter. Legacy to daughter Jean Deards. Captain John Dubrows, a creditor and Francis Reonalds are mentioned.
Witnesses: John Robbisson, Thomas Skidmore, Samuel Skidmore.

HENDSON, WILLIAM. Phila. Bricklayer.
6/29/1694. September 3, 1694. A. 258.
Wife Ann sole Executrix and children John and Elizabeth.
Witnesses: John Hart, Mary Dunton, Jno. Parsons.

SWANSON, ANDREW. Wiccoco, Phila. Co.
January 8, 1687/8. September 25, 1694. A. 259.
Estate to wife Anna and children, eldest son Gunner, Christopher, Andrew, Catherine(?), Elizabeth, Christian and Margaret.
Executors: Swan and Wollow Swanson, Andreas Bankson, Lassy Cock and Peter Yocham.
Witnesses: Richard Rodes, Richd. Reynolds, Henry Flower.

GRISCOM, ANDREW. Phila. Carpenter.
7/4/1694. October 1, 1694. A. 261.
Estate to wife Sarah who is sole executrix and his children whose names are not given. Legacies to mother Grizell Morris and to wife's brother, John Dole. Mention is made of an estate held in German Town and of a lot adjoining Joseph Brown's lot.
Overseers: John Dole, Philip James and Joseph Willcox.
Witnesses: John Buzby, Mary Buzby, Francis Cooke.

PICKERING, CHARLES. Phila. Merchant.
January 25, 1693/4. April 20, 1694. A. 263.
Estate to wife Anne who is Executrix with Andrew Robeson and Joseph Willcox, Esqrs., and John Moore, gentleman, all of Phila. The last three named are also legatees. Legacies to John Hart; Rachell Preston; William Salloway, Esq.; brother Richard Pickering; sister Mary Lancaster; Richard Thompson of Chester Co.; and William Busey.
Witnesses: Humphrey Morrey, Tho: Hill, Tho. Willard, James Shattick.

FELLOWS, JOHN. Phila. Joyner.
October 3, 1694. October 12, 1694. A. 266.
Nuncupative will. Estate to wife Margaret and child whose name is not given.
Witnesses: Abraham Hooper, John Songhurst, Arthur Cooke.

LLOYD, THOMAS. Phila.
7/10/1694. October 22, 1694. A. 267.
Estate to wife Patience and his own children Mordecay, Thomas, Hannah, Rachell, Mary, Eliz: and Deborah. His wife's children Enoch and Marcy Story. His negroes Mingo, Wissen, Julious, Marria and Sarah.
Executors: His wife, son Mordecay Lloyd, son-in-law Isaac Norris and kinsman David Lloyd.
Witnesses: Sam: Carpenter, Alexandr. Beardsley, John Jones.

BRIGHTWEN, WM. Phila. Butcher.
6/20/1694. October 26, 1694. A. 267b.
Nuncupative will. Whole estate to wife Susannah who is sole Executrix.

Witnesses: Declared in the presence of Griffith Owen, Wm. Hudson and Margrett Cook.

BASSNETT, RICHARD. Burlington, West New Jersey.
October 8, 1694. October 13, 1694. A. 268.
Wife Elizabeth and children William; daughter May wife of Edward Hunlock and her daughter Sarah; daughters Elizabeth and Hannah; son-in-law Thomas Frampton; daughters-in-law Elizabeth and Sarah Frampton.
Executors: His wife with James Marshall, Francis Davenport and James Hill.
Witnesses: Benjamin Wheat, Bernard Devonish, Phill: Richards.

PEARLE, RICHARD. Now of Burlington, West New Jersey.
November 14, 1694. November 19, 1694. A. 270.
Legacies to widow Guest of Phila; George Peacock now of Burlington; John Lowell and Benjamin Stanley, both of Phila.
Executor: George Peacock.
Witnesses: Thomas Bibb, Samll. Oldale, Jno. Hickman.

HAWKES, WILLIAM. Chichester Township, Chester Co., PA
11/30/1693/4. November 20, 1694. A. 272.
Estate to wife Jane who is sole Executrix. Legacies to son-in-law George Chandler; daughter-in-law Jane Jeffries; sons and daughters-in-law Sivethin Chandler, Wm. Chandler, Thomas Chandler, Charity Chandler and Ann Chandler.
Witnesses: Robert Jeffries (was blotted out of the will by the will of the testator), Jacob Chandler, Edward Foard.

WILLCOX, GEORGE. Phila. Merchant.
February 17, 1693/4. November 24, 1694. A. 274.
Intending (God willing) shortly a voyage to sea. Estate to brother Joseph Wilcox who is sole Executor, Ester Wilcox, Abigall Wilcox and Rachel Willcox. Legacies to sisters Rachell and Abigall Wilcox, sister Hannah Roads and brother Joseph Wilcox's children whose names are not given.
Witnesses: Griffith Jones, John Duplloueys, J. Moore, Albertus Brandt.

LAMBERT, THOMAS. Nottingham, Burlington Co., West New Jersey. Tanner.
9/23/1693. December 8, 1694. A. 276.
Estate to wife Elizabeth and children, eldest son Thomas, Samuel, Hannah, Mary, Elizabeth and Ruth. Sons James and Olliver Lambert deceased. Legacy to son John Lambert. Brother Olliver Hooton, Olliver Hooton the younger, batchelor, deceased, Henry Grubb and a place called Asenpinck are mentioned.
Executors: His wife and son Thomas.
Advisor: Francis Davenport to whom a legacy is given.
6/3/1694 - An addition to the will is made regarding an estate in Phila., and the legacy of a negro woman called Phillis to his wife.
Witnesses: Jno. Lambert, Senr., Elizabeth Wright, Mary Embley.

RODNEY, JOHN. Phila. Gentleman.
September 15, 1694. December 12, 1694. A. 279.
Estate to wife Ann who is sole Executrix and to son Ceaser Rodney who is also given the negro boy called Nero. Legacies to daughter Penelopy Roach, nephew Wm. Rodeny of Jones Co., friend Thomas Boleman.
Overseers: Kinsman Wm. Rodeny, Phillip Richards and John Jones of Phila., merchant, to each of whom a legacy is given.
Witnesses: John Wilkinson, John Stephens, Alexander Deveren, Esther Wilkinson.

MORE, SAMUEL. Phila.
November 6, 1694. December 14, 1694. A. 281.
Son and heir of Nicholas More my late father, Esq., deceased. Wife's name is not given. Estate to mother whose name is not given, brother Nicholas More and sister Sarah More. Legacies to father-in-law John Holme and Adam Burch.
Executor: Father-in-law John Holme.
Witnesses: Wm. Salway, John Duploueys, Tho: Fairman.

BRISTONE, JOHN. Chester Township, PA Edge-tool Maker.
6/27/1694. December 15, 1694. A. 283.
Estate to children John, William and Hester, and at their death to brother Richard Bristow living at the City of Bristoll in England. Wife's name is not given. Legacies to kinswoman Mary Whitaker, and to the finishing of the Meeting House at Chester. Cripel's land

bought of Albert Hendrickson and lime hills purchased of Jasper Cause, tanner of ye City of Bristoll are mentioned.
Executors: Joseph Wilcox of Phila. and Caleb Pusey of Chester Co.
Witnesses: Henry Worley, Sarah Howell.

ROBESON, ANDREW. Phila. Merchant.
November 12, 1694. December 24, 1694. A. 286.
Estate to wife Elizabeth who is sole Executrix.
Overseers: Robert Turner and John Moore.
Witnesses: Thomas Tresse, James Murrall, James Poulter.
November 16, 1694 - Codicil: Legacy to Andrew Robeson of West Jersey, yeoman of land lying upon Raccoon Creek in West Jersey "and adjoining to the fishing place." Legacies to Robert Turner and John Moore.
Witnesses: Griffith Jones, Joseph Wilcox, John Duploueys.

ROSSELL, FRANCIS. Bucks Co., PA
8/5/1694. January 1, 1694/5. A. 288.
His body is to be buried at Burlington. Legacies to sister Jane wife of --- Wells, surgeon of London; Jane wife of Tho: Brock and her daughter Mary Huff; John Towne; Deborah wife of John Town; servant Wm. Smith of land in Bucks Co. that adjoins an Indian Town; to the children of John Hough whose names are not given; to the poor of the Quakers in Bucks Co. and to the other poor of the said County; to the sons of Saml. Burgis whose names are not given; Phineas Pemberton and Ralph Boone of Bucks Co. His loving friend and partner, Samuel Carpenter is sole Executor.
Witnesses: Isaiah Labahy, Louis Lavalles, Susanah Collins.
8/5/1694 - Codicil: Legacy to Richard Wilson of Bucks Co. and Samuel Carpenter residuary legatee.
Witnesses: Louis Lavalles, Isaiah Lebahy, Richard Mather, Susanah Collins.

DEAN, KATHERINE. Widow and relict of Richard Deane, late of Phila. Nailer.
9/12/1694. January 3, 1694/5. A. 291.
Estate to children Nathaniell and Deborah.
Guardians and Executors: Saml. Carpenter, Alexander Beardsley and Wm. Forrest.
Witnesses: Dad. Lloyd, Thomas Morris, Henry Clifton, Richard Gove.

WADDY, HENRY. Waddeys Grange of Oxford, Phila. Co.
9/20/1694. January 5, 1695. A. 293.
Estate to Richard Cony, hosier, living in Holborn, England and to Ann Cony his wife, my sole daughter whome I appoint Executor and Executrix. Legacy to the deserving poor such as my trustees may see fit.
Trustees: Jno. Goodson of Phila. and Joseph Paul of Oxford, Phila. Co.
9/20/1694 - Legacy to Daniel Hall "my ungratfull kinsman" to be paid him by March 28, 1696, but if he die before then it shall go to his daughter and her husband (whose names are not given).
Witnesses: Daniel Hall, Richard Jones.
9/20/1694 - And further to confirm this my within mentioned will I do sign and seal it in the presence of John Fletcher, Robert Adams, William Preston.
9/24/1694 - Codicil: Additional legacy to Daniel Hall.
Witnesses: James Dilworth, Olive Wells, Gunsey Cock.

MCKOUINE, DAVID.
December 26, 1694. January 7, 1694/5. A. 297.
"As for my estate in Barbados, I leave it according to my testament made there." Legacy to wife Ann who is living in Barbados, to Richard Keies and to Edward Smout. Joseph Allford of Barbados; Richard Potts; James Stanfeild; John Sedgewick; Edward Farmer; widow Waterman and George Bersar are mentioned.
Executors: Richard Keies and Edward Smout.
Witnesses: James Johnstown, Richard Potts.

ROYDON, WILLIAM. Late of London, England, now of Phila. Merchant.
September 8, 1694. January 31, 1694/5. A. 300.
A codicil declaring his last will and testament already made wherein John Tizick of London, merchant is Executor, and moreover ratifying this and appointing Andrew Robeson, merchant, and Joshua Carpenter, brewer, trustees or agents under the aforesaid Executor. Legacies are given to each trustee.
Witnesses: Peter Reverdey, J. Moore, Margarett Cooper, Mary Carpenter.

SALWAY, WILLIAM. PA Merchant.
November 12, 1694. February 1, 1694/5. A. 302.
Wife's name is not given. Estate to son Samuel and daughters Mary and Hanna Salway and niece Margaret Salway. Mary White is mentioned in connection with a conveyance.
Trustees and Guardians: Andrew Robeson, Joseph Growdon, Pat. Robinson and John Parsons to each of whom is given a legacy.
Witnesses: Jno. King, Jno. Mc Comb, Anthony Taylor.
November 13, 1694 - Codicil: Legacy to niece Margaret Salway.
Witnesses: M. McComb, Jno. Crapp, James Standfield.

WALL, RICHARD.
December 27, 1694. February 10, 1694/5. A. 306.
Wife's name is not given. Estate to children, Richard and the two youngest, Mary and John Wall. He held an estate in Kent Co., PA and a lot on Society Hill near ye lot of Saml. Roland in Phila.
Executrix: Mrs. Rachell Hill, widow.
Witnesses: Thomas Hartley, Thomas Herris.

HOLME, THOMAS. Dublin Township. Phila. Co.
12/10/1694. April 8, 1695. A. 308.
Aged full seventy years. Wife's name is not given. Daughters Elinor Mosse and Hester, wife of Silas Crispin. Daughter Sarah, wife of Richard Horcomb who had children whose names are not given. Niece Susannah James. Grand-children, Sarah, Rebecca, Mary, William, Thomas, Elinor and Hester, who were the children of Hester and Silas Crispin. Kinsman John Fletcher "who came over with me out of England." John Osborne "that come over with me." Pat. Robinson. Pyne Spring plantation in Upper Dublin Township, Phila. Co. and Well Spring plantation in Phila. Co. are mentioned.
Executor: Son-in-law Silas Crispin.
Witnesses: Samuel Jones, George Eaton, Edmond McQeagh.

TAYLOR, ROBERT. Springfield, Chester Co.
2/21/1695. May 14/1695. A. 311.
Estate to wife Mary and children Thomas, Jonathan, Martha, John, Jacob and four others whose names are not given. He held an estate in England.
Executors: Wife and brother Jonathan Heyes.
Witnesses: Walter Fausit, John Maris.

WILLIAMS, EDWARD. Late of Haverford, Chester Co. Tailor.
1/22/1694/5. May 15, 1695. A. 312.
Nuncupative will. Being at my house at work was taken sick and if pleased ye Lord that he died there. Whole estate to his aunt Catherin Davies and her children whose names are not given. He said he had no other relations in this country.
Witnesses: Josiah Taylor, Henry David.

GREEN, JOHN.
December 14, 1691. May 16, 1695. A. 313.
Estate to mother Margaret Greene who is sole Executrix.
Witnesses: Richard Lawrence, George Lawrence.

CREWS, WILLIAM. Phila. Potter.
9/4/1694. May 20, 1695. A. 314.
Estate to sons John, who is sole Executor, and James. Legacy to wife Elizabeth. He held an estate called Cowby Lane End in Walford Parish, Hereford Co at Castles Brooke.
Overseers: Wife, Everard Bolton and John Kinsey.
Witnesses: Everard Bolton, Jno. Kinsy, David Powell.

HUNT, WILLIAM. Phila.
9/4/1694. June 1, 1695. A. 316.
Friends Mary Serey and her sister Abigaill Serey. His master John Parsons is sole Executor. Captain Waterman is mentioned.
Witnesses: Daniel Radley, Jacob Taylor.

THOMAS, GRACE. Phila. Widow.
7/25/1694/5. June 1, 1695. A. 318.
Brother-in-law James Thomas. Sons Mycah Thomas, Gabriell Thomas and James Thomas, the latter of whom is sole Executor. Daughters Elizabeth Thomas, Mary Snead and Rachell Wharton and two other children whose names are not given. Jane, wife of Even Olive. Morgane Jones and Mary Hilliers are mentioned.
Witnesses: Henry Cliffton, Robert Burrow, Mary Helliard.

HOGAN, THOMAS. Late of ye Island of Barbados, now of Phila. Merchant.
March 17, 1694/5. July 4, 1695. A. 319.

Estate to wife and children whose names are not given, and who seem to have been living in Barbados. Samuel Carpenter of Phila., merchant, is Executor of his estate in PA Edward Smout is mentioned.
Witnesses: Dad. Lloyd, James Chick, John Willis.

ATCHLEY, THOMAS. Phila.
July 5, 1695. July 16, 1695. A. 321.
Estate to wife Martha. Legacy to son Thomas.
Executors: Wife and friend, Thomas Tress.
Witnesses: Tho: Makin, Francis Jarvis, Elizabeth Walker.

BUTLER, CHARLES.
March 26, 1695. September 18, 1695. A. 322.
Nuncupative will. Estate to friend Charles Bagley living within a mile and a half or two miles of Cohansey Town.
Witnesses: William Henson and his brother Isaac Goodin.

HOWELL, KATHERINE. Phila. Widow of Thomas Howell, lately deceased of West New Jersey.
August 17, 1695. October 4, 1695. A. 324.
Estate to youngest daughter Katherine, wife of James Robinson, the latter of whom is Executor. Legacies to eldest son Daniel Howell; second son Mordacay Howell; eldest daughter Miriam, wife of Henry Johnson; grand daughter Katherin Shout; son Daniel's daughter Hannah Howell.
Witnesses: Joshua Tittery, Millisent Hodgkins, Prudence West.

ARSE, JOHN.
11/2/1694. November 20, 1695. A. 325.
Estate to wife Mary who is Executrix and to son James. Legacies to daughters Hanna, Sarah and Mary Arse.
Witnesses: Joseph Fisher, Robert Adams, Peter Taylor.

LOFTUS, JOHN. Late of Chester Co., now of Phila. Planter.
6/31/1695. December 2, 1695. A. 324.
Legacies to John Hart late of Phila. but now of Bucks Co., yeoman; to James Jacobs of Phila., cordwainer; to Ann Pickering, widow, and to Rachell Furnis the daughter of Henry Furnis. Thomas Tress, Thomas

Pert, James Poulter and William Snowdon, John Gardiner of Phila. Co. and Robert Whitten of Chester Co.
Executors: Thomas Powell of Chester Co. and James Jacobs.
Witnesses: Samuell Robeson, Henry Furnis, James Wood.

LESTER, WILLIAM. Manor of Rockland, New Castle Co.
9/24/1691. November 5, 1695. A. 329.
Legacy to kinsman George Lester; friend Dorothy Cartwell; cousin Peter Lester. Friends Jacob Chandler and Valentin Hollingsworth. Daughter Mary Hunt. He gives Joan Richardson's estate left him to Henry Hollingsworth and George Robinson.
Overseers and Executors: Valentin Hollingsworth, Jacob Chandler and Henry Hollingsworth.
Witnesses: Thomas Hollingsworth, Samuell Hollingsworth, Wosa Torsey.

LESTER, GEORGE.
10/5/1694. December 14, 1695. A. 331.
Estate to kinsman Peter Lester who is sole Executor. Legacy to friend Mary Sharpley.
Witnesses: Mary Sharpley, Cor. Empson.

BEAKES, MARY. Widow of William of Bucks Co., PA
12/5/1694. February 28, 1695/6. A. 333.
Estate to four sons, William, Stephen, Samuel and Abraham Beakes.
Executors: Sons Stephen and Abraham.
Witnesses: Edward Lucas, Joseph Kirkbride, William Biles.

DAY, JOHN. Phila. Merchant.
8/15/1692. April 15, 1696. A. 334.
"Going to sea," estate to wife Hannah who gets the brick house standing in Delaware Front Street in which he lived. Oldest daughter Hannah a house and lot near Jarmartown, Phila., and a lot in front on the High Street, lying between the Sixth and Seventh Street from Delaware, and another lot on High Street between the Third and Fourth Street; daughter Grace and youngest daughter Sarah. Sister Margaret Cock and her daughter Mary, both in England, and cousin Hannah Gardiner's daughter Hannah. Land to the Quarterly Meeting to which he belonged on which to build a

Meeting House or a School. Land on Taconie Creek; Moore's Manor and Thomas Holme are mentioned.
Executors: John Parsons and wife, Hannah Day.
Witnesses: Richard Sutton, Margaret Scott.

PASCHALL, WILLIAM. Phila. Silversmith.
12/16/1695/6. April 29, 1696. A. 337.
Estate to wife Susanna nee Budd who is Executrix and son William. Legacies to parents Thomas and Joana Paschall. Mary and Rose Budd; John Budd, Senr. and Mary his wife; John Morrey's two sons, Humphrey and Thomas.
Witnesses: Henry Flower, Jno. Budd, Jr., Francis Cooke.

MALIN, WILLIAM. Upper Providence, Chester Co.
April 12, 1696. April 20, 1696. A. 339.
He was a Quaker. He died April 18, 1696. Nuncupative will. Estate to wife Ann and daughter Ann.
Trustees: Randle Malin and George Smedley.
Witnesses: Randle Malin, George Smedley, Wm. Edwards, all of whom were of Chester Co.

BOONE, ANDRES SWANSON. Phila. Co.
April 18, 1694. June 1, 1696. A. 339.
He desired to be buried at Wisoco. Estate to wife Anneka and children Sevan, Peter, Hance, Catherin, Neeles, Wolla, Margaret, Bridgett, Andres and Ambo. Calcoone Hook, Carcus Hook, Joseph Wood of Darby Township and Book Creek are mentioned.
Executors: His sons Swan and Peter.
Witnesses: Swan Boone, Peter Boone, Richard Longshore.

HOWELL, MARGARET. Merion Township, Phila. Co. Widow.
September 12, 1696. September 25, 1696. A. 341.
Brother James Mertimer; nephew James Mertimer; sister Margaret Thomas; cousin Betty Thomas; brothers-in-law David Jones and David Haubot; cousin James Mertimer(?); Lewis David; John Hastings; Kathrin Pris, her maid, "the residue of her time to be free;" Lewis Waker; to my negro, name not given; John Simons; Nathan Thomas; Owen Thomas; John, William and Ann Habart; Elizabeth and Katherine Thomas; Betty and Margaret Lewis; David Pugh; Mary Waker; Joan Pris; Mary, wife of Ben. Humphrey and her son Jon.

Humphrey; Mary, wife of David Moris; John Humphrey, Senr. and John Humphrey, Jr.; and legacies also to the meeting houses in Merion and Haverford.
Executors: Morris Lewellin and James Thomas, Jr.
Witnesses: Edward Jones, David Habard, John Humphreyes.

HOWELL, FRANCIS. Merion Township, Phila. Co. Yeoman.
1/15/1695. September 25, 1696. A. 344.
Wife Margaret who is sole Executrix. Brother Thomas, sisters Elizabeth, Margaret, Mary and Susan. Legacy to James Mortimer.
Witnesses: John Bevan, William Howell, John Humphreys.

SWANSON, SWAN. Wiecacoe, Phila. Co. Husbandman.
July 21, 1696. October 6, 1696. A. 346.
He desired to be buried at Wiecacoe. Wife Katherine to whom a legacy is given. Estate to daughters Bretta, wife of Swan Boon, Margaret, wife of John Cock, Jr., and two youngest daughters Barbara and Katherine Swanson who are yet unmarried. Two grandsons, Andrees Boon and Swan Cock. Legacy to the Swede's congregation at Wiecacoe of a piece of ground for a burying-place forever.
Overseers: Lassie Cock, Andrew Bankson, Neels Jones and Andrew Rambo.
Executors: Sons-in-law Swan Boon and John Cock, Jr.
Witnesses: Wm. Burge, Saml. Robeson, Pat. Robinson. Lasse Cock, John Swanson.

TERWOOD, THOMAS. Phila. Co. Yeoman.
December 13, 1696. January 12, 1696/7. A. 349.
Estate to Joseph Fisher, Jr. and to Mary and Martha Fisher. Legacies to William Beavan; John Barns and his wife whose name is not given; Joseph Wright, John Sankless; John Lewis and Joseph Fisher, Senr.
Executor: Friend Joseph Fisher, Senr.
Witnesses: Joseph Wright, George Fisher, Edward Farman.

WHITPAINE, JOHN.
February 8, 1696/7. February 15, 1696/7. A. 351.
"Minutes taken from John Whitpaine in order the making his will."
Estate to wife Content who is sole Executrix. Legacies to the three

children, whose names are not given, of brother Zachariah Whitpaine, deceased. Father, Richard Whitpaine.
Trustees: David Lloyd and John Budd, Jr.
Witnesses: John Budd, Thomas Mourry.

LYTELL, PETER, alias NEALLSON. Shakamakson, Phila. Co.
11/23/1691/2. March 10, 1696/7. A. 352.
Wife's name is not given. Estate to sons Andwiss and Hance Lytell. Legacies to daughters Anneca, Mallee and Breitta. Son Andrew.
Executors: brother Mybell Lytell, Otta Ernst Cock and my son Neals Lytell.
Witnesses: Swan Swanson, Wm. Preston.

DAVID, MORGAN. Merion Township, Phila. Co. Yeoman.
12/15/1694/5. 7/18/1695. A. 354.
Wife Catherine sole Executrix. Estate to two oldest sons John and Evan. Son David. Legacies to daughters Katherine and Elizabeth and to Meeting House in Haverford. Chistnot-well and Beech-well are mentioned.
Overseers: William Howell, Morris Llewelin, Francis Howell and David Laurence.
Witnesses: Robert Owen, Rowland Powell, John Humphreys.

WALKER, WILLIAM.
11/6/1693. May 24, 1697. A. 356.
"Intending to take a voyage to England." Estate to wife Elizabeth who is sole Executrix and to daughter Elizabeth.
Witnesses: Richard Johns, Thomas Duckett, Saml. Jenings.

COPE, OLIVER. Now of New Castle Co.
3/25/1697. June 10, 1697. A. 357.
Estate to wife Rebeca who is sole Executrix and to children Elisabeth and Ruth, William and John.
Trustees: John Buckley and Richard Buffington.
Witnesses: Jeremiah Collett, Hance Justice, John Childe, John Prien, Joan Pren, Rebecca Cope.

WALKER, ELIZABETH. Phila. Widow.
5/24/1697. August 14, 1697. A. 361.

Estate to her only daughter Elizabeth Walker. Legacies to brother William Reynolds of Winsberry in Cherbury Parish, County Shropshire; to the children, whose names are not given, of my other brother John Reynolds; and the children, whose names are not given, of my sister Joan Llewelin; and my sister Susanah Baskus' children, whose names are not given, and to the Monthly Meeting of Phila. for "the service of truth." Also to Samuel, John and Hannah Carpenter, children of Samuel Carpenter of Phila. my ancestor.
Executors: Samuel Carpenter and James Fox, both of Phila.
Witnesses: Joan Forrest, Ann Hasketh.

WALKER, JOSEPH. Phila. Skinner.
August 10, 1697. September 1, 1697. A. 363.
Estate to wife Margaret and to children Joseph and Sarah. Legacy to Thomas Boyer of Phila., turner.
Executors: His wife and son Joseph.
Overseers: Francis Cook and Able Noble.
Witnesses: Seemercy Adams, John Moore, Michal Ganolin, Hugh Bawdin.

BEARDSLY, ALEXANDER. Phila.
12/18/1696/7. October 12, 1697. A. 365.
Estate to wife Margaret who is sole Executrix, and to grandson George Gray the oldest son of my daughter Mary Gray and to grandson Joseph Gray.
Witnesses: Rachell Preston, Robert Owen, David Lloyd.

HAYS, RICHARD, SENR. Haverford Township, Chester Co., PA
8/4/1697. October 30, 1697. A. 366.
Estate to wife Issat and to son Richard who are the Executors. Legacies to son John; cousin Sarah James and to the Meeting House in Haverford.
Trustees: David Lawrence and Roland Powell.
Witnesses: William Jenkins, Adam Roades, William Howell, Henry Lewis, Samuel Lewis.

MURROW, GABRAEL. Bucks Co., PA Widow and relict of Peter Murrow.
October 15, 1697. November 10, 1697. A. 368.

Estate to son Peter and daughter Hannah Morrow, and to friends Peter Resnier, shipwright, and Thomas Bibb, blacksmith, both of Burlington. Legacies to daughters Elizabeth Poynsett and Mary Carter.
Executors: Peter Resnier and Thomas Bibb.
Witnesses: Embling Dugliss, Mary Bowne.

EWER, ROBERT. Phila. Merchant.
5/5/1697. December 11, 1697. A. 370.
Whole estate to wife Mary who is Executrix with her father Daniel Wills and Nathan Stanberry, who are joint Executors. Legacies to the poor of the Quakers of Phila. to be disposed of by the Monthly Meeting; to Little Rose, the Dutch girl and to her mother whose name is not given, and to Joseph Phips' three children whose names are not given.
Witnesses: Edward Shippen, Albertus Brandt.

THATCHER, RICHARD. Bucks Co., PA Husbandman.
October 13, 1690. December 24, 1697. A. 372.
Wife's name is not given. Estate to sons Bartholomew, Joseph and Amos. Legacies to eldest son Richard and to daughters Sarah, Rachel, Martha and Mary Thatcher. Phineas Pemberton is mentioned.
Executors: Sons Bartholomew, Joseph and Amos Thatcher.
Witnesses: Thomas Stackhouse and Israel Taylor.

WHITEHEAD, BENJAMIN. Phila.
February 13,1697/8. February 18, 1697/8. A. 374.
Estate to daughter Esther and youngest daughter, Elizabeth. Wife's name is not given.
Executors: John Arrowsmith and John Murry.
Witnesses: Thomas Tresse, Anthony Taylor, Jacob Willis.

FREELAND, WILLIAM. Phila.
12/23/1697/8. March 18, 1697/8. A. 376.
Estate to wife Esther who is sole Executrix and to daughters Susanna and Rebecca Freeland. Brother Joseph Willcox of Phila. is adviser to wife.
Witnesses: Charles Sober, John Craven, John McComb, Joseph Willcox.

GOSS, CHARLES. Phila. Merchant.
June 21, 1697. March 18, 1697/8. A. 378.
Estate to Elizabeth Hooten, widow, who is sole Executrix. Legacies to Mary Bradshall, widow, and to John Crapp.
Witnesses: John Test, Samuel Holt, Charles French, Thomas Tresse.

BOWEN, JOHN. Phila.
11/3/1697. March 19, 1697/8. A. 379.
Estate to cousin Margaret Mathews who is sole Executrix. Legacy to cousin Henry Bowen. Joseph Growden is mentioned.
Witnesses: John Jennett, Robert Tate, Nathaniel Harding, Jno. Persones.

MORA, GILES. Phila. Widow of James Mora.
February 9, 1697. March 20, 1697/8. A. 381.
Estate to Thomas Tress, James Porter and John McComb who are also the Executors. Dorcus Johnson is mentioned.
Witnesses: Jacob Turner, John Bowyer, Dorcus Johnstown, Elizabeth Tate.

MEDLICOTT, DAVID. Near Haverford, PA
7/16/1688. March 20, 1697/8. A. 382.
Estate to wife Martha who is sole Executrix and to daughter Mary Medlicott. He held an estate "near Skoolkill beyond the gulff."
Overseers: Edward Jones, Francis Howell to whom legacies are given.
Witnesses: Stephen Evans, John Roberts, Daniel Meredith.

BUDD, THOMAS. Phila. Merchant.
February 9, 1697/8. March 25, 1697/8. A. 384.
Estate to wife Susannah and to children Thomas Budd, Mary Budd £200, Rose Budd £200, and John Budd.
Executors: Wife and son John.
Witnesses: John Langstaff, Thomas Atkinsen, Sarah Atkinsen, William Budd.

LYNAM, JOHN. Phila.
1/29/1698. April 8, 1698. A. 386.
Estate to John Kinsy, carpenter and Ralph Jackson, locksmith, both of Phila. who are the Executors. Legacies to the Monthly Meeting of

Phila. for a free school for the children of poor Quakers; Richard Hoskins, Thomas Ducket; William Forest; Jane Brintnall; Thomas Fitzwater; John Lynam my brother's name not given; son, Thomas Lynam and his sister Elizabeth; Thomas Zachary; William Gabitas; and Hannah Emlen.
Witnesses: John Davis, Elnathan Zane.

LEAKIN, ANN. Phila. Widow.
January 29, 1697/8. April 12, 1698. A. 390.
Whole estate to grand-daughter Elizabeth Casson, late of England and now of this Province, spinster. Letters of administration were granted to Elizabeth Cason.
Witnesses: Thomas Paschall, Ambrose Brandfield, Pat. Robinson.

WATTS, JOHN. Phila. Butcher.
1/22/1697/8. April 14, 1698. A. 392.
Whole estate to wife Hester who is sole Executrix. Legacy to Mary Johnson, daughter of Richard Johnson of Salem Town. Jasper Yeates of Upland is mentioned. He held estates in New Castle County and in West Jersey.
Witnesses: Isaiah Degan, Grace Edgar, William Alloway.

KING, JOHN. Mohomensing, Phila. Co. Mariner.
2/7/1698. April 15, 1698. A. 393.
Estate to wife Mary who is sole Executrix and to children John and Love King. Legacies to kinsman Thomas King and to Nathaniel Puckle and his wife Ann. [There is a detailed estimate of testator's estate appended to the will.]
Advisers: Samuel Harrison, John Crapp and Joseph Pidgeon.
Witnesses: Jos. Pidgeon, Jno. Crapp, Thomas Budd.

ANDREWS, THOMAS. Phila.
1/29/1698. April 20, 1698. A. 397.
Estate to wife Elizabeth who is sole Executrix and to children Simon and Ellen. Jane Moore, a property owner, is mentioned.
Overseer: Brother Edward Rees.
Witnesses: Jane Moore, Anthony Moore, Thomas Jones.

CROSSE, THOMAS.
April 7, 1698. April 19, 1698. A. 399.

Legacies to Thomas Kendall and Joseph Adams for the use "of our Meeting at Burlington;" daughter-in-law Abigail; sons-in-law Jonathan and Thomas Curtis, and to the children, whose names are not given, of William Atkinson. [The original will is filed at Trenton, N. J.]
Executors: George Deacon and Daniel Leeds, who also receive legacies.
Witnesses: Thomas Brian, Joseph Collins, William Atkinson.

HUTCHESON, GEORGE. Phila. Merchant.
2/29/1698. May 9, 1698. A. 400.
Wife's name is not given. Estate to daughter Rachell who is young and unmarried; daughter Mary Standfield of Phila.; daughter Elizabeth Peeres of Burlington and her two children named Mary and Martha; daughter Martha's child named Mary; son James Stanfield of Phila., and to the children, whose names are not given, of my son Samuel in England. Friends Susanah Turner and Elizabeth Bacon, widow, of West Jersey are mentioned. [Charles Read formally withdrew as Executor for reasons given.]
Executors: Son James Stanfield and friend Charles Read.
Witnesses: Francis Cooke, Joseph Willcox, Thomas Budd, Mary Brodwell, Mary Pearse.

STIDMAN, JOSEPH. Springfield, Chester Co., PA Husbandman.
10/8/1694. May 12, 1698. A. 403.
Estate to wife Margaret who is sole Executrix. Legacies to brother John Stidman; brother-in-law Thomas Pullford my wife's brother; sister Sarah, wife of Peter Thomas; natural mother Elizabeth Stidman. Servant William Beans, Bartholomew Coppock is mentioned.
Witnesses: John Hood, Senr., George Maris, Bartholomew Coppock.

DEACON, JOHN. Phila., late of Barbados.
3/9/1698. May 20, 1698. A. 405.
Estate to wife Ann who is sole Executrix. Cousin William Deacon, wife's daughter Ann Curtis. He held a plantation called All-Corn in Christ Church Parish in Barbados. [The original will is missing.]
Witnesses: Richard Sandford, Herbert Corric, Stephen Coleman.

TRENT, JAMES. Inverness, Murryshire, Scotland. Merchant.
October 30, 1697. July 29, 1698. A. 407.
At present in the Province of PA, intending a voyage to sea. Whole estate to brother William Trent of Phila. who is sole Executor. Edward Burwash, commander of the ship Charles; Thomas Courts of London, merchant; Patrick Coutts of Edinburgh, Scotland, merchant, and David Amya of Gottenburgh, Sweden, merchant are mentioned. [The original will is missing.]
Witnesses: John Farmer, John Moore, John Jones, Rebeckah Moore.

HODGSKINSON, JOHN. Chester Co. Tailor.
11/2/1694/5. August 15, 1698. A. 409.
Estate to wife Mary and children John and Hannah Hodgskinson. Legacies to sister Frances Hodgskinson; wife's sister Hannah Ashton; friend John Wood of West Jersey.
Executors: Wife with John Simcock, the elder; Thomas Vernon, the elder; Walter Faucett and Caleb Pusey, all of Chester Co.
Witnesses: Geo. Forman, Robert Barbar.

WADE, ROBERT. Essex House (the name of his plantation), Chester Co., PA
5/9/1698. August 15, 1698. A. 412.
Whole estate to wife Lidia who is sole Executrix. Legacies to the Free School at Phila. to be paid to the Monthly Meeting in Phila.; to brothers Thomas and John Wade; to the children, whose names are not given, of Thomas Wade excepting Robert and Lidia Wade (children of the said Thomas Wade) "who are sent for into this Province of Penns.;" to sister Rachell's two daughters, whose names are not given, in England.
Overseers: Kinsman John Jones of Phila., merchant; and friend Jacob Chandler of Chichester Township, Chester Co.; to both of whom legacies are given.
Witnesses: John Martin, Thomas England.

HICKMAN, ELIZABETH. Thornbury Township, Chester Co. Widow.
2/18/1698. September 16, 1698. A. 414.
Estate to sons Joseph, who is sole Executor, and Benjamin Hickman. Legacies to son Robert Chamberlyne; to daughter Sarah and her husband Richard Arnold; to daughter Mary and her husband Joseph

Edwards; to daughter Hannah and her husband Robert Way; to daughter Joan and her husband Charles Joanes, and to son-in-law Richard Rigeway.
Trustees: Friends George Peirse and Nicholas Pyle.
Witnesses: John Mendenhall, George Strode.

WATTS, HESTER. Phila. Widow.
6/27/1698. October 1, 1698. A. 416.
Estate to son John Murrey. Legacies to her brother William Alloway and his wife Elizabeth and their children William and Sarah Alloway; to friends Rodger Wootton of New Castle and John Parsons.
Executors and Trustees: Brother William Alloway and friend John Parsons.
Witnesses: William Johnson, Jemimum Moore, Ann Barrat.

COX, ABRAHAM.
8/26/1697. October 10, 1698. A. 418.
Estate to wife Sarah, who is sole Executrix, and to sons Abraham and Thomas Cox.
Trustees: Edmund Lovett and Joseph Kirkbride.
Witnesses: Edmund Lovett, Martha Lovett, Joseph Kirkbride.

PRICHARD, THOMAS. Phila. Cordwainer.
1/29/1698. November 1, 1698. A. 419.
Estate to wife Barbara and sons Mathew and Benjamin Prichard. Legacies to son John and daughters Ann, Jane and Martha. A lot fronting in Strawberry Alley is mentioned.
Executors: Wife and son Mathew.
Witnesses: Mathew Bellis, Jon. Kinsy.

RICHARDS, PHILIP. Phila. Merchant.
January 2, 1697/8. November 9, 1698. A. 421.
Estate to wife Mary who is sole Executrix and to my children by my said wife Mary, Joseph, Mary and Elizabeth. Charles Reade is mentioned.
Overseers: James Fox and Nathan Stanbury.
Witnesses: Phillip James, David Lloyd, Caspar Hoedt.

RAMBO, PETER, SENR. Phila.
August 30, 1694. November 19, 1698. A. 423.

To be buried at Wisoco. Wife's name is not given. Estate to children Gunner, John, Andres and Peter Rambo; Gertrue wife of Andres Banckson; Katherin wife of Peter Dalbo. Lands in West New Jersey on Homons Creek and in Little Mantass Creek, and land lying opposite to Pasayunck Township on the west side of the Schuylkill are mentioned.
Sole Executor: Son Andres Rambo.
Witnesses: Lasse Cock, Mathias Holstein, R. Longshore.

BOURDETT, PETER.
November 7, 1698. November 29, 1698 - New York, and December 5, 1698 - Phila. A. 426.
Estate to father Stephen Bourdett and to brother Samuel who is sole Executor. Other brothers and their children, all of whose names are not given, are mentioned. [This will does not seem to have been signed nor witnessed. The original will is missing.]

WRIGHT, ELIZABETH. Late of Ashford in the Water, Darbyshire, England, now of PA Widow.
July 28, 1698. December 14, 1698. A. 427.
Whole estate to friend John Moon of Phila., brewer who is sole heir and Executor.
Witnesses: Samuel Lambert, Samuel Weaver, Senr.

LIVZEY, JONATHAN. Dublin Township, Phila. Co.
8/31/1698. December 17, 1698. A. 429.
Estate to wife Rachell, who is Executrix, and to children Thomas, Jonathan and David Livzey. Legacies to daughters Mary, Martha and Rachell Livzey. Father, Thomas Livzey.
Trustees: Arthur Cooke, William Preston and Edmond Orpwood.
Witnesses: Richard Worell, John Mierick.

WARDEN, WILLIAM. Phila. Merchant.
December 26, 1698. January 7, 1698/9. A. 433.
Legacies to mother Mary Warden; to sisters Mary and Orian Warden; to brother Benjamin Hamden; to Charles Sober and his wife Ann and their children Thomas, John and Ann Sober; to Sarah Daniell; to Sarah Dwesbury and her sister Elizabeth Dwesbury; to William Tapshare; Richard Sandford; to Mrs. Rebecka Gibbs and her sister Jones; to Frances daughter of Robert Hall; Thomas Clayton.

Sole Executor: Friend Charles Sober.
Witnesses: William Tapshore, Joseph Cooke, Richard Sandford.

METCALFE, JAMES. Now of Island of Barbados. Merchant.
June 11, 1697. October 26, 1697 - Barbados, and January 9, 1698/9 - Phila. A. 436.
Whole estate in America to wife Elizabeth who is Executrix of that portion. Legacies to brother Nicholas Metcalfe of Glandford-Bridge, Lincolnshire, England who is Executor in England; to nephew William Sibsy, son of sister Elizabeth and William Sibsy late of Lincolne, deceased, her husband who had two other children whose names are not given; to sister Ann Bristoll; to nephews William, James and Peter, sons of brother William Metcalfe of Glandford-Bridge, Lincolnshire, England; to sister Hannah; to sister Mary Sibsy and to Benjamin Knight. George McKinzie of Barbados, merchant; George Joland(?) of Glandford-Bridge, Lincolnshire; William Bolton; Slevp Dolphin, Nicholas Andrews, Master; Joseph Geates of PA, merchant. Ship Unity and sloop Philadelphia whose masters are not given, are mentioned. [The original will is missing.]
Witnesses: Elizabeth Dearsley, John Rye, Bridget Edgerton.

YOUNG, JACOB. Late of Shackamanon, Phila. Co. Schoolmaster.
April 11, 1686. May 12, 1698. A. 439.
Nuncupative will. Deceased on or about April 11, 1686. Katharine, the companion or reputed wife of Jacob Young, who married soon after Jacob Young's death, John Tank. Whole estate "to our girl Hester Young whom I have brought up," who afterward married Robert Wilkins.
Witnesses: Michell Nelson alias Leyken, Guner Rambo.

FLECKNE, JOHN. Phila. Carpenter.
January 14, 1698/9. January 21, 1698/9. A. 442.
Whole estate to wife Elizabeth who is sole Executrix.
Adviser: Friend John Hayword.
Witnesses: Richard Iles, Thomas Hall, Samuel Weaver, Senr.

COEBURNE, THOMAS. Middletown, Chester Co., PA Carpenter.
3/21/1697. March 6, 1698/9. A. 444.
Wife's name is not given. Son Joseph Coeburne and Susanna his wife who had two sons and a daughter whose names are not given;

daughter Ann Butler in Virginia; daughter Martha and her husband Daniel Ridge and their son Thomas; son Thomas Coeburne in Ireland; daughter Cisely and her husband Francis Baldwin and son William and four other children whose names are not given; son William Coeburne and Mary his wife and son Samuel and three other children whose names are not given; daughter Mary and her husband William Cureton and their two daughters whose names are not given. Caleb Pusey and Joseph Baker are mentioned in connection with property sales.
Executors: Sons William and Joseph Coeburne.
Overseers: Jacob Chandler and John Beal to both of whom a legacy is given.
Witnesses: William Browne, Richard Woodward, Dinah Chuckman.

MILTON, THOMAS. Late of New York, now in London.
October 6, 1697. October 15, 1698 - New York and October 19, 1698 - Phila. A. 445.
Estate to wife Christian who is sole Executrix. Legacies to eldest brother Peter Milton and brother William Milton. [No witnesses are given, and the original will is missing.]

NEWLIN, NICHOLAS. Concord Township, Chester Co. Yeoman.
2/8/1699. June 5, 1699. A. 446.
Wife Elizabeth; son Nathaniel Newlin; son Nicholas Newlin who had a son Nicholas. Legacies to daughter Elisabeth who seems to be living elsewhere; daughter Rachell; sons-in-law Ephraim Jackson and William Paggett. Estate to son Nathaniel who is sole Executor.
Witnesses: Edward Kinnison, Nicoles Pile, Thomas King.

LAWRENCE, DAVID. Haverford Township, PA
2/12/1699. July 1, 1699. A. 449.
Estate to wife Ellinor and eldest son Daniel who are the Executors. Sons Henry and Thomas Lawrence, and daughters Margaret, Ellinor and Rachell Lawrence.
Overseers: Brothers Ellis Ellis, Humphry Ellis and William Howell.
Witnesses: John Roberts, Rowland Powell, John Bevan.

ROWE, WILLIAM. Haverford Township, Chester Co.
3/8/1699. July 1, 1699. A. 452.
Wife's name is not given. Estate to daughter Grace Rowe. Legacies to Haverford Meeting House; to Daniel Lawrence and to Rowland Howell.
Executors: Friends Rowland Ellis and Thomas Paschal.
Guardians of daughter: John Lewis, David Maurice and Henry Lewis.
Witnesses: John Roberts, Daniel Humphrey, Lewis Waker.

MAHONY, CORNELIUS. Phila., late of Maryland. Merchant.
2/9/1699. August 4, 1699. A. 454.
Estate to the Free School, the poor and the Meeting House as Friends shall see convenient. Legacies to Stephen Coleman of Phila., glover, who is Executor, and Sarah his wife and their daughters Rebecca and Sarah Coleman; to Henry Hosier son of Henry Hosier of Kent Co., Maryland, and his daughters Joanna, Mary and Rebecca, the latter being the youngest; and to Joyce Quincy of Cecil Co., Maryland, widow.
Witnesses: Randall Spakeman, James Jacob, John Paine.

THOMAS, JAMES. Merion Township, Phila. Co.
2/8/1699. August 10, 1699. A. 456.
Estate to wife Margaret and sons Thomas and Nathan. Legacies to son Owen and daughters Elizabeth and Catherine; to grand-children Nathan and Ann;' to brother-in-law David Jones and to the Meeting House at Haverford, at Merion and at Radnor. Brother-in-law Thomas Howell, and Duffsyn Maur are mentioned.
Executors: Wife Margaret and son Nathan Thomas.
Witnesses: Lewis David, Rowland Ellis.

ADIE, PATRICK. Late of Boston, now of Phila. Merchant.
April 7, 1699. August 15, 1699. A. 459.
"Being bound to the Island of Barbados," estate to wife Catherine now in London, who is Executrix of his estate in England and to son James.
Executors: William Geddes of Barbados, merchant, for his estate there, and Pat. Robinson for his estate in PA
Witnesses: David Giffing, Duncan Garrock.

COLEMAN, STEPHEN. Phila. Glover.
6/15/1699. August 21, 1699. A. 460.
Whole estate to wife Sarah who is sole Executrix, and legacies to two young children whose names are not given.
Advisers: The Friends of the Monthly Meeting of Phila.
Witnesses: Samuel Carpenter, John Buzby, Robert Burrow, George Fox, David Brintnall.

JONES, ROBERT. Phila. Blacksmith.
August 15, 1699. August 25, 1699. A. 463.
Estate to wife Charity who is sole Executrix and daughter Charity, and in the event of the latter's death to the sons, whose names are not given, of his brothers John and Samuel Jones living near West Chester in England. Legacy to the Public School of the Monthly Meeting in Phila. Friend Hannah Delavale, widow, is mentioned.
Guardians of daughter: Isaac Norris, Abraham Hooper and John Williamson.
Supervisors: Friends John Williamson and Henry Mellows.
Witnesses: Samuel Carpenter, Nicholas Nixon, Margaret Morris, Samuel Weaver, Senr. and James Cooper.

ASHTON, ISAAC. Phila. Cooper.
6/13/1699. September 1, 1699. A. 468.
Estate to "intended wife" Elizabeth Richardson and her brother William Hudson of Phila., tanner, who are the Executors. (The latter afterward renounced his executorship.) Legacy to his mother whose name is not given.
Witnesses: Joseph Jones, Eliz. Killcop, Francis Cooke.

BURDETT, MATHEW. Late of Neither Denbrigh, Yorkshire, England.
August 1, 1699. September 5, 1699. A. 470.
Estate to friend Thomas Corbine of Liverpool now boatswain of the Brittania bound for PA Legacy to friend Richard Smyth, late of Yorkshire, England.
Executors: Richard Smyth and Thomas Musgreave.
Witnesses: Timothy Hudson, Benjamin Smithson, Henry Cooper, Richard Wright.

ATKINSON, CHRISTOPHER. Late of Scotforth, Lancashire. Husbandman.
July 1, 1699. September 6, 1699. A. 472.
Estate to wife Margaret who is sole Executrix and children William Hannah, Margaret and Isabell Atkinson and a child unborn. He held property in the vessel Britania.
Witnesses: Thomas Musgreave, John Scott, George Godsalie.

FOX, GEORGE. Phila. Merchant.
7/3/1699. September 7, 1699. A. 474.
Estate to wife Susannah and son Joseph. Legacy to "the Publick School lately erected or ordered so to be at Phila."
Executors: His wife Susannah and his father James Fox.
Witnesses: Justinian Fox, Eliz. Hibert, James Fox, Junr.

FOX, THOMAS. Darby, Chester Co. Yeoman.
6/31/1699. September 8, 1699. A. 477.
Estate to nephew William Cooke and to nieces Grace Hollingsworth, Elizabeth Gregg and Hanna Holborn all being the children of his sister Elisabeth Parke and all of whom with their mother are Executors. He had "an interest in a certain Island lying in Darby Creek," and widow Bartram are mentioned.
Trustees: Thomas Smith, yeoman, and James Cooper, clothmaker, both of Darby.
Witnesses: John Bethall, Richard Parker.

SMITH, JOHN. Chippin.
July 29, 1699. September 9, 1699. A. 479.
Estate to wife Ellen and children Joseph, Ruth, Isaac, Timothy, Robert, Ann and Margaret Smith.
Executors: James Dillworth of Phila. and John Scott lately of the Hill in Yorkshire, England, and now on board the Britania.
Witnesses: Timothy Hudson, George Clough, William Braken.

SMITH, THOMAS. Phila. Merchant.
7/3/1699. September 8, 1699. A. 482.
Estate to son Thomas Smith who is sole Executor. Legacies to daughter Ann Mears and to grand-daughter Mary Mears; to daughter-in-law Sarah Harding; to Francis Harding son of Nathaniel Harding. He held an estate in Chester Co.

Witnesses: Samuel Powell, Emanuell Walker, Margaret Walke[r], John Parsons.

HARDING, NATHANIEL. Phila. Basket-maker.
6/13/1699. September 9, 1699. A. 484.
Estate to wife Sarah who is sole Executrix and to son Francis. Legacies to wife's son Jacob Usher and to the Free School of the Monthly Meeting of Phila. He held an estate on the Delaware River near the mouth of Neshaminy Creek in Bucks Co., PA
Witnesses: Eliz. Knowles, Thomas Smith, Junr., John Parsons.

SMITH, THOMAS.
7/9/1699. September 9, 1699. A. 487.
Son and sole Executor of my father Thomas Smith, deceased. Estate to sister-in-law Sarah Harding who is sole Executrix. Legacies to sister Ann Meers; to Francis Harding and to the Monthly Meeting of Friends.
Witnesses: Isaac Norris, Anthony Morris, Jacob Usher, Daniell Radley.

MORRIS, DANIEL AND ELCE.
6/29/1699. September 13, 1699. A. 489.
He and his wife being members of the Church of Warrington. He lately died at sea on board the Britannia, Richard Nicholas, Commander, while on a voyage from Liverpool to Phila. The will is in the form of a letter. He named no Executors. Estate to his children (there seem to have been two) whose names are not given, or to his father-in-law John Hilldidge of Morton, Cheshire, or in the event of their death to the Church at Warrington. Letters of administration were granted to Thomas Bibb and Nathaniel Douglas.
Guardians of children: John Brookes, Richard Smith and Alexander Baines.
Witnesses: Samuel Eaton, Jonathan Higginson.

COOKE, DANIEL. Phila. Carpenter.
September 8, 1699. September 13, 1699. A. 492.
Wife's name is not given. Estate to son Thomas Cooke or in the event of his death to his wife's son John Emlen in England. Legacies to John Watts and to my man James Sheaphard.

Executors: John Farmer, watchmaker, and Joseph Kirle, Mariner, both of Phila. and to whom a legacy is given.
Witnesses: William Hearn, Nicholas Rideout, Thomas Rogers.

DUCKETT, THOMAS. Phila. Malster.
3/20/1699. June 24, 1700. A. 494.
Estate to wife Ruth who is sole Executrix, to daughter Jane Duckett and to daughter-in-law Ruth Wood. Legacies to sons-in-law James and John Wood; to Lucy Hendricks; to cousin Mary the daughter of Nathaniel Duckett and to the Monthly Meeting of Phila. for building and maintaining a free school in Phila. David Lloyd, Isaac Norris, William Salway and property in Shippen and fronting on Schulkill River are mentioned.
Witnesses: Joseph Kirkhide, Jonathan Scaife, John Smith, Phineas Pemberton.

LEE, LAWRENCE. Late of Crosstone, Yorkshire, England.
7/8/1699. September 15, 1699. A. 497.
Wife's name is not given. Estate to cousin Elisabeth Pickup. Wife's brother Antony Dixon of Crosstone, Yorkshire. William Southebe's wife is mentioned but her name is not given.
Executors: Friends William Southebe, Thomas Redman and "my servant" Robert Shaw to each of whom a legacy is given beside the freedom of the last named Executor.
Witnesses: Thomas Langstone, William Fisher.

BONSALL, RICHARD. Darby, Chester Co., PA Yeoman.
7/12/1699. September 15, 1699. A. 500.
He died September 13, 1699. Nuncupative will. Estate to his children whose names are not given. [The original will is missing.]
Witnesses: John Wood, Michael Blunston, John Hood, Senr., Thomas Smith.

COX, ANN. Phila. Widow.
August 3, 1699. September 18, 1699. A. 502.
Estate to her daughter Elizabeth Shephard, widow who is sole Executrix. Legacies to son William Trotter; to daughter Ann Thompson wife of George Thompson; to Thomas Clayton of Phila., clerk; to John Arrowsmith of Phila.; to Elizabeth Hooton of Phila., widow; to Mary Broadshaw, widow; to John Duplouvys, merchant and

to John Farmer, watchmaker. The last two named are appointed Trustees. [The original will is missing.]
Witnesses: Robert Snead, Samuel Robeson, Thomas Clarke.

STANFIELD, JAMES. Phila. Merchant.
September 1, 1699. September 27, 1699. A. 505.
Estate to sisters Mary, Sarah, Elisabeth, Grace, Hannah and Deborah. Legacy to Rachell Hutcheson daughter of George Hutcheson my father-in-law, deceased; to the two children, whose names are not given, of Thomas Budd of Phila., cooper; to Mary daughter of John Pearce of Burlington; to Thomas Clayton of Phila., minister; to friend Mary King, widow; to Dinah Burden "who is now attending me;" to friends Charles Read, Joseph Willcox and John Budd, Jr., all of Phila. who are the Overseers.
Executor: Brother Francis Chads of Chester Co., PA
Witnesses: Seemercy Adams, Peter Boss, Jr., Thomas Budd.

DUPLOUVYS, JOHN. Phila. Merchant.
September 14, 1699. September 27, 1699. A. 508.
Estate to wife Wainkey who is executrix and after her decease John Vanlear of Phila., barber, is to be the Executor. Brother Abraham and sister Mary Duplouvys in Holland. Sophia Bokrenagen.
Witnesses: John Crapp, William Hall, H. Grahame.

BUDD, THOMAS. Phila. Cooper.
September 19, 1699. October 5, 1699. A. 511.
Estate to wife Martha who is Executrix and children Mary and George Budd and a child unborn.
Trustees: Brother John Budd, Charles Reade and Joseph Willcox.
Witnesses: John Crapp, H. Grahame, Charles Plumly.

COOK, ARTHUR. Phila. Co.
7/30/1699. 8/7/1699. A. 573.
Estate to wife Margaret who is sole Executrix and children eldest son John and his five children whose names are not given, sons Thomas, Joseph and Benjamin, and daughters Sarah and Priscilla. He held an estate at Little Egg Harbour in West Jersey.
Witnesses: Griffith Jones, Jane Jones, William Preston.

MORRIS, MARY. Widow of Anthony Morris of Phila., and formerly widow of Thomas Coddington of Rhoad Island.
7/25/1699. October 7, 1699. A. 516.
Daughter Mary Coddington; son William Coddington, deceased; brother John Howard of Phila.
Executor: Brother Edward Shippen of Phila.
Witnesses: Rebekah Shippen, Elisabeth Knowles, Rachel Reeves.

COX, SARAH. Phila. Widow.
7/11/1699. October 8, 1699. A. 518.
Estate to sons Abraham and Thomas who are the Executors. During the minority of her sons, Pentecost Teague and John Buzby are to be the Executors. Legacy to the Monthly Meeting in Phila. "for the maintenance of the Publick School intended to be set up."
Witnesses: William Forrest, William Hudson, Samuel Carpenter.

RICHARDS, MARY. Phila. Widow.
7/23/1699. October 9, 1699. A. 521.
Estate to children Joseph and Mary. Legacy to sister Elizabeth Bassett and to the Quakers in Phila. for the maintenance of the Publick School lately erected by them. Anthony Morris, Joshua Carpenter and William Dugglass, merchant are mentioned in connection with property in Phila.
Executors: Friends Edward Shippen, Isaac Norris and Nathan Stanbury, and a legacy to the first two named.
Witnesses: Thomas Makin, Caspar Hoot, Elizabeth Fox.
September 27, 1699 - Codicil. Legacy to each of the three children, whose names are not given, of her sister Elizabeth Bassett.
Witnesses: Susanna Harwood, Sarah Densey, David Lloyd.

FOX, JAMES. Phila. Baker.
7/4/1699. October 10, 1699. A. 525.
Estate to wife Elizabeth and children James, Francis and Elizabeth. Legacy to daughter Sarah; to grandson Joseph son of George and Susannah Fox; to the Publick School of the Phila. Monthly Meeting. [The original will is missing.]
Executors: Wife and son James.
Overseers: Friends Samuel Carpenter, David Lloyd and Isaac Norris.
Witnesses: William Harwood, Ralph Jackson, Thomas Wharton.
7/8/1699 - Codicil. His son George's just debts are to be paid.

BRUER, ROBERT. Late of Bumley, Lancashire. Blacksmith.
August 2, 1699. October 10, 1699. A. 528.
Nephew Henry Whitiker of Liverpool who belongs to the sugar-house, who had children John, eldest daughter Margaret Whitiker and youngest daughter Mary Whitiker. Legacy for poor widows and fatherless children "of the people who are for scorn called Quakers." Signed on board the Bretaine of Liverpool [for Phila.]
Executors: Thomas Musgrave, Lawrance Lee, George Clough, Benjamin Smithson and Richard Smith.
Witnesses: Jonathan Higginson, Thomas Lare, Sampson Ford.

SMITHSON, BENJAMIN. Late of Areton, Yorkshire.
6/18/1699. October 11, 1699. A. 530.
Legacy to Mary Hindes of what was left him by Alice Kinerley lately deceased; to Mary Atkinson; to Elisabeth Musgrave; to his servant Jane Shelton and to Richard Smith who is the Executor. Kinsman Thomas Smithson at Langbur near Skipton in Craven. Signed on board the Britannia of Liverpool, Richard Nicholas, commander, bound for Pennsylvania.
Witnesses: Timothy Hudson, Jonathan Couper, Richard Smith.

ALLOWAY, WILLIAM. Phila. Tallow-chandler.
6/30/1699. October 12, 1699. A. 532.
Estate to wife Elizabeth and oldest son William, son John and daughter Sarah. Legacy to the Monthly Meeting of Quakers in Phila.
Executors: Friends William Southbee and John Parsons.
Witnesses: Samuel Powell, Francis Richardson, Rachell Minshell.

BUZBY, JOHN. Phila. Weaver.
8/3/1699. October 12, 1699. A. 535.
Estate to his father and mother John and Mary Buzby; to brothers William, Edward, Richard and Nicholas Buzby; to sisters Mary Hunt, Elizabeth Davis, Sarah Tomlinson and my wife's brother Joseph Taylor. Wife's name is not given.
Executors: Brothers William, Edward and Richard Buzby.
Witnesses: Pentycost Teage, William Forrest, Elizabeth Knowles, Samuel Siddon, Sue Bellonge.

CHICK, JAMES. Phila. Joiner.
September 21, 1699. October 13, 1699. A. 537.

Estate to wife Damaris who is Executrix, and daughter Lydia and a child unborn; and in the event of their death to brother Robert Chick of Cullumpton in Devonshire.
Overseers: Thomas Pearce, Nicholas Pearce and John Harrison.
Witnesses: Richard Sutton, Arthur Welles, Henry Preston.

ROBESON, SAMUEL. Phila.
September 21, 1699. October 15, 1699. A. 539.
Estate to uncles or father's brothers Thomas and David Robeson living in Scotland. Legacy to Mrs. Sarah Dyer; to Elizabeth daughter of Elizabeth Shepherd; to friend Nicholas Webb; to Septimus the youngest son of Patrick Robinson of Phila. and to Mary Hart my maid. [The original will is missing.]
Executors: Friend Patrick Robinson and cousin Andrew Robeson of West Jersey.
Witnesses: Robert Snead, Hugh Grahame.

SANDERS, CHARLES. Phila. Merchant.
7/30/1698. October 16, 1699. A. 544.
Estate to wife Sarah who is sole Executrix and to child or children unborn. Nephews Charles and John Sanders sons of his brother William Sanders of London.
Trustees: Friends William Clark, Patrick Robinson and Samuel Buckley.
Witnesses: Robert Webb, Thomas Mourry.

SWANSON, WOLLEY. Wiecacoe, Phila. Co. Yeoman.
3/11/1692. 6/13/1692. A. 549.
Estate to wife whose name is not given, and oldest son, John, sons Peter and Swan, and daughters Mary, Brithtey, Lydia, Katherine and Juday. He held an estate in Gloster Co., West Jersey.
Executors: Brother Swan Swanson, kinsman Nels Jonson and friend John Stitley.
Witnesses: Lasse Cock, Charles Pickering.

JENNETT, JOHN. Philadelphia. Tailor.
September 10, 1699. November 30, 1699. B. 1.
Children Richard, Lydia, Hester and Sarah. Brother's children Joseph (apprentice to William Dillwyn) and Hester Jennett. Friends

Thomas Courtney, Daniel Smith, William Freeman and John Songhurst.
Executrix: Wife Bridgett.
Overseers: Robert Turner, John Barnes, Joseph Wilcocks.
Witnesses: William Humphrys, John Barnes, Francis Cooke, William Rakestraw, James West.

GREENE, DANIEL.
October 22, 1699. November 1, 1699. B. 3.
Whole estate to his Executor Thomas Asson, who renounced both in favor of James Poulter of Philadelphia., wheelwright.
Witnesses: Joseph Yeates, Samuel Richardson, David Lloyd and James Fox.

FITZWATER, THOMAS.
---. October 2, 1699. B. 5.
Wife Elizabeth, sons Thomas and George, Executors. Daughter-in-law Elizabeth Jackson.
Witnesses: Anthony Morris, George Gray, William Southebe.

MALTBY, WILLIAM. Philadelphia. Baker.
8/11/1699. ---. B. 7.
Children mentioned but names not given. Wife's brother Adam Rhoads.
Executrix: Wife Mary.
Witnesses: William Fillpot, Richard Gove, John Rhodes.

LONDSDALE, MARGARET. Late of Yellan, in the Parish of Warton, Lancashire. Widow of Thomas.
8/7/1699. November 6, 1699. B. 8.
Daughter Elinor sole heir with remainder over to Testatrix's sister Elizabeth Addinell living in England.
Executor: David Brientnall.
Overseers: Robert Burrow and George Glough.
Witnesses: Timothy Hudson, Richard Gove, William Hudson.

OYSTERHAVEN, LEONARD. Philadelphia.
October 1, 1699. November 8, 1699. B. 10.
Son Henry.
Executrix: Wife Susannah.

Witnesses: Thomas Lassetts, John Therry, Thomas Harris.

HAMS, HENRY. Marple, PA Shoemaker.
September 9, 1699. November 10, 1699. B. 12.
Son Francis.
Executors: Wife Rebecca and Jacob Simcox.
Witnesses: John Howell, John Fincher, Josiah Taylor.

WHITE, ELIZABETH. Middletown, Bucks Co.
September 11, 1699. November 7, 1699. B. 13.
Sons John, Peter, William, Francis, Joseph and Benjamin. Daughters Sarah Huett and Elizabeth Nowell.
Executors: Sons John and Peter.
Witnesses: Samuel Baker, Thomas Yardley, Job Bunting.

CULCOPP, ELIZABETH. Philadelphia. Widow.
October 27, 1699. November 12, 1699. B. 17.
Daughters Elizabeth and Mary. Sister Ann Westby's children.
Cousin John Culcopp. Friends Robert Burrow and Thomas Howell of Maryland, tailor.
Executrix: Daughter Elizabeth.
Witnesses: Richard Sutton, Samuel Powell, Ann Hasketh.

JOHNSON, WILLIAM. Philadelphia. Tailor.
August 28, 1699. November 25, 1699. B. 20.
Wife Hannah, daughter of John Dominick, living in Leinster, England.
Son Samuel. Friends Margaret Morris, Sarah Jeffries and William Findlow.
Executor: Thomas Makin.
Witnesses: William Alloway, John Vanlear, Sarah Jeffries.

WILSON, THOMAS. Late of Lancaster, England.
---. November 25, 1699. B. 22.
Children mentioned but names not given.
Executors: John Scott, late of Wilt, Yorkshire, and Anthony Morris of Philadelphia.
Witnesses: Thomas Makin, David Breintnall, Robert Burrow.

TRUMAIN, ALICE. Aston, PA Widow.
2/7/1699. November 8, 1699. B. 24.

John Hitt kinsman of her late husband. Friends William Brown, Ann Brown, John Baldon his wife and daughter Ruth, all of Aston; Mary Farr of Concord; Joan Brintnall, Robert Pyle, Brockholt(?); Edward Carter, Margaret Carter, Robert Carter and his children John, Hannah, Lydia and Prudence. Edward Carter's son Robert, John Tush's Scotch lad.
Witnesses: Rebecca Faucit, Robert Pyle, Hannah Sharpless.

BOYDEN, JAMES. Neshaminy, Bucks Co.
August 1, 1699. November 30, 1699. B. 26.
Son James. Grandchildren Daniel Boyden and John Radney.
Executrix: Wife Margaret.
Witnesses: Henry Bowen, Joseph Ball, John Conn.

COCK, LAWRENCE. Passyunk.
October 1, 1699. 10/1/1699. B. 28.
Children Peter, John, Andreas, Catherine, Robert, Mouns, Lawrence, Gabriel, Margaret, and Deborah.
Executrix: Wife Martha.
Overseers: William Carter, Thomas Herris.
Witnesses: Richard Rodes, Thomas Herris.

NIXON, RICHARD. Macclesfield, England.
9/30/1699. January 22, 1699/1700. B. 30.
Cousin John Hough; Richard Hough and his children; Richard Hough and his son John; and George Lowe. Joseph Stanious' children. James Nixon's children Thomas, Elizabeth and Sarah. George Clarke's daughter Mary.
Executors: John Hough of Macclesfield, England, and Richard Hough of Pennsylvania.
Witnesses: Abel James, Mary James, Richard Hough.

PRICHARD, BARBARA. Philadelphia. Widow.
September 30, 1699. February 10, 1699/1700. B. 32.
Children John, Benjamin, Matthew, Ann, Jane and Martha.
Executor: Son Matthew.
Witnesses: Ralph Jackson, George Fitzwater, Eliz. Jackson, Henry Edgcomb.

SIMONDS, JOHN. Philadelphia. Glover.

October 2, 1699. March 1, 1699/1700. B. 35.
Wife Grizegon. Children Grize, Thomas and Mary. Kinsman John, son of James Kite. Kinswoman Grize, daughter of James Kite. Friends John and Elizabeth Jones.
Witnesses: William Hall, Mary Hall, Elizabeth Jones, J. Jones.

CADMAN, HENRY. Upper Providence, Chester Co.
---. May 1, 1700. B. 38.
Friends Thomas Powell, Mary wife of John Howell, Mary eldest daughter of Walter Martin, and William Buckingham.
Witnesses: Peter Taylor and Samuel Robinett.

STEVENSON, ROBERT.
Not recorded and original lost.

STEVENSON, ALLEN.
Not recorded and original lost.

PRESS, REES. Philadelphia. Carpenter.
---. June 25, 1700. B. 50.
Children David, William, Richard, Thomas, Joseph, and Elizabeth.
Executrix: Wife Elizabeth.
Witnesses: Robert Edwards, Samuel Meales, David Powell.

ROBESON, SAMUEL. Philadelphia.
September 21, 1699. October 15, 1699. B. 52.
To be buried beside his father and mother. His father's brothers Thomas and David Robeson in Scotland. Friends Sarah Dyer, Elizabeth daughter of Elizabeth Shepherd, Col. Nicholas Webb, Septimus son of Patrick Robinson and Mary Hart.
Executors: Cousin Andrew Robeson of West Jersey and friend Patrick Robinson of Philadelphia.
Witnesses: Robt. Snead, Hugh Graham.

GODSALL, GEORGE. Late of Lancaster, England.
July 25, 1699. May 18, 1700. B. 54.
Brother William. His three sisters whose names are not given. William Hugan and his wife Alice. John son of William Godsall. The son of Christopher Holkins.

Executors: George Clough, Thomas Musgrave, William Godsall of Lancaster, England, and William Stoute.
Witnesses: Thomas Langdale, William Bracken, John Daves.

DUTTON, EDMUND. Philadelphia. Carpenter.
September 12, 1699. August 1, 1700. B. 56.
His mother living in England. Friends Joseph Knight, James Poulter, John Moore, Joshua Carpenter, Henry Mallows and Samuel Weaver.
Witnesses: Samuel Richardson, Thomas England, Samuel Weaver.

TATHAM, JOHN. Burlington, N. J.
July 15, 1700. July 26, 1700. B. 59.
Children mentioned but names not given except a daughter Dorothy Hickman who is disinherited. Original filed at Burlington.
Executrix: Wife Elizabeth.
Witnesses: Thomas Revell, Joshua Newbold, Joseph White.

TODD, JOSEPH. Eling, Southamptonshire, England.
March 2,1698. August 31, 1700. B. 63.
Son by first wife Joseph. Children by second wife Joshua, Caleb, Thomas, Elizabeth and Mary. Brother Daniel and his son David. Sister Elizabeth Bradshaw and her children James and Hester. Friends John Swift, Sr., John Swift, Jr., Henry Abbott and Peter Chamberlyne.
Executrix: Wife Joane.
Witnesses: John Worsham, Richard Chambers, Andrew Worsom.

HUMPHREY, JOHN. Welshtract, PA
September 22, 1699. August 31, 1700. B. 65.
Nephew Benjamin Humphrey (sole Executor) and his wife Mary and son John. Friends Rowland Ellis, Sr., and his daughter Jane; Joshua Owen; John Owen; John Robert's children; Robert Owen's son John and other children whose names are not given. Cousin Tabitha, Ann and Joseph Humphrey. James Trate.
Witnesses: John Roberts, David Llewelyn.

TAYLOR, JOSIAH. Marple, PA
6/16/1700. September 10, 1700. B. 69.
Wife Sarah and unborn child. Children Robert, Phebe and Hannah.
Executors: Wife and Thomas Masey.

Witnesses: John Worrell, Evan Phillips.

BROOKES, JOHN. Philadelphia.
September 12, 1700. September 26, 1700. B. 71.
Children John, William and daughters whose names are not given.
Executors: William Lee and James Poulter.
Witnesses: Samuel Richardson, Mary Shipard, Samuel Sheppard.

EVANS, JACOB. Philadelphia.
7/30/1699. September 27, 1700. B. 73.
Daughter Elizabeth. Friend Joseph Wilcox.
Executrix: Wife Mary.
Witnesses: Samuel Richardson, James Morgan, William Preston.
*N. B. This will was afterwards set aside as a forgery.

HALL, JACOB. Tacony, PA Gentleman.
September 29, 1699. September 28, 1700. B. 75.
Sons Jacob, Joseph and Solomon. Daughter Sarah Taylor.
Executrix: Sarah Charlesworth, his children's aunt.
Witnesses: Abraham Senior, John East, Samuel Weaver.

WALLICOT, WILLIAM.
September 8, 1699. October 1, 1700. B. 78.
Executors: Wife Margaret and John Fellows the elder of her two children by a former husband.
Witnesses: John Redman, Sr., Thomas Harding, John Sanders.

RICHARDS, NATHANIEL. Aston, Chester Co. Blacksmith.
12/16/1699/1700. October 10, 1700. B. 80.
Father Joseph Richards. Children William, Nathaniel, Elizabeth and Mary.
Trustees: George Harland, James Lonns and Robert Pyle.
Witnesses: John Parries, Ann Scarlet, Humphrey Scarlet.

BRINTON, WILLIAM. Brimingham, Chester Co.
6/20/1699. December 1, 1700. B. 82.
Daughters Elizabeth wife of Hugh Narry, Esther wife of John Willis and Ann wife of John Bennet.
Executors: Son William and son-in-law John Bennet.
Overseer: George Harlan.

Witnesses: Richard Gove, Hannah Way, Jacob Chandler.

DILWORTH, JAMES. Bristol Township, Philadelphia. Co.
7/8/1699. December 10, 1700. B. 85.
Children William, Richard, Jane, Hannah, Jennette, Rebecca and James. Brother-in-law Nicholas Waln. Friend Edmond Orpwood.
Executrix: Wife Ann.
Witnesses: William Preston, Richard Tomlinson, Arthur Cooke, Griffith Jones.

BURGESS, ELIZABETH. Bucks Co.
May 6, 1700. December 16, 1700. B. 87.
Executor: Father Henry Packston, sole heir.
Witnesses: John Tatham, Benjamin Wheat, Thomas Plumly.

BOLT, JOHN. Philadelphia. Butcher.
October 11, 1700. February 15, 1700/1. B. 89.
Daughters Alice wife of Charles Woolfe at Lyme, Connecticut, and Mary Bolt.
Executrix: Wife Mary.
Overseers: John Farmer and Thomas Paschall, Sr.
Witnesses: Thomas Potts, Joseph Ranstead, Jacob Cofing, J. Jones.

SCOTT, JOHN. Bucks Co.
October 17, 1700. April 1, 1701. B. 92.
Children mentioned but names not given.
Executrix: Wife Jane.
Witnesses: John Surket, Richard Large.

LEWIS, HARRY. Radnor, PA
7/12/1699. April 1, 1700. B. 94.
Wife Abigail. Children Harry (sole Executor), Mary and Elinor. Friend Richard Faddery.
Witnesses: David Davis, Benjamin Humphrey, David Lewis, Ben. Lewis.

BOYDON, MARGARET. Late of Neshaminy, now of Philadelphia. Widow.
October 22, 1700. April 10, 1701. B. 96.

Son James and his sons Daniel and James. Grandsons John and Daniel, sons of Daniel Radley (who is sole Executor).
Witnesses: John Songhuret, Elizabeth Griffith, John Parsons.

FOX, JAMES. Philadelphia.
January 22, 1700/1. April 10, 1701. B. 98.
Wife Anne and unborn child. Father James Fox. Brother Nathan Stanberry.
Witnesses: John Cadwalader, John Jones, Thomas Story.

BEARDSLEY, MARGARET. Philadelphia. Widow of Alexander.
7/18/1699. April 15, 1701. B. 101.
Daughter Mary Gray and her children Joseph, Samuel and George Gray. Sister Martha Minion living in London. Brother-in-law Joseph Beardsley and his son Alexander and his other children whose names are not given. Friends Margaret Morris of Philadelphia, widow; Thomas Denniss of West Jersey; Hannah Carpenter; Hannah Delavall; and Anthony Morris.
Executors: Isaac Norris and Samuel Carpenter.
Witnesses: Thos. Story, Robert Burrow, Mary Dickson, Joan Forrest.

COX, ANN. Philadelphia. Widow.
August 3, 1699. September 18, 1699. B. 107.
Son William Trotter. Daughter Ann wife of George Thompson. Friends Rev. Thomas Clayton of Philadelphia., Rev. John Arrowsmith of Philadelphia., Elizabeth Hooton, widow, Mary Broadshaw, widow, John Duplouvys, merchant, and John Farmer.
Executrix: Daughter Elizabeth Sheppard, widow.
Witnesses: Robert Snead, Samuel Robinson, Thomas Clarke.

BEAKIS, STEPHEN. Bucks Co.
3/5/1699. May 17, 1700. B. 110.
Children John, Mary, Grace and Elizabeth.
Executrix: Wife Elizabeth.
Witnesses: Edward Lucas, Isaac Atkinson, Abigail Pemberton.

PENNOCK, CHRISTOPHER. Philadelphia. Bardmaker.
April 15, 1701. August 15, 1701. B. 114.
Wife Mary. Son Joseph P. and daughter Hannah Goslin living in Ireland. Granddaughter Hannah Galloway.

Executors: James Atkinson, William Southeby and Richard Sutton.
Witnesses: Randall Speakman, Grace Speakman.

GRAISBERRY, JAMES. Philadelphia. Mariner.
February 1, 1700. February 20, 1700/1.
Proved in Barbados. Wife Elizabeth and unborn child. Children Joseph and Mary. Land in West Jersey. Brother Joseph Graisberry. Sister Catherine Graisberry. Nephews Benjamin and Francis Graisberry. Nieces Mary and Elizabeth Graisberry. Father James Graisberry.
Executors: Wife and brother James Graisberry.
Witnesses: Nicholas Braddick, Hugh Rowland, John Woodward.

MUSGRAVE, THOMAS. Late of Halifax, Yorkshire.
August 1, 1699. July 25, 1701. B. 120.
Children Thomas, Abraham, Elizabeth and William.
Executrix: Wife Hannah.
Overseers: Joseph Growden, David Lloyd, Phineas Pemberton and Samuel Carpenter.
Witnesses: John Hughes, Samuel Eton, Richard Wright.

TOMLINSON, ELIZABETH. Late of Middletown, Bucks Co.
February 12, 1699/1700. February 10, 1701/2. B. 122.
Children John, Henry, Joseph, Thomas and Elizabeth.
Executor: John Cowgill.
Overseers: Thomas Baines and Gabriel Baines.
Witnesses: Thos. Stackhouse, Wm. Hayhurst, Robert Neaton, John Croasdell.

DECOW, ABRAHAM. Late of Newcastle [on Delaware].
1/1/1700/1. May 14, 1701. B. 124.
Brother-in-law Edward Blake. Sister-in-law Sarah Blake. Friends George Hogg, Jr. of Newcastle, John Land, Thomas Hogg, John, Joseph and Ann children of Robert Ashton, Prudence Holt, Thomas Makin and Sarah his wife.
Executors: Sister Hannah and her husband Thomas England.
Witnesses: Thomas Makin, John Roberts, William White.

BREWER, RICHARD. Late of Port Royal, Jamaica.
May 27, 1701. August 14, 1701. B. 126.

Friends Col. Edward Stanton and his wife, Col. Nicholas Richardson and wife, Dr. Arthur Muttas and wife, Edward Sands' son. Mary Smith living in London, and Mary Dickinson. Sisters Jane, Rachell, Joan and Hannah.
Executors: Anthony Major and Thomas Mitchael, Jr. of Port Royal, and Jonathan Dickinson of Philadelphia.
Witnesses: Charles Read, Robert Wheeler, Isaac Norris and William Fishbourn.

JENNER, MARGARET. "Kinsessin," Philadelphia. Widow.
8/15/1701. November 19, 1701. B. 129.
Children Euclid and Alice Longshore and Mary Jenner.
Executors: James Cooper of Darby, cloth worker, and Paul Saunders of Chester, tanner.
Witnesses: Peter Cock and Andrew Longaker.

* N. B. This will was contested by John Cock [brother of the testatrix] Peter Cock, Gabriel Cock and others of the family of Margaret Genard [sic] deceased. With their protest are filed original depositions of Hannah Cooper, Robert Smith, William Smith, Rose Bethell and Paul Saunders.

MOLL, JOHN. Philadelphia. Merchant.
May 17, 1701. July 1, 1701. B. 134.
Wife Katharine [2d wife] sole Executrix. Son John and his wife Elizabeth. Other children Cornelius, Jacob and Katharine.
Trustees: Thomas Paschall, Francis Cook, Johannis Kelynis(?).

NAYLOR, THOMAS.
July 9, 1701. July 25, 1701. B. 139.
Wife Mary (sole Executrix) and unborn child. Mother Mary. Sister Hannah.
Witnesses: Nathaniel Puckle, John Crapp, John Budd.

WADE, LYDIA. Chester, PA Widow of Robert.
4/30/1701. August 28, 1701. B. 141.
William Crouch of London merchant. Kinsman John Peirs or Peirce of Billreke, Essex, England. Kinsmen the sons of John Allen. Kinsman John Jones and his children Richard, Grace and Samuel. Kinsman John Wade. Kinswoman Lydia Walker, Sr. Jeremy Langley

a pauper now at Randall Vernon's house. Robert Goforth of Chester. Valentine Hollingsworth, Sr. Lydia daughter of Caleb and Anne Pusey. Henry Hollingsworth of Chester. Jane wife of James Bayles of Chester township.
Executor: Kinsman John Jones of Philadelphia., merchant.
Witnesses: Jonathan Hoskins, Joseph Edge and Edward Dangger.

LEWIS, JOHN. Philadelphia Co.
September 29, 1700. July 16, 1701. B. 145.
Whole estate to the poor.
Executors: William Preston and Edward Williams.
Witnesses: Jeffrey Wainwright, Mary Williams.

STACY, ROBERT. Philadelphia. Tanner.
2/11/1699. October 18, 1701. B. 147.
Daughters Mary, Elizabeth and her children, Judith and Ellen and her son.
Executor: Son John.
Witnesses: Samuel Siddon, Francis Cooke.

SIDDON, SAMUEL. Philadelphia.
8/4/1701. October 16, 1701. B. 149.
Friends Francis Cooke, Pentecost Teague, John Kinsey and Samuel Carpenter.
Executor: Brother Thomas Siddon.
Witnesses: Nathaniel Edgecomb, Rosina Bringhurst.

ROADES, JOHN. Darby, PA Cordwainer.
8/20/1701. November 22, 1701. B. 151.
Other children Jacob, John, Mary [widow of Won.], Maltly, and Elizabeth Daws. Servant Charles Robinson.
Executors: Sons Joseph and Adam.
Witnesses: Josiah Gratton, John Hood, Sr.

TATHAM, ELIZABETH. Burlington, N. J. Widow of John.
October 15, 1700. May 21, 1701. B. 154.
Children John, Elizabeth, Dorothy wife of --- Hickman and unborn child. Dr. Dunsdale, Thomas and Mary children of the late widow Hooton of Philadelphia. Matthew Robinson of London and his two sons. Servant James Stevens.

Overseers: Thomas Revell of Burlington, Patrick Robinson of Philadelphia.
Witnesses: George Deacon, Henry Grubb, Daniel Sutton.

BRYANT, ROBERT. Newcastle [on Delaware]. Merchant.
September 2, 1701. December 17, 1701. B. 16-.
Children Robert, Ann, Mary wife of John Lann.
Executors: Robert Bryant, Ann Bryant, and Margaret Heath.
Overseer: Richard Holliwell.
Witnesses: J. Jones, Jacob Glen, James Claypoole.

DECOW, JACOB. New Castle Co.
2/2/1688. February 7, 1701/2. B. 162.
Wife Hannah. Children Abraham and Hannah, wife of Thomas England.
Executors: Wife, son and daughter.
Trustees: Robert Ashton, Cornelius Empson, Valentine Hollingsworth.
Witnesses: Mary Barras, Jacob Decow, Jr.

VASTALL, WILLIAM. Westtown, Chester Co.
January 19, 1701/2. February 25, 1701/2. B. 164.
Children William, George and Mary.
Executors: Wife Alice and Thomas Powell of Providence.
Witnesses: John Wood, Nathaniel King, Robert Way, Robert Jeffreys.

DONALDSON, JOHN. Newcastle Co.
February 12, 1701/2. April 8, 1702. B. 166.
Children Mary and Catherine. Brother William. Friend Dorcas wife of George Hogg. Robert French and Richard Halliwell, both of Newcastle, merchants, and Thunis DeKey of New York, merchant.
Witnesses: Thomas Janvier, Wm. Douglas, Jas Claypoole.

LEWIS, HARRY. Radnor, Chester Co.
March 20, 1701/2. April 13, 1702. B. 169.
Sister Mary Worrell and Elinor Lewis. Servant Richard Faddery.
Executor: Brother-in-law John Worrell.
Witnesses: Peter Worrell, Edward Thomas, David Evan.

GIBBINS, HENRY. Darby, Chester Co.
12/28/1701/2. April 25, 1702. B. 172.
Daughters, Mary wife of Robert Scothorn and Ann Sellers and her children. Son Henry and daughter Sarah, wife of John Johnson of Nottingham, disinherited.
Executor: Son-in-law Robert Scothorn.
Witnesses: Richard Parker, James Cooper.

WALL, RICHARD.
1/15/1697/8. February 9, 1701/2. B. 174.
Friend Wm. Bubb.
Executrix: Granddaughter Sarah, wife of George Shoemaker.
Witnesses: Samuel Richardson, Evan Morris, Richard Townsend.

BRANDT, ALBERTUS. Philadelphia. Merchant.
September 16, 1701. February 10, 1701/2. B. 177.
Executrix: Wife Susannah, sole heir.
Witnesses: Jedidiah Andrews, Elizabeth Knight, Chr. Philipson.

FURNIS, HENRY. Philadelphia. Saddler.
December 30, 1701. January 20, 1701/2. B. 179.
Wife Jane. Children Samuel and his four oldest children; John; Sarah and her two oldest children; Mary and her two oldest children; Rachel and Brigett. Cousin Jane Burland in England. Executors: Son-in-law William Robinson and James Poulter of Philadelphia., wheelwright.
Witnesses: John Bowyer, James Parrock, Ralph Ward, Wm. Dillwyn.

PEMBERTON, PHINEAS. Bucks Co. Yeoman.
10/6/1701. March 12, 1701/2. B. 183.
Wife Alice. Children Israel, Joseph, Abigail and Priscilla. Brother-in-law Robert Hodgon. Father Ralph Pemberton.
Executors: Son Israel and Samuel Carpenter.
Witnesses: Richard Hough, Samuel Smith, John Surkett.

HARDIMAN, ABRAHAM. Philadelphia.
6/28/1699. September 10, 1702. B. 189.
Children Mary, Hannah, Deborah and Rebecca. Friends William Biles, Samuel Beakes and George Biles. James Fox, Isaac Norris and

John Kinsey. Brother Samuel Carpenter. Cousin John and Rebecca Harris. Cousin Rebecca Williams.
Executrix: Wife Rebecca.
Witnesses: David Lloyd, Abraham Decow, Isaac Waterman.

HUGH, DAVID CADWALADER ap.
November 23, 1700. October 23, 1701. B. 192.
Nephew Hugh ap Edward. Numerous debtors all Welshmen mentioned. Original missing.
Overseers: Brother Evan ap Hugh and Edward Foulke.
Witnesses: Robert John, Edward Griffith, Edward Foulke.

TOWNSEND, JOHN. Philadelphia. Whitesmith.
5/2/1701. May 2, 1702. B. 194.
Children Richard, John and Mary. Grandchildren mentioned but names not given.
Executrix: Wife Grace.
Overseers: Joshua Carpenter, William Lee.
Witnesses: Thomas Story, David Brientnall, William Till.

CHISWELL, ANTHONY. New York. Merchant.
May 31, 1702. August 17, 1702. B. 197.
Signed in Jamaica, W. I. Original filed in New York.
Executors: Brother John of London and sister Ann of New York.
Witnesses: Joseph Short, Charles Crommelien, George Forest, Jacob Mayle.

JAMES, PHILIP. Philadelphia. Merchant.
March 31, 1702. July 1, 1702. B. 200.
Daughters Abigail and Sarah. Brother Joseph Wilcox. Friends John Kaighn and Charles Read.
Executrix: Wife Esther.
Witnesses: John Guest, Samuel Powell, David Lloyd.

WEST, PRUDENCE. Philadelphia. Widow of James West, shipwright.
6/5/1702. August 14, 1702. B. 203.
Children James, Charles, Mary and Jonathan. Kinsman Robert Harrow.

Executors: Wm. Southebe, John Kinsey, Pentecost Teague, Joseph Kirl.
Witnesses: Jas. Parrock, John Morton.

YOCUM, PETER. Arunnamunk, Kingsessing.
2/4/1700. June 4, 1702. B. 206.
Sons Peter, Charles, Mounce, Swan, Jonas, Andreas and John.
Executors: Wife Judith and brother John Hance.
Witnesses: Nils Jonson, Jonas Brurstrom, Benjamin Chambers.

LIGHTFOOT, THOMAS. Late of England. Tailor.
July 30, 1702. August 19, 1702. B. 208.
Nuncupative will. John Neally of Apoquininunk sole heir.
Witnesses: James Smithers, aged about 50 years, and William Williamson aged 28 years.

WELLS, ARTHUR.
April 7, 1702. June 29, 1702. B. 209.
Sons Thomas and Arthur.
Executrix: Wife Rebecca.
Witnesses: James Boyden, George Fitzwater, James Wood.

FOX, ELIZABETH. Philadelphia. Widow.
2/13/1702. July 27, 1702. B. 211.
Children Elizabeth, Sarah and Francis. Granddaughter Mary daughter of James Fox. Susannah Fox. The three daughters of Anthony Taylor. Nathan Stanberry, Samuel Carpenter, Isaac Norris.
Witnesses: Thomas Story, John Jones, Elizabeth Janney.

HOGBIN, RICHARD.
December 25, 1697. March 17, 1701/2. B. 214.
Executrix: Wife Elizabeth, sole heir.
Witnesses: John Redman, William Hearn, George Guest.

ROBINET, ALLEN, Sr.
4/4/1694. May 26, 1702. B. 216.
Children Sarah, Samuel, Allen and his wife, and Susannah wife of Robert Ward and their daughter Elizabeth.
Witnesses: Richard Woodward, Mary wife of Randall Malin, John Salvert or Falvert.

ROLLS, WILLIAM. Bucks Co. Yeoman.
1/12/1702/3. April 5, 1703. B. 217.
Wife Dorothy. Daughter-in-law Sarah widow of his son William. Daughter Mary wife of Peter Child and her daughter Mary. Son-in-law William Gregory, sole Executor, and his children William, John, George, Mary and Sarah. Grandchild Lacy Rolls. Friends James Bond, Mary daughter of Robert Mason, Samuel Preston of Philadelphia. and Mordecai Moor of Maryland.
Witnesses: Thomas Harding, John Shaw, Henry Strike.

STURGES, ANTHONY. Philadelphia. Feltmaker.
June 16, 1702. August 22, 1702. B. 221.
Wife Dorothy. Other children Sarah wife of Matthew Holgate, Esther Nunsaman, son-in-law Peter Long. Grandchildren children of Sarah Holdgate and Esther Huntsman. Friend John Hart the Keithian Speaker. Son-in-law Matthew Holdgate's daughter by his first wife. Stephen Lobb.
Executor: Son Cornelius.
Witnesses: Anthony Taylor, Samuel Nicholas, Thomas Berden, Daniel Hodgson.

RIGHTON, WILLIAM. Philadelphia. Mariner.
February 5, 1701/2. May 4, 1702. B. 223.
Signed in Jamaica. Wife Sarah. Mother name not given. Sisters --- Claypoole, --- Janney (Masters) and Frances Righton. Brother Stephen. Jane Ambler of Newcastle-upon-Tyne, widow of Joseph Ambler, my mate who died in Barbadoes. Jane Macklin.
Executors: Wife and Thomas Masters.
Witnesses: Alexander Blair, William Heughes, Israel Robbs, Thomas Biddle.

WALKER, MARGARET. Philadelphia. Widow.
October 9, 1702. October 12, 1702. B. 226.
Her daughter name not given. Sister --- Naylor. Children, names not given, of John Naylor.
Executors: Brother John Naylor and John Sissom.
Witnesses: Abel Noble, Francis Cooke.

PLUMLY, JAMES. Middletown, Bucks Co.
8/16/1702. November 14, 1702. B. 228.

Son John. Brother Charles and other brothers whose names are not given. Uncle William Budd.
Executrix: Wife Mary.
Witnesses: Thomas Plumly, aged 30 years, Hannah Slade, Hannah Tusbee, John Hart.

SWENSON, GUNNER.
March 2, 1701/2. May 18, 1702. B. 231.
His mother name not given. Brothers Ulrich, Christopher and Andrew. Friends Valentine Cock; Andrew Wheeler and his son John; and Mauns Gustason and his son John.
Executors: Peter Cock, Jr. and Peter Bengtzon.
Witnesses: Peter Cock, Andrew Rudman, Peter Bengtzon.

DAILE (DIALE), PETER. Pennypack Mills.
6/1/1703. December 3, 1703. B. 235.
Brother-in-law William Palmer. Friends Charles Read, Joseph Wilcox and Charles Saunders.
Executrix: Wife Martha.
Witnesses: Charles Sober, John Welles, John Smallwood.

HOOD, JOHN, JR. Darby, Chester Co. Husbandman.
4/12/1702. November 27, 1702. B. 239.
Wife name not given and unborn child. Children John, Elizabeth and Samuel.
Executors: Father John Hood of Darby and Henry Lewis of Haverford.
Witnesses: Katherine Bynon, Samuel Hood, Thomas Huews.

HEUGHES, WILLIAM.
June 1, 1702. July 13, 1702. B. 242.
Children Mary and Ann.
Executrix: Wife Ann.
Witnesses: Daniel Hodgson, Anthony Sturgis, James Boyden.

CLOUD, WILLIAM, SR. Concord, Chester Co.
7/20/1700. August 25, 1702. B. 244.
Sons William, Jeremiah, Joseph, John and Robert. Daughter Susannah Lukens living in England. Granddaughter Hannah, daughter of Jeremiah Cloud.

Witnesses: Robert Pyle, Ann Pyle, Sarah Pyle.

BURLING, JOHN. Philadelphia. Co. Wheelwright.
3/30/1702. August 15, 1702. B. 246.
Brother Elias. Nephew Edward son of deceased brother Edward.
Executors: Ephraim Bouldin and Samuel Richardson.
Witnesses: David Potts, Peter Clevers, F. D. Pustronius.

MARTIN, JOHN. Philadelphia. Tailor.
November 8, 1702. November 20, 1702. B. 249.
Executors and Legatees: Friends Thomas Chalkley of Philadelphia, sawyer, Ralph Jackson, smith, George Jackson and John Meathiner, yeoman.
Witnesses: Thomas Bradford, John Parsons, Nathaniel Evornden.

ROBERT, JOHN. Chester Co. Blacksmith.
7/26/1702. January 5, 1702/3. B. 251.
Daughter Margaret wife of Thomas Kenderdine and her children Richard, Thomas, John, Margaret and Mary. Son John and daughter Elinor Jenkins living in Wales. Friend Joan Potts, widow, and John Kinsey.
Executors: John Bevan and John Rees.
Witnesses: William Howell, Mary Badcock, John Kinsey.

HOULDSTONE, JOHN. Edgemont, Chester Co.
4/17/1698. March 14, 1701/2. B. 254.
Father and mother living. Four sisters names not given. Cousin James Serrill and cousin Mary Serrill and their two children. Children of Peter Taylor and William Gregory names not given. A protest signed by Joseph Baker, John Worrilaw, John Bowater, David Ogden, Edward Jones, Frances Bowater, Eliz. Houldstone, Francis Worrall, Sarah Taylor and Rebecca Gregory was filed in August 1701 and the will was eventually set aside by the Orphans' Ct.
Executors: Wife Ann and son John.
Witnesses: John Goulding, John Musgrave, Edward Jones and Peter Taylor.

ELTON, WILLIAM. Philadelphia. Shipwright.
June 22, 1702. December 15, 1702. B. 258.

Brother Edward Smout, brother Anthony Elton and his wife Susannah and their children Revell, Robert, Anthony, Mary, Elizabeth and Hannah Elton. Sister Jane wife of Edward Smout and their children Edward, Elton and Sylvanus. Mother [Susannah]. Friends John Watts and John Eaglesfield.
Executor: Brother Edward Smout.
Witnesses: Chr. Danson, Samuel Weaver, Elizabeth Harding.

ELTON, SUSANNAH.
December 9, 1702. December 17, 1702. B. 261.
Daughter Jane Smout. Granddaughter Elizabeth Elton. Daughter-in-law Elizabeth Elton. Grandchildren the children of her son Anthony Elton and her daughter Jane wife of Edward Smout. Granddaughter Mary wife of Samuel Cole. Friends James Morgan, Jane Morgan, Joshua Humphreys and Ann wife of Thomas Kendall.
Executor: Joshua Humphreys of West New Jersey.
Witnesses: Ann Kendall, John Wills.

DYER, ELIZABETH. Newcastle [on Delaware]. Widow.
October 20, 1702. January 4, 1702/3. B. 263.
Children Robert and Elizabeth Dyer [the latter died before the will was probated.] Friend George Dakeyne.
Witnesses: Richard Clarke, Dorothy Hall, Elizabeth Weber.

ROBERT, HUGH. Merion.
5/20/1702. December 7, 1702. B. 265.
Children Robert, Owen, Elizabeth and Edward. Servants Morris Robert and John Robert.
Executors: His three sons.
Overseers: John Robert, Cadwalader Morgan, Griffith John, Griffith Owen.
Witnesses: Samuel Bowne, Griffith Owen, Samuel Jenings.

HOUSE, FRANCIS. Philadelphia. Brewer.
March 10, 1697/8. January 18, 1702/3. B. 268.
Children John, George, Ruth and Elizabeth.
Executrix: Wife Susannah.
Witnesses: Nicholas Rideout, Able Noble, Francis Cooke.

EDWARD, JOHN ap.
8/16, 1683. 2/8/[1683/4?]. B. 270.
See ante p. 16.

WARD, JOSEPH. Middletown, Bucks Co.
8/4/1702. February 1, 1702/3. B. 272.
Brother-in-law Thomas Bears.
Executors: Wife Ann and son John.
Witnesses: Matthew Wildman, Joseph Wildman.

NORBURY, THOMAS. Newtown, Chester co.
5/16/1702. August 10, 1702. B. 274.
Children Stephen, Jacob, Deborah, Thomas, Philip, John, Benjamin, Mary, Hannah, Sarah and Rachel.
Executors: Daniel Williamson and Evan Lewis.
Witnesses: Bartholomew Coppuck, Jonathan Taylor.

NORCROSS, WILLIAM. Austen-cum-Nutherston, Parish of Ribchester, England.
6/12/1699. ---. B. On file, but not recorded.
Other children Jane, William and Thomas. Signed on board the Britannia of Liverpool. Bond of Elizabeth Sands, late Norcross (as administratrix), Stephen Sands and Jonathan Cockshaw, dated September 17, 1703.
Executors: Wife Elizabeth and son John.

PAYNTER, HENRY.
October 12, 1702. February 12, 1702/3. B. 276.
Children Henry and Ann. Son-in-law [step-son?] Andrew Dunk. Daughter-in-law Sarah Dunk, her late father Andrew Dunk.
Executrix: Wife Mary.
Witnesses: John Carver, James Beilder, Mary Carver, William Rolls.

PETERSON, ADAM. Newcastle on Delaware.
December 6, 1702. February 17, 1702/3. B. 279.
Children Garrett, Adam, Andrew, Armentie, Eleanor and Elizabeth.
Brother and sister Isaac and Eletie Vigoreu.
Executors: Sons Garrett and Andrew.
Witnesses: Roger Wotton, William Desbournes, Sarah Outhout.

WILLIAM, JOHN REES (REES JOHN). Merion, Philadelphia. Co.
11/24/1697/8. March 4, 1702/3. B. 282.
Sons Richard Jones, Evan Jones and John Jones.
Executrix: Wife Hannah Jones.
Overseers: Cadwalader Morgan, Abel Thomas, Edward Jones, Griffith Jones, John Roberts.
Witnesses: Griffith John and Abel Thomas.

BUNTING, JOB. Bristol Twp., Bucks Co.
9/14/1702. March 10, 1702/3. B. No page number.
Children Samuel, Job, John, Rebecca and Sarah.
Executrix: Wife Rachel.
Witnesses: Thomas Watson, Lawrence Pearson.

YARDLEY, THOMAS. Bristol, Bucks Co.
11/27/1702/3. March 10, 1702/3. B. 287.
Son William.
Executrix: Wife Esther.
Witnesses: Nathan Baker, William Yardley, Rachel Bunting.

DOYLES, EDWARD. Bucks Co. Husbandman.
September 16, 1702. March 12, 1702/3. B. 289.
Children Clement and Edward. George Knight, Tobias Dymoche, Wm. Surket.
Executrix: Wife Rebecca.

YARDLEY, WILLIAM. Bucks Co.
12/12/1702/3. March 10, 1702/3. B. 291.
Brother Thomas's son. Brother Enoch and his children. Mary Triggo. Servant Nathaniel Hare.
Executors: Brother Thomas and cousin Jacob Janney.
Witnesses: John Carliett, Thomas Story, Mary Yardley, Reuben Powell, Alice Bingham.

WHEELER, GILBERT. Bucks Co. Yeoman.
April 21, 1698. March 11, 1702/3. B. 294.
Executors: Wife Sarah, son-in-law John Clark of Burlington, N.J. and friend John Pidcock of Bucks Co.
Witnesses: Richard Bull, Sarah Bull, Willis Taylor, Wm. Emlen.

PEGG, DANIEL.
February 11, 1702/3. March 1, 1702/3. B. 296.
Wife Barbara. Children Elizabeth, Jane, Nathan, Elias and Daniel.
Executors: John Stacy, Elias Jones and John Redman.
Witnesses: John Hart, Nathaniel Poole, Samuel Parker.

SIMCOCK, JOHN. Ridley, Chester Co.
5/25/1702. April 24, 1703. B. 300.
Other children John, Hannah and Elizabeth. Children of deceased daughter Mary, wife of John Cook, viz., Arthur, John, Thomas, Margaret and Mary Cook. Son-in-law Ralph Fishbourn.
Executors: Wife Elizabeth and son Jacob.
Witnesses: Walter Faucit, Randall Vernon, Paul Saunders.

CARTLIDGE, EDMUND. Darby, Chester Co.
2/21/1703. June 12, 1703. B. 304.
Daughter Mary. Sister Mary, wife of Richard Smith and her children Thomas, Richard and Matthew Smith. Sister Helen Black.
Executors: Wife Mary, son John, brother-in-law Joseph Need and Michael Blunton.
Overseers: Isaac Bartram and his brother William Bartram.
Witnesses: John Smith, John Halliwell, John Hood.

HOWELL, JOHN. Marple, Chester Co.
11/31/1702/3. June 19, 1703. B. 307.
Wife Mary. Daughters Mary, Barbara and Hannah, wife of Thomas Taylor and her children John and Mary Taylor. Sister Mary living in England. Brother-in-law Daniel Williamson. Servant Alexander Nicholas.
Executors: Jacob Simcock and Charles Whitaker
Witnesses: Joseph Selby, Thomas Massey.

RADLEY, JOHN. Birmingham, Chester Co. Worsted comber.
11/26/1701. July 26, 1703. B. 311.
Wife Frances. Eldest son John living in England. Sons Daniel and Thomas.
Executor: Son William.
Witnesses: Hugh Harris, John Willis, George Strode.

HOSKINS, RICHARD. Pennsylvania, now residing in London. Merchant.
May 4, 1700. [July 25,] 1701. B. 314.
Children Aurelius, Martha, Mercy, Mary and Ann.
Executors: Friends Philip Collins, planter, and John Gronoo (Groves?), merchant, both of Barbadoes, executors in Barbadoes. Sam. Carpenter, David Lloyd, and Edward Shippen executors in Philadelphia. Theodore Eccleston executor in London.
Witnesses: John Ellis, Charles Owen, John Booker.

HOSKINS, ELIZABETH.
7/30/1699. August 11, 1701. B. 319.
Brother Aurelius, sisters Martha, Mary, Mercy and Ann.
Witnesses: Joseph Forrest, Elizabeth Fox, Rachel Preston.

CUTOUT, SARAH. New Castle [on Delaware]. Widow.
---. ---. B. 321.
Granddaughter Helena Peterson. Elizabeth Peterson, Sarah de Haas. Lydia Williams, Joanna Williams, Elizabeth Williams, Jacobus Williams. John Williams, Henrieus Williams. Fabius Towson, his brother and two sisters names not given. Elinor Gibson.
Executors: Robert Halliwell and Richard French.
Witnesses: Hypo: Lifevre, Henry Williams, Lydia Williams "neer ringh."

TAUTON, HENRICK. Amosland, Chester Co.
September 17, 1703. October 18, 1703. B. 324.
Sons Henrick, Andrew and Hance. Friend Annie Coleman, widow. Rev. Jonas Oureen [Auren] of Philadelphia.
Executors: Charles Whitaker of Ridley and John Orchard of Amosland.
Witnesses: John Hood, Andrew Morton, Henrick Brunjohn.

CORNISH, JAMES.
October 5, 1703. December 1, 1703. B. 328.
Children James, Ebenezer, Thomas and Lydia. Friends Jasper Yeates and James Sandilands.
Executrix: Wife Mary.
Witnesses: Jasper Yeates, Isaac Taylor, Henry Hollingsworth.

LUCAS, ROBERT. Bucks Co.
10/6/1687. December 21, 1703. B. 330.
Wife Elizabeth. Sons Edward, Robert, Oriles and John. Younger children names not given.
Witnesses: George Browne, Daniel Sleng(?).

SCOTT, THOMAS. Bensalem, Bucks Co.
12/27/1702/3. December 31, 1703. B. 332.
Children Thomas living in England, Samuel, Richard, Benjamin and two daughters names not given.
Executrix: Wife Amy.
Witnesses: George Dunkan, Mary Dunkan.

WHITE, JOHN. New Bristol, Bucks Co.
December 16, 1703. January 4, 1703/4. B. 335.
Wife Mary. Children George and Elizabeth.
Executors: John Rowland and John Balden.
Witnesses: Thomas Revell, Joseph White, Charles Lavalley.

HINTON, WILLIAM. Philadelphia. Distiller.
January 28, 1702/3. January 26, 1703/4. B. 339.
Wife Margaret living in Bristol, England. Children William and Eleanor. Friend Thomas Berkins of Bristol, Eng. His mother and brother Philip living in the parish of Chitern, Wilthsire. Sisters Mary Randall, Elizabeth Hinton and Deborah Hinton.
Executors: Israel Hobbs and Joseph Appleton.
Witnesses: Jacob Isaacs van Bebber, Matthew van Bebber, Samuel Weaver.

ROBINSON, ELIZABETH. Philadelphia. Widow.
December 22, 1694. February 25, 1703/4. B. 341.
Son Samuel. Friend Andrew Robeson.
Executors: Robert Turner and John Moore.
Witnesses: Thomas Tresse, James Murray, James Poulter, Mary Jeffes.

ROBERTS, JOHN. Merion, Philadelphia. Co. Miller.
12/18/1703/4. ---. B. 343.
Children John, Matthew and Rebecca. Nephews Robert, Joseph and Edward Roberts.

Executors: Brothers Edward Roberts, Matthew Roberts and John Owen.
Overseers: Brother Joshua Owen, friends Thomas John and Benjamin Humphreys.
Witnesses: James Thomas, Nathan Thomas, John Roberts, Jr.

LOCIER, ELIZABETH. New Castle Co. Widow of Nicholas.
December 16, 1702. December 19, 1702. B. 346.
Nuncupative will. Garrett, Andrew, Hermanchy, Helicha, Adam and Elizabeth children of Adam Peterson.
Witnesses: Cornelius Kettle, Anne Kettle, Hillety Vyeggero.

KING, JOHN. New Castle [on Delaware].
February 14, 1703/4. May 16, 1704. B. 347.
James Butterworth, sole heir.
Witnesses: John Steel, John Guardner, John Holthan, Joseph Steel.

STURGIS, CORNELIUS. Philadelphia.
2/13/1704. May 20, 1704. B. 348.
Children names not given.
Executrix: Wife Elizabeth.
Witnesses: Francis Cooke, Philip Roman, Mary Scull, Thomas Millard, Sr.

STEVENS, THOMAS. Philadelphia. Cordwainer.
August 26, 1703. June 2, 1704. B. 350.
Brother Anthony Stevens.
Executrix: Wife Elizabeth.
Witnesses: Thomas Tresse, John Sorton, Samuel Weaver.

HOUGH, EVAN ap.
May 21, 1703. June 7, 1704. B. 352.
Wife Anne, Son David. Other children, names not given. Nephew Hugh Edward.
Overseers: John Humphreys, Edward Foulke, Robert John.
Witnesses: Thomas Edward, Humphrey Bate, John Roberts.

HURLEY(?), JOSEPH. Bucks Co. Yeoman.
10/31/1703. June 15, 1704. B. 355.
Daughter Elizabeth. Friend Isabel, daughter of Mary Haywood.

Executors: John Clark and William Emley of Burlington, N.J.
Witnesses: Samuel Beake, John Mattock, Mary Howard.

GREGORY, WILLIAM. Edgmond, Chester Co. Yeoman.
6/20/1703. June 19, 1704. B. 357.
Wife Rebecca. Children John, William, Simon, Edmund, Elizabeth, Mary, Sarah and Martha.
Executors: Wife, John Worrall and Peter Taylor.
Witnesses: David Ogden, John Goulding.

JACOBSON, HENDRICK. Cranshook, Pa.
May 5, 1704. June 6, 1704. B. 359.
Other children Jacob, Catherine and Ann.
Executor: Son Hendrick.
Witnesses: Armond Stedham, Charles Springer.

STEDHAM, LULOFF. New Castle on Del.
May 5, 1704. June 6, 1704. B. 362.
Children Timothy, Luloff, Sarah, Margaret, Ingeborg and Ann.
Stepdaughter Katherine ---. Brother Asmond Stedham.
Executors: Wife Catherine and Charles Springer.
Witnesses: John Stallcop, Andrew Cock, Charles Springer.

MARKHAM, WILLIAM. Philadelphia. Esquire.
December 13, 1703. July 3, 1704. B. 364.
Daughter Ann Brown and her sons James and William. Daughter-in-law Elizabeth Regnier.
Executrix: Wife Joanna.
Witnesses: Nehemiah Alen, Charles Plumly, Henry Flower.

BARLOW, JOSEPH. Haverford, Chester Co.
6/14/1704. September 4, 1704. B. 368.
Son Joseph. Friend Rowland Powell, David Morris of Marple, Richard Hayes, David Llewellen, John Reese of Haverford and Evan James.
Executors: John Blunstone of Darby and David Morrice [aie] of Marple.
Witnesses: John Reese, David Llewellyn, Evan James.

MILLS, JAMES. Chester, PA
September 1, 1704. September 6, 1704. B. 370.
Son James. Wife's children by her first husband, viz., Thomas, Eben. and Lydia Cornish; their grandmother Ann Kay of Boston, N. E. and their uncle Elihu Kay of Philadelphia.
Executors: Henry Hollingsworth, Paul Saunders.
Witnesses: Henry Nicholls, Baptist minister, Eben Kay, Mary Gregg.

DIX, PETER. Birmingham, Chester Co.
12/12/1703/4. September 8, 1704. B. 374.
Signed also by his wife. Children Nathan, Peter, Elizabeth, Sarah, Esther and Deborah. Daughter Hannah Thatcher. Friends John Bennett and Nicholas Pyle.
Executrix: Wife Esther.
Witnesses: Francis Chads, Thomas King.

FAUCIT, WALTER. Chester, PA Cordwainer.
7/2/1703. July 8, 1704. B. 378.
Children John, Nathan, Rebecca, Mary and Sarah. Cousin Mary, daughter of Thomas Sharp. Servants Caleb Harrison and William Bruce.
Executrix: Wife Rebecca.
Overseers: Caleb Pusey, Robert Barber.
Witnesses: George Moris, Paul Saunders, Randall Vernon, David Lloyd.

MEREWEATHER, MARY. Philadelphia. Widow of Richard.
August 25, 1701. September 20, 1704. B. 381.
Children James and Jane. Daughter Mary, wife of Joseph Abbot and her children Joseph and Richard Abbott.
Executor: John Swift of Bucks Co.
Witnesses: John Cockerell, Thomas Tresse, John Swift, Jr.

KIRLE, JOSEPH. Philadelphia.
2/4/1702. October 16, 1702. B. 384.
Children John, Brett [a son] and Mary. Sister Hannah Leafavour [Lefevre] and her daughters Mary and Hannah. Sister Susan Cambridge living in England and her children.
Executrix: Wife Mary.
Trustees: Isaac Norris, Thomas Masters.

Witnesses: James Wood, Thomas Willard, John Wood.

TREGENY, HENRY. Philadelphia. Merchant.
September 18, 1704. December 1, 1704. B. 388.
Children Henry, Richard, Brian, Mary and Elizabeth wife of John Urin. Granddaughter Rebecca Urin.
Executors: Wife Elizabeth and Joseph Pidgeon, merchant.
Witnesses: William Hall, William Powell, J. Moore.

LEWIS, JOHN. Haverford, Chester Co.
9/2/1704. December 2, 1704. B. 392.
Daughter Elizabeth wife of John Rees. Kinsmen John Havard, Nathan Thomas.
Executrixes: Wife Elizabeth and daughter Margaret Lewis.
Witnesses: Nathan Thomas, John Havard, William Sinkler, David Powell.

BUDD, JOHN. Philadelphia. Upholsterer.
February 5, 1701/2. December 11, 1704. B. 394.
"To each of my present wife's children." Brother William of West Jersey and his son John. James Budd living in Ireland and his son John of Philadelphia, cooper. Children of brothers William and Thomas Budd. Cousin Rebecca Wheeler.
Executrix: Wife Ann.
Witnesses: Cesar Gheselin, Thomas Withers, Charles Read.

TEETON, THOMAS. Philadelphia. Skinner.
December 18, 1704. January 3, 1704/5. B. 391.
Wife Mary living in Hardingstone, Northamptonshire and her children. Brother-in-law William Roberts.
Executors: William Hudson and William Corker.
Witnesses: Thomas Makin, John Cawdry, John Parker.

DE WITT, MARINUS. Appoquinimick, New Castle Co. Cordwainer.
June 9, 1696. November 22, 1704. B. 400.
Ann, widow of Peter King, sole Executrix, and she and her children are the only legatees.
Witnesses: James Read, Joost Stoll, James Claypoole.

TWINING, WILLIAM. Newtown, Bucks Co.

4/26/1697. April 6, 1705. B. 402.
Other children Anna, wife of --- Biles and her daughters Anna and Elizabeth; Elizabeth wife of John Rogers; Joanna and Mehitabel. Grandson William son of Stephen Twining.
Executors: Wife name not given and sons Stephen and William
Witnesses: Jonathan Scaife, Ann Scaife.

MORTON, WILLIAM. Kent Co.
January 12, 1700. November 14, 1704. B. 405.
John Richardson, son of his lately deceased wife, at John French's school. William and Margaret children of Simon and Perues Hirons. Servants Samuel Smith, Patrick and James Herriot and Thomas Oberille. Friend Esther, widow of William Freeland. A protest was entered on the ground that after the execution of the will the testator had married a young woman.
Executors: Simon Hirons, Samuel Berry, John French and Robert Porter.
Witnesses: John Evans, William Winsmore and Nath. Willson.

CRUTE (alias CROUT), THOMAS.
March 21, 1704/5. April 16, 1705. B. 412.
Signed on board the ship Catherine bound for PA Sister Jane Crout living at Dawlish in Devonshire. Estate in Barbadoes to Alice J., daughter of Robert Harwood.
Executor: John Vonla [Vanlear].
Witnesses: Thomas Hurat and Samuel Bourdet.

COATE, JAMES. Philadelphia. Carpenter.
December 16, 1704. April 19, 1705. B. 414.
Children John, Ann and others whose names are not given. Brothers Archibald Meikle and Abraham Carliell.
Executrix: Wife Mary.
Witnesses: William Crisp, Abraham Carliell, Richard Heath.

GODFREY, JOSEPH. Philadelphia. Co. Yeoman.
2/11/1705. April 23, 1705. B. 417.
Nuncupative will. Wife name not given and unborn child. Son Thomas.
Executor: Father Thomas Godfrey.
Witnesses: Samuel Richardson, Griffith Miles, John Lucken.

HEATH, JOHN. Philadelphia. Tobacconist.
April 17, 1705. ---. B. 420.
Estate in Mansfield, Nottinghamshire, to Moses Price and Benjamin Bould in trust for Nathaniel Bates of that place.
Executor: George Lowther of Philadelphia.
Witnesses: Robert Assheton, Josiah Appleton.

OWEN, ROBERT. Merion, Philadelphia. Co.
10/2/1697. May 16, 1705. B. 422.
Son Evan and other children names not given.
Executor: Cousin Griffith John.
Trustees: John Humphrey, Hugh Roberts, John Roberts, Robert Roberts, Griffith John, Robert Jones, Robert Lloyd and Rowland Ellis.
Witnesses: John Owen, Rowland Ellis, Robert Jones.

KIRKBRIDE, MATTHEW. Bucks Co.
2/17/1705. May 14, 1705. B. 425.
Children Sarah, Eles and Martha.
Executors: Wife Jane and brother Thomas K.
Witnesses: John Snowdon, Thomas Watson, Constantine Overton.

BAKER, HENRY. Bucks Co.
3/7/1698. May 23, 1705. B. 427.
Children Margaret, Phebe, Hester, Nathan and Samuel. Daughter Rachel Bunting's children. Daughter Sarah Wilson and her three children. Daughter Rebecca Willford. Cousin Sarah Canby. Friends Thomas Canby, James Yeats and William Ellet.
Executors: Son Samuel and Enoch Yardley.
Overseers: Phineas Pemberton, Richard Hough.
Witnesses: Enoch Yardley, Richard Radcliffe, Richard Hough.

WORRALL, PETER. Bucks Co. Wheelwright.
3/25/1703. May 23, 1705. B. 430.
The will was contested by the testator's niece Elizabeth Crous.
Executrix: Wife Mary, sole heir.
Witness: Samuel Beaks.

SMITH, MATTHEW. Late of Maryland, now of Philadelphia. Brewer.
May 29, 1705. June 6, 1705. B. 433.

To Charles Rumsey of Bohemia Manor and his daughter Grace. To the daughter of Murtagh and Elizabeth Hauny of Miles River, Md. to Catherine Blaney of Philadelphia., widow. Friend Thomas Hopkins and his children by his wife the daughter of Winlock Christianson.
Executor: Richard Sutton of Philadelphia., Soapboiler.
Overseer: Caspar Hoodt of Philadelphia., tailor.
Witnesses: Josiah Appleton, Manuel Dawson, Samuel Weaver.

BAKER, JOHN. Moreland, Philadelphia. Co.
July 8, 1704. July 5, 1705. B. 436.
Daughter wife of George Gwinnup, her son George and her other children names not given. Friends Thomas Kimber and Mary Lester.
Executors: David Marple and John Butcher.
Witnesses: Edm. McVeagh and Henry Strike.

HOUGH, RICHARD. Bucks Co. Husbandman.
3/1/1704. June 11, 1705. B. 439.
Children Richard, John, Joseph, Sarah and Mary, wife of --- Atkinson. Friends William Ellet and Joseph Hanbury.
Executors: Wife Margery, son Richard and brother William Biles.
Witnesses: Jacob Janney, Abel Janney.

LEEDS, MARGARET. Philadelphia. Widow.
6/18/1703. October 11, 1703. B. 443.
Joan Gamblin, widow, and poor Quakers, sole legatees.
Administrator: John Parsons.
Witnesses: Ann Parsons, Joan Gamblin, Anthony Morris.

WHITE, WILLIAM. New Castle Co. Wheelwright.
December 22, 1702. September 14, 1703. B. 445.
Children Samuel, John and Elizabeth. Son-in-law Ralph Semson (Thomson).
Executrix: Wife Miriam.
Overseer: John Bayley.
Witnesses: John Grubb, Frances Grubb, Hugh Bawdon.

LOVE, RICHARD. Philadelphia. Cordwainer.
6/20/1703. June 2, 1704. B. 448.
Priscilla, daughter of Robert Lane of New Castle-upon-Lyne. Cecil, wife of William Love of Bristol, Eng. and Susannah, wife of John

Andrews of the same place, daughters of brother Anthony Love of Penmark, Glamorganshire. Friends Henry Grubb, Thomas Rapier of Burlington, N. J., Ann widow of Thos. Thackeray of Gloucester, N. J., Margaret Leeds of Philadelphia., George and Hannah Watson. John Love and the other children of brother Thomas Love of Penmark. Charles Hartford and Cornelius Sergeant of England.
Executors: Pentecost Teague, Dr. John Goodsonn, Thomas Story, John Parsons and Anthony Morris.
Witnesses: James Atkinson, Randall Sparkman, Rees Peters, Thomas Story.

MORGAN, OWEN. Merion, Philadelphia. Co.
9/23/1703. February 26, 1703/4. B. 451.
Wife Blanche. Son Humphrey Morgan. Daughter Mary Carpey. Friends Edward Morgan and John Lloyd.
Executrix: Daughter Katherine Morgan.
Overseers: William Lewis, Ralph Lewis, Ellis Ellis, John Bevan.
Witnesses: Daniel Thomas, John Moore, John Bevan.

PERKINS, EBENEZER. New Castle [on Delaware].
July 27, 1703. October 16, 1703. B. 456.
Children Isaac, Ebenezer, Daniel, David, Jonathan, Abigail and Elizabeth. Letters from Dorothy Cartmell, Nathaniel Cartmell, Cornelius Empson, Hugh Bawdon about the will.
Executrix: Wife Mary.
Witnesses: Derek Janson, Theunis Kunders?

SCULL, NICHOLAS. Springfield Manor, Philadelphia. Planter.
3/5/1703. September 23, 1703. B. 456.
Five other sons names not given.
Executors: Wife Mary and son Nicholas.
Overseers: Edward Farmer, Thomas Farmer, Francis D. Pastorius, Arent Klinken.
Witnesses: Peter Shoemaker, Derek Janson, Theunis Kunders?

SIDELL, JOHN. Bucks Co. Yeoman.
2/9/1704. May 5, 1704. B. 458.
Children Martha, James, John and Abigail.
Executrix: Wife Abigail.
Guardian: Joseph Kirkbride.

Witnesses: James Moon, Thomas Kirkbride, John Moon, Joseph Kirkbride.

WILLIAMSON, DUNK. Bucks Co.
February 18, 1697/8. March 6, 1699/1700. B. 462.
Wife Wallery. Sons William and John. Daughters Hannah, wife of John Gound and Margaret, wife John Johnson.
Administrator: Son William Williamson.
Witnesses: Leonard Vandegrift, Nicholas Vandegrift, Thomas Renshaw.

WALKER, GEORGE. Philadelphia.
12/22/1700. December 28, 1703. B. 465.
Sons Joseph who had two children, and Emmanuel. Daughter Rachel Reeves.
Executrix: Wife Ann.
Witnesses: Francis Cooke, John Kinsey.

ROBINSON, EDWARD. Philadelphia. Merchant.
September 7, 1699. November 4, 1699. B. 467.
Wife Elizabeth. Friend Lieut. Cor. William Markham and his wife Joanna. Friends Wm. Pritchett living in London and Mary Bradshour of Philadelphia., widow. [Original missing.]
Executor: Friend Samuel Robinson of Philadelphia., merchant. [He died before the testator and the widow administered.]
Witnesses: Charles Sober, Robert Webb, Thomas Clarke.

MUIRHEAD, HENRY.
October 10, 1699. February 1, 1699/1700. B. 470.
Brothers James, John, Gawin and William living in Scotland.
Executor: James Coutts of Philadelphia., merchant, renounced and Hercules Coutts administered.
Witnesses: Jedidiah Andrews, Patrick Robinson, Hugh Graham, Mary Jeffes.

LANGSTON, THOMAS.
October 1, 1699. November 1, 1699. B. 475.
Daughter Sarah.
Administrator: Wife Sarah.
Witnesses: William Southebe, William Fisher, Thomas Sisom.

CHANDLER, JOHN. Chichester, Chester Co.
11/30/1699. September 30, 1703. B. 476.
Kinsman George Chandler and his wife Ruth. Friends Richard Edmunds of Warr in Wiltshire, Ann Chandler, William Chandler, James Baylis, Jane Jefferes.
Executors: Kinsmen Swethen Chandler and Thomas Chandler.
Overseers: Jacob Chandler and Walter Martin.
Witnesses: Humphrey Johnson and Mary Bezer who as the wife of Ezekial Hardin deposed as to the execution of the will on 4/21/1703.
John Chandler administered October 6, 1703.

FOX, JAMES. Philadelphia. Baker.
7/8/1699. October 10, 1699. B. 479.
Daughter Sarah. Son Francis, son George and his wife Susannah and their son Joseph.
Executors: Wife Elizabeth and son James.
Witnesses: Wm. Harwood, Ralph Jackson, Thomas Wharton.

HUGH, DAVID.
---. October 23, 1701. B. 484.
Not recorded and original missing. Proved October 23, 1701 by Robert Jones and Edward Foulke, two of the witnesses. Letters testamentary to Evan Hugh, the Executor.

REES, HARRY. Radnor, Chester Co.
February 1, 1704/5. June 30, 1705. C. 1.
Wife Elizabeth. Children David, Gwen and Margaret.
Witnesses: Richard Moore, David Evan.

PARSONS, JOHN. Philadelphia.
7/1/1699. August 22, 1705. C. 3.
Brother Thomas and his children John, Thomas, James and Sarah. Brother-in-law William Tyler and his children William, John, Mary and Joane Tyler.
Executrix: Wife Anne.
Overseers: Wife's nephew Samuel Powell and Samuel Carpenter.
Witnesses: Samuel Carpenter, Abraham Hopper, Elizabeth Badcock.

READ, CHARLES. Philadelphia. Merchant.
January 4, 1704/5. August 6, 1705. C. 4.

Son Charles. Daughters Rachel and Sarah. Sisters-in-law Elizabeth Bustell and Martha Dunier.
Executrix: Wife Amy.
Overseers: Friends the wife of John Tomkins and her children, Rev. Evan Evans, Joseph Wilcox and Francis Cooke.
Witnesses: Thomas Atkins, Abraham Bickley, Nicholas Pearse.

GUEST, ALICE. Philadelphia. Widow.
6/30/1705. September 5, 1705. C. 7.
Other children John, Elizabeth wife of Arthur Holton and Phebe wife of Anthony Morris. Sister Elizabeth Hard widow. Grandson William Say, Jr. Other grandchildren Marshall and Phebe Guest, Mary Holton and Mary Guest. Deceased daughter wife of William Say, Sr.

Executor: Son George.
Overseers: Pentecost Teague and John Redman, Sr.
Witnesses: Nathaniel Edgcome, John Jones, Robert Pound.

BOWATER, JOHN. Westown, Chester Co.
5/20/1705. September 17, 1705. C. 10.
Children Mary, Elizabeth, Anne, Alice and Phebe.
Executrix: Wife Frances.
Overseers: John Bennett of Birmingham and Joseph Baker, Sr. of Edgmond.
Witnesses: John Turner, Robert Baker, Joseph Baker, Jr.

WEIR, JOHN. Late of Charlestown, S.C., now of Philadelphia. Mariner.
October 28, 1700. September 22, 1705. C. 12.
Executrix: Wife Mary, sole heir.
Witnesses: John Buckley, John Collins and Joseph Kay.

READ, AMY. Widow.
October 4, 1705. October 12, 1705. C. 13.
Daughters Rachel and Sarah. Son-in-law [step-son] Charles Read.
Executors: Francis Cooke, Pentecost Teague.
Witnesses: Abraham Buckley, Mary Senior, Sarah Ratliffe.

OGDEN, DAVID. Middletown, Chester Co.
5/16/1705. November 17, 1705. C. 14.

Children Jonathan, Martha, Sarah, Nehemiah, Samuel, John, Aaron, Hannah and Steven.
Executrix: Wife Martha.
Witnesses: Joseph Baker and John Goulding.

KIRK, JOHN. Darby, Chester Co.
8/25/1705. November 17, 1705. C. 16.
Wife Joan. Children Godfrey, William, John, Samuel, Joseph, Isaac, Thomas, Anne, Mary, Elizabeth, and Sarah.
Executors: Brother-in-law John Elliott and John Marshall.
Overseers: Adam Roads and Robert Smith.
Witnesses: John Wood, Benjamin Cliffe.

SPENCER, SAMUEL. Late of Barbados, now of Philadelphia. Merchant.
November 26, 1705. December 20, 1705. C. 17.
Sons Samuel and William. Friend Mary, daughter of Thomas Maddox.
Executor: Thomas Maddox.
Witnesses: Thomas Millard and Edward Farmar.

WELCH, SARAH. Philadelphia. Widow.
September 12, 1702. January 29, 1705/6. Codicil January 26, 1703/4. C. 18.
Daughter Susannah, wife John Guest, Esq.. Friends Alexander Paxton, William Hall, Rev. George Keith, Rev. Evan Evans, Rev. John Thomas, John Moore, David Lloyd and Charles Read. Mrs. Sarah Quarry, Margaret Tench, Rebecca Moore, the four children of Joseph Pidgeon and the six children of Francis Rawle.
Executors: William Trent, Joshua Carpenter.
Witnesses: Ralph Ward, Thomas Taesse, Charles Read, Thomas Pearb, Daniel Ridg.

SMITH, THOMAS. Darby, Chester Co.
February 11, 1705/6. March 2, 1705/6. C. 21.
Wife Sarah. Children Dorothy, Grace and Anne wife Robert Smith who had children Thomas, Richard, Sarah, Robert, Elizabeth, Mary and William Smith. Brothers John and William and their children.
Overseers: Brother John and brother-in-law John Marshall.
Witnesses: John Archer, Anthony Lee, Benjamin Cliffe.

JANSEN, REINER. Philadelphia. Printer.
11/26/1705/6. March 6, 1705/6. C. 22.
Children Stephen living in Amsterdam, Tiberius, Jinity wife of Matthias Melaen, Joseph and Alice wife of John Piggot.
Executors: Richard Hill, Isaac Norris, Pentecost Teague and Robert Burrwer [Brewer?].
Witnesses: Thomas Story, Samuel Borden, John Davis.

PARKEN, LASSEY. Ridley, Chester Co. Batchelor.
October 11, 1705. October 26, 26, 1705. C. 24.
Nuncupative will. "Who died 8/13/1705." Nephew Jacob Archer. Mother, name not given.
Witnesses: Enoch Enochovn aged 35 years, Elizabeth Peterson aged 17 years, Frederic Uring, Elizabeth Pritchett aged 50 years, Mary Broome aged 16 years and John Archer aged 56 years.

WILLARD, GEORGE. Warminster, Bucks Co.
11/24/1705/6. March 30, 1706. C. 25.
Susannah, Elizabeth, James, John, Joseph and George children of John Shaw. Philip son of Ralph Dracutt and Nicholas Randall.
Executors: John Shaw and nephew George Willard.
Witnesses: John Webster, William Hayhurst.

REECE, DAVID. Newtown, Chester Co. Yeoman.
11/14/1705/6. March 30, 1706. C. 26.
Wife Eleanor. Son Lewis.
Executor: Son Thomas.
Overseers: David Morrice of Marple, Henry Lewis of Haverford, and Richard Hayes.
Witnesses: Evan David, John Reece.

ELLIS, ELLIS. Haverford, Chester Co.
6/13/1705. April 6/1706. C. 28.
Son Thomas and other children names not given.
Executrix: Wife name not given.
Overseers: Rowland Ellis, John Richard, Rees ---, Benjamin Humphrey.

EVAN, DAVID. Haverford, Chester Co.
1/16/1698. April 20, 1706. C. 29.

Children Harry, Sarah and Elizabeth David.
Witnesses: John Bevan, Evan Bevan and Elinor Bevan.

STEWART, GEORGE. Philadelphia. Mariner.
1/13/1705/6. April 23, 1706. C. 30.
Friends James Wallis of Maryland, merchant, and Robert Finley.
Executors: Samuel Perry of Philadelphia., merchant, and Dr. Hugh Graham.
Witnesses: Christopher Blackburne, John Browne, John Cadwalader.

DYMOCK, THOMAS. Bucks Co. Yeoman.
2/15/1706. May 20, 1706. C. 31.
Executrix: Wife Sarah, sole heir.
Witnesses: Joseph Kirkbride, Edward Mayes, Hester Willson.

HUDDLESTONE, HENRY. Middletown, Bucks Co.
2/16/1706. May 17, 1706. C. 32.
Wife Elizabeth and unborn child. Children William and Elizabeth.
Executor: Father-in-law William Cooper.
Witnesses: Henry Johnson Van Dyke, Robert Heaton and John Cutler.

HALL, DANIEL. Philadelphia. Yeoman.
11/4/1705/6. May 24, 1706. C. 33.
Executors: Sister Margery and her husband Peter Stretch of Philadelphia., watchmaker.
Witnesses: Joseph Mayfield and Maurice Lisle.

SANDERS, ELIZABETH. Philadelphia. Widow of John.
April 27, 1706. May 26, 1706. C. 34.
Children names not given. Friend George Booker.
Executors: Edward Stuffen and Nathan Stanbury.
Witnesses: James Peller, Abraham Carliell, David Lloyd.

PICKLEO, WILLIAM.
May 24, 1706. July 3, 1706. C. 35.
Wife and two children names not given.
Executors: Thomas Powell and Jasper Yeates.
Witnesses: Henry Nicols, Paul Saunders, Richard Kenderdine.

HARDY, WILLIAM. Mariner.
September --, 1705. July 3, 1706. C. 35.
Mother Mary living at Lyme Regis, England. Friend Abigail Spencer.
Executor: Henry Stephens.
Witnesses: Robert Trustrum, Joseph Keble, Henry Robinson.

DARBY, WILLIAM. Bucks Co. Husbandman.
2/28/1706. July 29, 1706.
Children William, John, Sarah and Mary.
Executrix: Wife Elizabeth.
Witnesses: Joseph Kirkbride, Samuel Parke, Thomas Kirkbride.

WOOD, GEORGE. Darby, Chester Co. Yeoman.
5/20/1696. August 24, 1706. C. 37.
Daughters Mary, Elizabeth and Eleanor.
Executor: Son John.
Overseers: John Blunstone, Thomas Wouth?
Witnesses: Benjamin Cliffe, Josias Fearne.

KITCHING, THOMAS. Dublin Township, Philadelphia Co. Yeoman.
July 16, 1706. August 24, 1706. C. 37.
Executrix: Wife Ann, sole heir.
Witnesses: Thomas Kimber, Joseph Barton, Henry Strike.

BANETSON, ANDREW. Philadelphia. Co.
August 30, 1694. September 2, 1706. C. 38.
Wife Gertrude. Children Banot, Andreas, John, Daniel, Peter, Jacob, Katharine and Bridget.
Executor: Son Andreas.
Trustees: Lawrence Cock and Andrew Rambo.
Witnesses: Swan Swanson, Lasse Cock, John Cock and Robert Longshore.
Codicil - Son Joseph born since the execution of the will.

STACKHOUSE, THOMAS. Belmont, Bensalem Township, Bucks Co. Yeoman.
9/26/1705. August 31, 1706. C. 40.
Brother John. Sisters Jennette and Ellen. Nephews John and Thomas Stackhouse.

Executrix: Wife Margaret.
Witnesses: Jeremiah Scaife, Jonathan Scaife, John Romford.

RUSSELL, MARY. Philadelphia.
7/3/1706. September 25, 1706. C. 41.
Daughter Elizabeth (sole Executrix), wife of Joseph Mather, their daughter Mary and five other children names not given. Daughter Ann Fuller.
Witnesses: Sarah Hearn, John Forrest and Jane Breintnall.

EATTON, GEORGE. Dublin Township, Philadelphia. Co.
September 14, 1706. October 16, 1706. C. 41.
Brother John and his son George Eatton. The children of John Watts, Joseph Eaton, Henry Stirke and of Patrick Kelly. Friends Mary, Sarah and Ann Davis; Samuel Jones, Thomas Powel, Evan Morgan, Joseph Wood. Servant Amos Parker.
Executors: Wife Jane and George Eatton.
Witnesses: Samuel Jones and Peter Taylor.

PUCKLE, NATHANIEL. Philadelphia. Merchant.
July 8, 1706. November 6, 1706. C. 43.
Wife's sister Mary Jobson wife of Michael Jobson and their two sons Samuel and Michael Jobson. Kinsman John King and his sister Love King, the children of Mary Jobson [by her first husband John King.] John Nailor son of Mary Jobson [by her second husband Thomas Naylor.] Aunt Deborah Puckle.
Executors: Wife Ann and daughter Deborah.
Trustees: Samuel Preston and Francis Cooke.
Witnesses: Joseph Pidgeon, John Hugg, Jr. and Elizabeth Harwood.

HARVEY, MATTHIAS. Maxfield, Bucks Co.
April 5, 1699. November 23, 1706. C. 43.
Children Matthias, Thomas, Benjamin, and Mary. The widow married John Jackson before the will was probated.
Executrix: Wife Sarah.
Overseers: Brother John Harrison and Joseph Milnor.
Witnesses: Richard Warder, Jr., William Southebe, William Boulding, Abraham Senior.

WOODWARD, RICHARD. Middletown, Chester Co. Yeoman.

September 6, 1706. January 8, 1706/7. C. 45.
Other children Thomas, Jane, Mary, Sarah and Martha, wife of --- Baker.
Executors: Wife Jane and son Joseph.
Overseers: Sons Richard and Edward.
Witnesses: Joseph Jarvis, John Worrilaw, James Cooper.

KING, THOMAS. Concord, Chester Co.
8/25/1706. January 9, 1706/7. C. 47.
Kinsman George, son of John King.
Executrix: Wife Mary.
Witnesses: Nicholas Pyle and Nathaniel Newlin.

BEVAN, WILLIAM. Philadelphia. Cordwainer.
January 4, 1706. January 25, 1706/7. C. 47.
Children William, John, Benjamin, Katharine and Margaret. Friends John Stacy, James Carroll, John Cock and Thomas Lacey.
Executrix: Wife Mary.
Trustees: Silas Crispin, Thomas Harding, William Coleman.
Witnesses: Alexander Mill, Michael Jobson, George Lowther.

WILLIAMS, REBECCA. Widow of Thomas of Philadelphia., carpenter.
December 28, 1706. February 20, 1706/7. C. 49.
Daughter Sarah Edwards and her daughter Rebecca. Daughter Rebecca School and her daughter Anne.
Executrix: Daughter Mary Williams.
Witnesses: Randall Speakman, William Snowden, Samuel Weaver.

BOWEN, NORTH. Philadelphia. Practitioner of Physick.
December 16, 1706. February 25, 1706/7. C. 49.
Daughter Elizabeth. Brothers Henry and Thomas Bowen. Sister Elizabeth. Father Thomas Bowen. Uncle Lewis Bowen. Cousin Theodorus Lord. Friends Peter Evans, George Paynter and James Wogan. Estate at Haverford-West, Pembrokeshire.
Executor: Son North Bowen.
Witnesses: Peter Stretch, Hannah England, Sarah Blake.

PRICE, ISAAC.
September 4, 1706. March 1, 1706/7. C. 51.

Children Isaac, Mary and Gwen.
Executrix: Wife name not given.
Overseers: Rowland Ellis, Thomas Rees and David William.
Witnesses: David William, Thomas Rees and Rowland Ellis.

MORGAN, ANNE. Dublin Township, Philadelphia. Co. Widow of David, who died in Maryland.
February 25, 1705/6. April 7/1707. C. 52.
Father Thomas King.
Executor: Brother Robert Mason.
Witnesses: Richard Saunders and Henry Strike.

STEVENS, EVAN. Late of Llanafonfawr, Brecknockshire, now of Philadelphia. Laborer.
October 9, 1706. September 25, 1707. C. 53.
Son Thomas Evans, daughter Eleanor Evans, brother James Evans, all of Wales. Friends Isaac son of David Williams of Whitemarsh and John Fox of Philadelphia., laborer.
Executors: David Williams and John Cadwalader.
Witnesses: John Thomas, Sarah Thomas, Elizabeth Price, Abigail Watson.

NORTHROP, GEORGE. Dublin Township, Philadelphia. Co. Yeoman.
May 12, 1707. May 26, 1707. C. 54.
Children George, Susannah, Alice, Elizabeth and Mary.
Executrix: Wife Susannah.
Trustees: Henry Stirke and Joseph Fisher.
Witnesses: John Thomas, William Owen, Dorothy Edwards.

JORDAN, JOHN. Philadelphia.
September 18, 1706. June 21, 1707. C. 55.
Executrix: Wife Thomasin, sole heir.
Witnesses: Ann Pound, John Bell, Robert Turnham.

HOOPPER, ABRAHAM. Philadelphia. Joiner.
December 28, 1706. March 5, 1706/7. C. 56.
Wife name not given. Children by her Abraham, John and Elizabeth. Children by a former wife Jacob and Mary.
Executors: Wife and son Jacob.

Trustees: Gabriel Baynes and Thomas Baynes.
Witnesses: John Ward, Thomas Carus and John Neptune Gray.

BUTCHER, JOHN. Morkland, Philadelphia. Co. Yeoman.
June 25, 1707. July 10, 1707. C. 57.
Children John, Samuel, Mary and Sarah. Legacy to Alexander Quee and Mary Parker payable on their marriage to each other.
Executrix: Wife Hannah.
Overseers: Henry Stirke and Samuel Jones.
Witnesses: Philip Honnsell, Robert McGee and Alexander Quee.

EVAN, THOMAS - JOHN. Radnor, Chester Co.
1/31/1707. September 23, 1707. C. 59.
Children John, Joseph and Elizabeth. Friends Rowland Ellis, Sr., Joshua Owen and Rowland Ellis, Jr.
Executrix: Wife Lowry-John Evans.
Witnesses: Rowland Ellis and Joshua Owen.

NEELSON, RICHARD.
August 30, 1707. September 26, 1707. C. 61.
William Horner, sole heir.
Executor: Abraham Pratt.
Witnesses: Thomas Pratt, Peter Taylor.

WARNER, WILLIAM. Blockley, Philadelphia. Co. Yeoman.
September 8, 1703. October 18, 1706. C. 61.
Other children John, William and Robert. Son-in-law James Kite had children James and Abraham. Brother Isaac Warner. Estate at Draycot, in the parish of Blockley, Worcestershire.
Executors: Wife Anne and son Isaac.
Witnesses: Ephraim Johnston, Francis Cooke, Eliz. Bringhurst.

WILLIAMS, JAMES. Chetenham, Philadelphia. Co. Blacksmith.
12/18/1706/7. October 18, 1707. C. 63.
Children names not given.
Executrix: Wife Anne.
Overseers: Rees Thomas, Rowland Powell and John Reece.
Witnesses: Richard Walter, David William, Reece Thomas, Rowland Powell and John Reece.

EVANS, JOHN. Radnor, Chester Co.
6/17/1703. November 22, 1707. C. 65.
Wife Delilah. Daughter Mary wife of David Evan. Daughter Sarah wife of John Morgan and their children Sarah and James Morgan. Daughter Jane. Daughter Margaret wife of Hugh Samuel. Daughter Phebe wife of Edward David and her three children. Sons Rees Jones and Thomas Jones. Brother Edward Evans and his daughter Elizabeth.
Executors: David Evan and John Morgan.
Witnesses: Abel Roberts, John Jarman, Evan Rees, David Lloyd and Philip Howell.

SAVAGE, SAMUEL, SR. Rocksberry, Philadelphia. Co. Mason.
November 12, 1707. November 26, 1707. C. 66.
Other children George, John, Esther and Mary.
Executors: Wife Ann and son Samuel.
Witnesses: Thomas Rutter and Abel Noble.

SIBTHORP, CHRISTOPHER. Philadelphia. Yeoman.
10/25/1707. January 24, 1707/8. C. 67.
Wife Ann. Children names not given. Sister Elizabeth Whitworth and her daughter Mary. Friends Joshua Fischer, Barbara Wright and her daughter Barbara, and Rebecca Corker.
Witnesses: Samuel Richardson, Nicholas Walln and William Roberts.

JOHN, GRIFFITH. Merion, Philadelphia. Co.
4/26/1707. January 31, 1707/8. C. 69.
Sons John and Evan.
Executor: Son-in-law Thomas Jones.
Witnesses: John Roberts and Robert Jones.

PAPEN, HYVERT.
January 30, 1707/8. February 19, 1707/8. C. 70.
Wife Elizabeth. Children Styntje, Mary, Gaertruyd, Margaret and Elizabeth.
Executors: Abraham Teunis, Claes Ruttinghuysen and William Streepers.
Witnesses: Daniel Geislering, Johannes Kosters and Richard Vanderwerf.

KLINCKEN, ARET.
12/10/1707/8. February 20, 1707/8. C. 71.
Wife Nislee. Son Anthony. Daughters Ellin Williams and Eunike wife Kunrad Kunders.
Executors: Nephew Dirck Jansen and Francis Daniel Pastorius.
Witnesses: Dennis Kunders, Abraham Teunis, Wm. Streepers and Peter Shoemaker.

KUSTER, PAUL. Germantown.
11/28/1707/8. February 23, 1707/8. C. 72.
Nuncupative will. Wife Gertrude. Children names not given.
Letters of administration were granted to Arnold Kusters, Hermanus Kusters and Johannes Kusters, the widow Gertrude being dead.
Witnesses: Arnold Kusters, Dennis Kunders, Harmanus Kusters, Johannes Kusters and Cornelius DeWees.

MILLS, JOHN. Philadelphia. Bricklayer.
February 9, 1707/8. February 11, 1707/8. C. 73.
Nuncupative will.
Administratrix: Wife Mary, sole heir.
Witnesses: Josiah Harper and Wm. Oram.

BETHELL, JOHN. Darby, Chester Co.
February 26, 1707/8. March 6, 1707/8. C. 74.
Wife Jane. Other children Samuel, Ann, John, Mary wife of Job Harvey and Sarah wife of Obadiah Bonsall.
Executors: Son William, son-in-law Job Harvey and brother-in-law Richard Parker.
Overseers: John Hood and Michael Blunstone, both of Darby.
Witnesses: Wm. Kelly, John Hood, William Kelly, Jr., and Obadiah Bonsall.

BADCOCK, THOMAS. Philadelphia. Pewterer.
January 2, 1707/8. March 9, 1707/8. C. 76.
Cousin Alexander Badcock. Friends Thomas Paschall of Philadelphia., Nicholas Rosogens and his wife, Mary wife of Robert Skeene.
Overseer: Cousin Henry Badcock of Philadelphia.
Witnesses: Martyn Jervis, Francis Cooke and William Lee.

LEWIS, WILLIAM. Newtown, Chester Co.
January 16, 1707/8. March 12, 1707/8. C. 77.
Other children David, Lewis and Evan. Grandchildren names not given.
Executors: Wife Ann (died before the probate of the will) and son William.
Witnesses: David Evan, Abraham Musgrave, George Leonard and William Lewis.

THOMAS, LEWIS. Whitemarsh, Philadelphia. Co. Yeoman.
August 14, 1707. March 20, 1707/8. C. 79.
Children Isaac, Rebecca, Sarah and Ann. David William of Whitemarsh and Thomas Reece of Haverford.
Executrix: Wife Ann.
Witnesses: John Cartlidge, Edmund Cartlidge and James Thomas.

TURNHAM, ROBERT. Philadelphia.
January 6, 1707/8. March 22, 1707/8. C. 80.
Granddaughter Frances Turnham living in Barbadoes. Friends John Vanlear and David Giffing.
Executors: Daughters Frances and Anne.
Overseers: Marvin Gaut and Edward Archer of Barbadoes.
Witnesses: Joseph Yard, Wm. Yard and Justinian Fox.

GRUBB, JOHN. Chester Co. Tanner.
February 12, 1707/8. March 28, 1708. C. 81.
Children Emmanuel, John, Joseph, Henry, Samuel, Nathaniel, Peter, Phebe and Charity wife of Richard Beeson.
Executrix: Wife Frances.
Witnesses: Thomas Pryor, Thomas Harding, Richard Heath and John Redman, Sr.

BARTRAM, ISAAC. Darby, Chester Co.
March 7, 1707/8. April 3, 1708. C. 82.
Mother Elizabeth. Brother William and his sons John and James.
Executors: Brother William and John Hood.
Witnesses: John Smith, Thomas Hood, William Smith and Obadiah Bonsall.

HODGES, THOMAS. Philadelphia. Yeoman.

1/21/1707/8. April 3, 1708. C. ---.
Children names not given.
Executors: Wife Hannah and father-in-law Nicholas Waln.
Witnesses: Jas. Morgan. Eliz. Morgan and John Michener.

LANGHAM, ROBERT. Chichester, Chester Co. Yeoman.
March 24, 1707/8. April 10, 1708. C. 84.
Wife Elizabeth and unborn child. Daughter Mary.
Witnesses: John Maxfield, Caleb Pusey, Thomas Hendrickson, and Thomas Bright.

HUNTLER, WILLIAM. Kennett, Chester Co.
1/1/1707/8. April 10, 1708. C. 85.
Children Francis, Mary, Deborah and Sarah. Friend Elizabeth wife of Thomas Hope.
Executrix: Wife Mary.
Overseers: Thomas Hope and Edward Bennett.
Witnesses: John Hope, Grace Chads and Hugh Bawden.

HOPE, THOMAS. Kennett, Chester Co.
March 24, 1707/8. April 10, 1708. C. 86.
Brothers John and Francis. Sister Susannah. Servants James King and John Houghkins. Friend Ralph Draket of Bucks Co.
Executrix: Wife Elizabeth.
Overseers: Brother-in-law Edward Bennett and George Harlan.
Witnesses: Richard Webb and Isaac Taylor.

CARPENTER, ABRAHAM. Philadelphia. Merchant.
March 26, 1707/8. April 14, 1708. C. 87.
Sister Mary Hogoflesh of Lambeth, England, widow and her children. Sister Damaris wife of David Hunt. The children of deceased brother John of Hersham, Sussex, Eng. The children of deceased sister Deborah Jupp. Brother Joshua and his wife Elizabeth and their son. Brother Samuel and his wife Hannah and their children John and Samuel. Cousin John Carpenter. Cousin Samuel son of William and Hannah Fishbourn. Cousin Sarah Fishbourn. Cousin Susannah daughter of John and Anne Welsh of Southwark. Cousin Robert Story. Cousin Samuel son of brother Joshua. Sister-in-law Elizabeth wife of brother John. Kinsman Thomas Mitchell of Philadelphia., cooper. Friends Abraham son of Anne Acton, Elizabeth daughter of

Enoch and Anne Story, Elizabeth Paine, Mary wife of George Fitzwater, Hannah Hurdiman, Deborah Hardiman and Anne daughter of Anne Seton.
Executors: Brother Samuel and his son Samuel.
Witnesses: Nehemiah Allen, Henry Flower and Richard Heath.

HENDRICK, AERENT.
April 2, 1708. April 14, 1708. C. 91.
Wife name not given. Children Henry, Agnes and Anneta.
Overseers: Clause Johnson, Peter Verbinnen and Henry Bauchols.
Witnesses: Ann Born, Edward Farmer, Klaes Jonsen, Henrich Bucholtz and Peter Verbinnen.

HARRISON, JOHN. Philadelphia. House carpenter.
January 5, 1703/4. April 14, 1708. C. 91.
Son Joseph and other children whose names are not given.
Executrix: Wife Mary.
Trustees: David Giffing and Charles Reed.
Witnesses: Francis Cooke and Joseph Yard.

SCOTHORN, ROBERT. Darby, Chester Co.
1/7/1708. April 24, 1708. C. 92.
Sons Samuel and Nathan.
Executrix: Wife Mary.
Overseers: Samuel Sellers, Jonathan Cockshaw.
Witnesses: Samuel Sellers, Benjamin Cliffe, and John Wood.

TAYLOR, ANTHONY. Philadelphia. Woolcomber.
1/2/1707/8. April 26, 1708. C. 93.
Children Jane, Mary and Elizabeth who was married and had children.
Executrix: Wife Jane.
Witnesses: Joseph Yard and Justinian Fox.

MILES, SAMUEL. Radnor, Chester Co.
4/24/1707. April 28, 1708. C. 94.
Children Phebe, Tamar and Ruth.
Executrix: Wife name not given.
Overseers: Brother Richard Miles, Stephen Bevan and Edward Reece.

Witnesses: Edward Rees, Richard Miles, David Thomas, William Davies and John Reece.

HOLSTEIN, MATTHIAS. Persyon, Philadelphia. Co. Yeoman.
December 4, 1706. May 24, 1708. C. 97.
Children Lawrence, Matthias, Andrew, Frederick, Peter and Henry.
Executrix: Wife Catherine.
Overseers: William Carter and Peter Mounts.
Witnesses: (Rev.) Andreas Sandel, Peter Cock and Thomas Makin.

FRISBY, WILLIAM. Philadelphia. Gunsmith.
April 20, 1708. April 28, 1708. C. 99.
Executor: Friend Thomas Tresse, sole heir.
Witnesses: Arthur Stevenes, Isaac Ashton and Thomas Tresse, Jr.

GREEN, ELIZABETH. Philadelphia. Widow.
January 29, 1705/6. April 28, 1708. C. 99.
Daughter Lydia Samways. Grandchildren John Green (now in England), Timothy Green, Lydia Green, Elizabeth Green and Sarah Wood. Son-in-law Thomas Asson and his son whose name is not given. Friends Robert Wood and Jedidiah Andrews.
Executors: Thomas Trease and John Harrison.
Witnesses: Arthur Stevenes, John Williams and Thomas Tresse, Jr.

DAVIES, JOHN. Philadelphia. House carpenter.
April 25, 1708. April 30, 1708. C. 100.
Children Rebecca and Hannah. Friend Joshua Johnson.
Executors: Wife Dinah, her brother Samuel Borden and Francis Cooke.
Witnesses: John Jones and David Gaunt.

BUSHALL (BOSHALL), JOSEPH. Concord, Chester Co.
12/8/1703. May 13, 1708. C. 101.
Daughter Jane wife of Walter Martin and their children Walter, Mary, Steven, John, Ann, Sarah and Elizabeth. Daughter Abigail wife of --- Pyle and their children Mary, Edith, Nicholas, Samuel and James.
Executrix: Wife Sarah.
Overseers: Caleb Pusey and Nathaniel Newlin.
Witnesses: Robert Pyle and John Vernon.

YEARSLEY, JOHN. Thornbury, Chester Co. Yeoman.
February 27, 1707/8. March 4, 1707/8. C. 103.
Son John. Daughters Ann wife of Jacob Vernon, Elizabeth wife of Moses Kay, Martha Yearsley and Hannah Yearsley.
Executrix: Wife name not given.
Overseers: Sons-in-law Jacob Vernon and Moses Kay, and Nicholas Pyle and John Lea.
Witnesses: John Willis and Randall Vernon.

JONES, JOHN. Philadelphia. Merchant.
2/28/1708. May 11, 1708. Codicil - May 2, 1708.
Wife Margaret and unborn child. Son John and his wife Margaret. Other children Richard, Grace, Samuel, Rebecca, Sarah, Jacob and Gibbs. Testators deceased wife Rebecca.
Executrix: Wife Margaret.
Trustees: Samuel Preston and Clement Plumsted.
Witnesses: John Webb, James Cooper, Thomas Story, Richard Jones, Martha --- Claypoole and Ann Webb.

RHEON, CAREON. Dublin Township, Philadelphia. Co. Batchelor.
May 6, 1708. May 18, 1708. C. 112.
Friends John Caheel and Rev. Mr. Clubb.
Executors: Thomas Kumber, Edward McVeagh, Patrick Kelly, Benj. Ashton and Henry Stirke.
Witnesses: Joseph Ashton, Jane Ashton, and Elizabeth Ashton.

GUEST, JOHN. Philadelphia. Esquire.
February 1, 1706. May 22, 1708. C. 113.
Brothers Thomas and Samuel.
Executrix: Wife Susannah.
Witnesses: Joseph Pidgeon, John McComb and William Hall.

DAWSON, EMMANUEL. Philadelphia. Mason.
March 31, 1708. May 26, 1708. C. 115.
Wife Hannah. Children William, Rebecca, Thomas, Charles and Susannah.
Executor: Henry Badcock.
Witnesses: Nehemiah Allen, Edward James and Richard Heath.

TUCKER, RICHARD. Philadelphia. Yeoman.
May 21, 1708. May 27, 1708. C. ---.
Son Nathaniel. Daughter Mary Wildren.
Executrix: Wife Jane.
Overseers: William Forrest, cordwainer, and Thomas Lassell, glazier.
Witnesses: John Brown, Richard Abrell and John Cadwalader.

FAUCITT, NATHAN. Philadelphia.
1/27/1708. May 29, 1708. C. 116.
Son John.
Executrix: Wife Jane.
Overseers: Father-in-law David Breintnall and John Wood.
Witnesses: William Mason, Benjamin Cliffe and John Croxton.

ASHTON, JOSEPH. Dublin Township, Philadelphia. Co. Yeoman.
May 15, 1708. June 18, 1708. C. 117.
Grandchildren Jane and Hannah daughters of Joseph, and John son of Benjamin.
Executors: Wife Jane and sons Joseph and Benjamin.
Witnesses: James Stone, John Prichard and Henry Stirke.

EVANS, JOHN. Radnor, Chester Co.
11/19/1707/8. June 19, 1708. C. 119.
Evan Johnes, Edward Johnes, Mary Johnes and Sarah Johnes.
Brother Edward Evans.
Executrix: Wife Mary.
Guardians: John Robert, William ap Edward, Edward Rees and Hugh William.
Witnesses: Wm. ap Edward, Hugh William.

PUGH, WILLIAM. Radnor, Chester Co. Yeoman.
June 19, 1705. June 19, 1708. C. 120.
Son Hugh Williams and his children William, Catherine, Susannah and Elizabeth. Grandson Hugh Jones and Joseph Jones. Friends Richard and Ann, brother and sister of John Roberts of Merioneth, and Jane daughter of Robert Ellis.
Witnesses: Daniel Harry, Susanna Williams and William Davies.

COEKER, JOSEPH. Philadelphia. Sawyer.
January 3, 1707/8. July 22, 1708. C. 122.

Wife Abigail.
Executor: Son Samuel.
Witnesses: Robert Tate, Hugh Hughes and Joshua Fincher.
Codicil - January 20, 1707/8. Estate at Waterford, Hertfordshire.
Friend Elizabeth Waley.
Administrator: Thomas Farman during the minority of Samuel Corker.
Overseers: John Bowyer and Elizabeth Panock.
Witnesses: Joshua Fincher, Robert Taites, Thomas Fairman.

HOUNSEL, PHILIP. Philadelphia. Co. Tailor.
June 5, 1708. July 31, 1708. C. 123.
Mary Butcher and her sister Sarah sole heirs.
Executors: Peter Lester and David James.
Witnesses: Thomas Savage, Henry Stirke and Hannah James.

JAMES, JAMES. Haverford, Chester Co. Yeoman.
6/18/1708. August 28, 1708. C. 124.
Children George, David and Sarah James. Son-in-law David Lewis and his children. Friends Rowland Powel and Adam Roades.
Executor: Son Thomas James.
Witnesses: Richard Hayes, Rowland Powell and Adam Roades.

SNEAD, WILLIAM. Philadelphia. Tailor.
5/20/1708. September 9, 1708. C. 125.
Executrix: Wife Mary.
Witnesses: Thomas Contes, Samuel Nicholas and John Cadwalader.

HARRIS, HUGH. Birmingham, Chester Co. Weaver.
1/27/1708. September 28, 1708. C. 126.
Children Evan, William, Hugh, John, Elizabeth, Ann, Jane, Lois and Olive.
Executrix: Wife Elizabeth.
Witnesses: Richard Webb, Jonathan Thatcher, William Brinton and John Bennett.

SMITH, JOHN. Bucks Co. Yeoman.
10/30/1706. September 28, 1708. C. 127.

Sisters Margery Pearson and Mary Williamson. Brothers-in-law Thomas Pearson and Daniel Williamson. Cousins Mary Pearson and Abigail Williamson.
Executrix: Wife Mary.
Witnesses: Abel Janney, John Watson and Thomas Janney.

DAVID, LEWIS. Late of Landewi, Pembrokeshire, now of Haverford, Chester Co.
3/26/1697. January 22, 1708. C. 128.
Son-in-law Peregrine Musgrove of Haverford West, Wales and his three children.
Executor: Son James Lewis.
Witnesses: Abraham Hardiman, David Lawrence and David Lloyd.
Codicil - February 26, 1707.
Witnesses: John Maris and David Jones.

JONES, EVAN. Merion, Philadelphia. Co.
1/28/1708. October 1, 1708. C. 129.
Mother's name not given. Brothers and sisters Lovely(?) Lloyd, Richard, John, Edward, Jane Sarah and Margaret Jones.
Executors: Brother Richard Jones and brother-in-law Robert Lloyd.
Overseers: Cadwalader Morgan and Abel Thomas.
Witnesses: Rowland Ellis, Richard Jones and Robert Lloyd.

BARBAR, ROBERT. Chester Co. Cordwainer.
July 13, 1708. October 2, 1708. C. 130.
Brothers Thomas, John and Richard in England and James Barbar. Nephews Thomas and Robert Barbar sons of brother John. Isaac Williams, wife's sister's son and his sisters Rachel and Hannah Williams. Lydia wife of Thomas Vernon. William Hudson, Paul Saunders. David Lloyd.
Executrix: Wife Hannah.
Overseers: William Hudson and James Lowns.
Witnesses: John Hoskins, George Woodyear, and George Simpson.

GREEN, MARGARET. Concord, Chester Co. Widow.
7/7/1708. October 6, 1708. C. 134.
Sons Robert and Thomas. Daughter Mary and her children whose names are not given. Son Thomas' children whose names are not given. Grandson Henry Green. Cousin Henry Guest. Benoni Moore

alias Peacock, Elizabeth Walker, Thomas Moore, Mary Stroad. Mary Fleming and her children names not given. Susanna Moor, George Moor.
Executors: Son Thomas Green and grandson John Moor.
Witnesses: Frances Pinick, William Pose, and Thomas Pierson.

FISHBOURN, RALPH. Chester, Chester Co.
1/12/1707/8. October 6, 1708. C. 135.
Son William and his children names not given.
Executrix: Wife Elizabeth.
Witnesses: George Simpson, Jacob Howell and Margaret Cooke.

PARSONS, ROBERT. Philadelphia.
August 2, 1708. October 11, 1708. C. 136.
Children William, Edith, Mary and Sarah.
Executrix: Wife Grace.
Witnesses: William Wossencraft, William Prigg, and Richard Heath.

JANNEY, JACOB. Bristol, Bucks Co. Yeoman.
8/2/1708. October 15, 1708. C. 137.
Son Thomas.
Executrix: Wife Mary.
Witnesses: John Rowland, William Croasdale and William Biles.

RUDMAN, ANDREW. Philadelphia. Clerck.
September 13, 1708. October 20, 1708. C. 138.
Daughters Magdalen and Ann-Katherine.
Executrix: Wife Elizabeth.
Overseers: Nicholas Pearse and John Crapp.
Witnesses: John Clubb, Andreas Sandel and Peter Evans.

CLAESEN, CORNELIUS.
September 30, 1708. October 23, 1708. C. 139.
Daughter Catherine Beerens of Philadelphia., widow and her four children names not given.
Administrator: Katherine Beerens.
Witnesses: Jacob Gaetschalck, Isaac van Sintern and Hannah Kasdorp.

RICE, CHARLES. Philadelphia.
June 28, 1707. October 25, 1708. C. 140.
Brother Peter Rice son of Jenkin Rice of Carmarthenshire. Estate in Barbadoes. Brother Richard Rice.
Executor: Abel Tudor.
Witnesses: John Vanlear and Jacob Perks.

HUNT, JOHN. Philadelphia., now in Virginia. Merchant.
October 7, 1706. December 24, 1706, York Co., Va.- November 8, 1708, Philadelphia. C. 141.
Body to be brought to Philadelphia for interment. Mother Elizabeth Hunt of Barbadoes. Son John. Kinswoman Elizabeth Palmer. Friend John Martin. Daughters Elizabeth and Rebecca. Friend Benjamin Ball. Executor-in-Chief: Friend Nathaniel Curtis of Barbadoes.
Executor in Virginia: Hon. Dudley Diggs.
Executor in Maryland: Richard Bennet.
Executor in Pennsylvania: Anthony Palmer.
Witnesses: John Thruston, Philip Moody, Benjamin Ball and William Tunley.

ROWLAND, THOMAS. Chester Co. Yeoman.
3/3/1708. November 16, 1708. C. 143.
Daughter Mary and her children whose names are not given. Friends John Robeson and Elizabeth Idings.
Executors: Wife Mary and friend John Dutton of Aston.
Overseers: George Harland and John Baldwin.
Witnesses: Michael Harland and John Renfro.

WATKINS, NOAH. Chester Co. Yeoman.
October 6, 1708. December 4, 1708. C. 144.
Nuncupative will.
Executor: Philip Yarnall, sole heir.
Witnesses: John Wade, David Roberts and Simon Akers.

MASSEY, THOMAS. Marple, Chester Co.
1/24/1707/8. December 4, 1708. C. 145.
Children Mordecai, James, Thomas, Esther, Hannah, Phoebe and Mary.
Executors: Wife Phoebe and Henry Lewis of Haverford, yeoman.

Witnesses: Jacob Taylor and Bartholomew Coppock.

SINEXSON, BRUER. Newcastle Co. Jaman [sic.]
November 25, 1708. December 15, 1708. C. 146.
Dorcas wife of son James and their eldest son Bruer. Friends Erricus Burcos and Erricus Anderson.
Executors: Wife Sophia and son James.
Witnesses: Justa Cock and John Richardson, Jr.

PLUMLY, CHARLES. Philadelphia. Joiner.
November 30, 1708. December 17, 1708. C. 147.
Son Charles. Daughter Sarah. Wife Rose. Brother George.
Executors: Brother John and father-in-law Henry Paxson.
Witnesses: Joseph Claypoole, Sarah Morrey and Richard Heath.

DEAN, MARY. Philadelphia. Spinster.
10/18/1708. December 30, 1708. C. 148.
Mary Sutton of Philadelphia. widow and her daughter Mary.
Executor: Friend John Webb of Philadelphia., tailor.
Witnesses: Thomas Nixson, Susanna Webb and William Monington.

WOLF, PAUL. Germantown. Weaver.
5/5/1708. January 6, 1708/9. C. 149.
Brother Ebbe Wolf's widow Mary. Sisters Mary, Engeborg, Dorothy, Ann, Christine and Katherine who were born in Tendern in the Duchy of Holstein. Wife's sister Trintie once wife of Hieronymus Bonus of Hamburg, Germany, deceased.
Executors: Francis Daniel Pastorius and Peter Shoemaker.
Witnesses: Dennis Kunders, Lenart Arets and Anthony Loof.

O'LASH, HUGH. Philadelphia.
July 29, 1708. January 11, 1708/9. C. 150.
[See No. 138 for a later will.]
Executor: Friend Thomas Tresee.
Witnesses: Anthony Stevens, Francis Jarvis and Thomas Tresse, Jr.

GRIGG, ALEXANDER. Philadelphia. Co. Laborer
December 29, 1708. January 3, 1708/9. C. 151.
Nuncupative will.
Administrator: John Collett, sole heir.

Witnesses: John Hiberd and Joseph Hart.

BOORE, LAWRENCE, SR. Dublin Township, Philadelphia. Co. Yeoman.
November 27, 1708. February 7, 1708/9. C. 152.
Other children Andrew, Mary and Elizabeth. Elizabeth the wife being dead at that time.
Executors: Wife Elizabeth and son Lawrence.
Witnesses: Daniel McDaniel, Peter Rambo and Swen Rambo.

ENES, ALEXANDER. Benton, Philadelphia. Co.
February 20, 1707/8. February 11, 1708/9. C. 153.
His master Peter Chamberland. John Hart, Sr., and David Griffith.
Executrix: Elizabeth Dayel.
Witnesses: John Swift, Peter Chamberlin and Isaac Knight.

PEARSON, JOHN. Newtown, Chester Co.
10/8/1708. March 17, 1708/9. C. 154.
Margery wife of brother Thomas and her children names not given. Cousin Daniel Williamson and his wife Mary and their children names not given. Cousin Robert Williamson and Hannah his wife. Brother Edward and his son Lawrence and other children names not given. John Fincher and Martha his wife and their children. James Dickson. Abraham Hill.
Executors: Brother Thomas and kinsman Daniel Williamson.
Witnesses: Joseph Worrell and Thomas Selby.

HODGSON, DANIEL. Philadelphia. Practitioner of Physic.
September 1, 1707. March 23, 1708/9. C. 155.
Executrix: Wife Sarah.
Witnesses: J. Graham, John Harrison and Francis Cooke.

MORGAN, EVAN. Dublin Township, Philadelphia. Co.
December 11, 1708. April 5, 1709. C. 156.
Daughter Frances.
Executrix: Wife Mary.
Witnesses: John Manners, Joshua Todd and John Swift, Jr.

WARD,HENRY. Late of Barbadoes, now of Philadelphia. Merchant.
April 9, 1709. April 27, 1709. C. 157.

Children Henry, Judith, Ruth, Mary and Sarah.
Executors: Edward Shippen, Sr., Andrew Hannis, John Hannis, David Griffin and Anchor Smith.
Witnesses: Jacob Warren, Austice Parrott and John Cadwalader.

MAYOO, EDWARD. Bristol, Bucks Co. Merchant.
1/24/1708/9. April 28, 1709. C. 158.
Children Edward and Mary. Thomas Smith grandfather of his daughter Mary. Luke Guyant; John Balding; George Clough, bolter; John Crosswhite, joiner.
Executrix: Wife Anne.
Witnesses: William Croasdale, Samuel Burges, Jr. and Samuel Carpenter.

CARTER, HENRY. Philadelphia. Brickmaker.
October 5, 1708. May 24, 1709. C. 159.
Children names not given.
Executors: Wife Susanna and Edward Church, cordwainer.
Witnesses: Francis Cooke, William Robinson and Thomas Carter.

HUGH, DAVID. Haverford, Chester Co.
April 27, 1709. June 9, 1709. C. 160.
Children David, Ruth, Mary, Jonathan, Samuel and Caleb.
Executrix: Wife Martha.
Overseers: Father-in-law Ralph Lewis and cousins David Lewis, William Lewis and Lewis David.
Witnesses: Daniel Lawrence, Thomas James, Robert Jones and Henry Lawrence.

NICHOLAS, SAMUEL. Philadelphia. Lawyer.
11/20/1708/9. July 29, 1709. C. 162.
Children names not given.
Executrix: Wife Margeret.
Overseers: John Stacy, tanner, and John Cadwalader, schoolmaster.
Witnesses: James Tewxberry, John Price and Elizabeth Tewxberry.

CARUS, THOMAS. Philadelphia. Joiner.
December 1, 1707. August 15, 1709. C. 163.

Aunt Ellen wife of John Sanders late of Thornton, Yorkshire, and her children names not given. Friends Richard Heath and Gabriel Baines.
Executor: John Cuttler, until the aforesaid aunt or her eldest son arrive in this province.
Witnesses: Thomas Armitt, John Ward and John Webster.

BENNETT, JOHN. Birmingham, Chester Co. Yeoman.
2/14/1709. September 20, 1709. C. 164.
Other children Ann, John, Olive Pyle and her son John and her husband William Pyle. Brother Edward.
Executors: Wife Ann and son William.
Overseers: Brother-in-law William Brinton and Nicholas Pyle.
Witnesses: Nathaniel Newlin, Robert Pyle, Jos. Edwards and Isaac Taylor.

MADDOX, THOMAS. Upper Dublin Township, Philadelphia. Co.
September 24, 1709. October 18, 1709. C. 166.
Wife name not given. Children John, Thomas, Tobey and Hester.
Executors: Edward Farmar and John Roads.
Witnesses: Robert Jones, Joseph Charles and Benjamin Charles.

TITTERY, JOSHUA. Philadelphia. Potter.
Her brother Edmund Wooley and his daughter Cicely. Brother Daniel and his children. Also my sister's children. Friends Col. Robert Quarry, Bridgett Gemel, Edward Hughes and Samuel Grimsditch.
Executrix: Wife Cicely.
Trustees: Francis Cooke and Pentecost Teague.
Witnesses: Samuel Cart, Thomas Canby and Richard Warder, Jr.

MOODY, JOHN. Philadelphia. Mariner.
April 14, 1709. September 16, 1709. C. 169.
William son of William Franklin of Antigua. Children of George Riscarick and Thomas Gordon both of East Jersey.
Executors: Hugh Graham and Alexander Arbuthnot.
Witnesses: Joseph Waddington and Jeremiah Rion.
Codicil - April 19, 1709. Brother John Barslay. Children of his four sisters names not given.
Witnesses: Margaret Warrington and Joseph Warrington.

LARGE, JOSEPH. Bristol, Bucks Co. Weaver.
12/9/1705/6. September 16, 1709. C. 170.
Son Ebenezer and other children whose names are not given.
Executrix: Wife Elizabeth.
Witnesses: Sarah Dymocke, Hester Wilson, Deborah Dungan and Tobias Dymocke.

TAYLOR, SAMUEL. Whitpain Township, Philadelphia. Co. Carpenter.
10/22/1708. August 24, 1709. C. 171.
Sons John, Benjamin and Samuel.
Executors: John Blunston, Jr. of Darby, yeoman, and John Cartledge of Plymouth, yeoman.
Witnesses: Robert Wilkins, Thomas McCarty and Ann McCarty.

TAYLOR, PHILIP. Oxford Township, Philadelphia. Co.
6/30/1709. September 3, 1709. C. 172.
Wife Julian. Children Peter, Benjamin, Elizabeth, Julian, Sarah, Martha and Ursela. Friend Abel Cottey.
Executor: Brother Peter Taylor.
Witnesses: Enoch Narman, Abel Cottey and Julian Taylor, Jr.

COUCH, WILLIAM. Philadelphia.
January 25, 1710/11. February 12, 1710/11. C. 173.
Friend Mary Clark.
Executrix: Susannah Harwood.
Witnesses: Johanna Harwood, Jane Malecam and Alexander Lindsey.

DUANY, ANDREW. Late of Jamaica, now of Philadelphia. Merchant.
March 10, 1708/9. March 30, 1709. C. 174.
Wife name not given. Son Andrew. Brother Owen Duany of Co. Sligo, Ireland. Friends Michael Karney, Brian Higgins and Margaret Warthinton. William Rawlin.
Executors: Edmond Karney and Michael Booth.
Witnesses: Nathaniel Sykes, H. Graham, Thomas Andrews and Peter Bard.

O'LASH, HUGH. Philadelphia.
September 15, 1708. September 30, 1709. C. 175.

Brothers Dennis, Cornelius and Daniel. [See ante No. 116]
Executor: Friend Thomas Tresse.
Witnesses: Elizabeth Grier, Hugh Graham and George Tankersley.

THOMAS, JAMES. Late of Philadelphia.
4/2/1706. Nov. 9, 1710 at Sussex on Delaware. C. 176.
Brother Michael Thomas and his children. Brother Gabriel Thomas. Sister Mary Snead and her children. Sister Rachel Wharton and her husband Thomas Wharton and their children. Uncle James Thomas. Nieces Elizabeth, Mary and Rachel Williams and their brother. Edward and Elizabeth Shiffen grandchildren of Edward Shippen, Sr. Margaret and Hannah daughters of Samuel Preston. [See infra No. 187.]
Executors: Edward Shippen, Sr. Executor and Samuel Preston.
Witnesses: Philip Russell, Walton Huling, Jonathan Bailey and Morris Edwards.

TAYLOR, JONATHAN. Marple, Chester Co.
7/20/1709. November 26, 1709. C. 177.
Children Hannah, Mary, Thomas and Jonathan.
Executors: Wife Martha and brother-in-law Henry Lewis of Haverford.
Witnesses: Bartholomew Coppock and Joseph Selby.

FISHBOURN, ELIZABETH. Chester, Chester Co. Widow.
October 25, 1709. November 28, 1709. C. 178.
Son-in-law William Fishbourn, late husband Ralph Fishbourn. Brother Jacob Simcock and his children Hannah, Sarah, Jacob and Benjamin. Brother John Simcock. Sister Hannah. Nieces Margaret and Mary Cooke and Elizabeth wife of John Dutton. Cousin Joseph Harvey's wife. Francis Whorley and Mary his wife. William Lee, John Rightson of Maryland, Elizabeth wife of Richard Webb. Hannah wife of John Lee. James Lowns. Henry Worley. John Taylor.
Executors: Guyan Stevens and Caleb Pusey.
Witnesses: Nicholas Fairlamb, John Hoskins and John Hood.

OTTER, JOHN. Philadelphia.
3/6/1709. December 5, 1709. C. 180.
William Coleman of Philadelphia., carpenter, and his three children. John Swift. Elizabeth Hard of Philadelphia., widow. Nehemiah

Allen's children by his first wife. Mary and other children names not given of Nehemiah Allen, Sr. Richard Tison. Elizabeth wife of Samuel Hooton. Mary Estaugh. The children of Joshua Sparrow, shipwright in Redarich Co., Surrey, and his wife Elizabeth. Elizabeth Webb, Hannah Ley, Thomas Chalkley and Martha his wife. John Salkill, Richard Gove, Samuel Spencer, Thomas Pryor, Henry Clifton, John Oxley.
Executors: Griffith Jones and John Webb.
Witnesses: William Wossoncraft, Rachel Wossoncraft and Joane Clifton.

PEARSE, NICHOLAS. Philadelphia. Shopkeeper.
July 21, 1709. December 6, 1709. C. 181.
Daughter Mary. The children of his deceased sister Joan Blunt of Plymouth, Eng. Wife's sister Elizabeth Curtis and her children of Plymouth, Eng.
Executrix: Wife Mary.
Overseers: Friends Leeson Loftus and Timothy Stevenson.
Witnesses: William Robinson, Ruth Prise and John Blayney.

PEART, JANE. Philadelphia. Widow of Bryan Peart, formerly of Thurok, Yorkshire and late of Philadelphia., whitesmith.
April 28, 1708. December 7, 1709. C. 182.
Children Benjamin, Ralph, Anne, Margaret, Rachel and William.
Executors: Thomas Raper of Burlington and son-in-law James Rush of Phila., smith.
Witnesses: David Lloyd, Richard Heath, Timothy Stevenson and Elizabeth Stevenson.

WORRILAW, THOMAS. Philadelphia. Yeoman.
May 23, 1709. December 9, 1709. C. 183.
Wife Susanna. Son John and his children whose names are not given. Grandsons Thomas Worrilaw, Walter Worrilaw and William Beakes.
Executors: Son-in-law Daniel Hoops and friend John Marris.
Witnesses: Richard Heath, Joseph Ranstead, William Green and Joshua Lawrence.

PRATT, ABRAHAM. Dublin Township, Philadelphia. Co.
October 24, 1709. December 21, 1709. C. 185.

Children Thomas, Joseph, John, Jeremy and Elizabeth. Isaac Waterman.
Executrix: Wife Jane.
Witnesses: Edward McKeach and Peter Taylor.

EATON, EDWARD. Abington, Philadelphia. Co. Shoemaker.
November 11, 1708. December 29, 1709. C. 186.
Daughters Mary and Sarah.
Executrix: Wife Sarah.
Witnesses: Joseph Phipps, George Shoemaker and John Roberts.

JANSEN, DIRK, SR. Germantown. Laborer.
December 12, 1709. January 3, 1709/10. C. 187.
Friends Henry Tibben, Maricke daughter of Arnold van Vossen. Brother Dirk Jansan and Magdalene his wife and their children in Germany. Sister Stintje and her children.
Executors: Dennis Kunders, William Streepers and Henry Tibben.
Witnesses: Johannes Rebenstock, Claus Braun and Francis Daniel Pastorius.

BROCK, THOMAS. New Bristol, Bucks Co.
November 16, 1709. January 3, 1709/10. C. 188.
Wife Julian.
Executors: Son-in-law Michael Huff and John Baldwin.
Witnesses: John Chenowith, Benjamin Collins and Nathaniel Clamants.

ALBERSON, WILLIAM. Bucks Co.
December 7, 1709. January 17, 1709/10. C. 189.
Children Benjamin, Josiah, William, Abraham, Ann, Cassandra, and Rebecca Sotterthoit. Grandchildren names not given. Sons-in-law Jervis Stockdale and John Keighn. Friends George Goldsmith and Walter Forrest.
Executrix: Wife Hannah.
Witnesses: Thomas Millard, Christ. Vandergraft and John Kaighn.

WAITE, WILLIAM. Philadelphia. Yeoman.
10/19/1709. January 21, 1709/10. C. 191.
Ralph Jackson, blacksmith. Daughters-in-law Rebecca and Mercy Nicholson. Daughter Sarah Waite coming from England. Cousin

Jane Cowin and her sister. Brother Richard Waite and Mary Waite of Cumberland, Eng. Brother John Waite's four daughters.
Executors: John Salkeld and Anthony Morris, Sr.
Witnesses: William Fishbourn, Abel Cottey and Ann Story.

JEFFES, MARY. Philadelphia. Widow.
December 20, 1702. January 30, 1709/10. C. 192.
Daughter Elizabeth Cory and her children John and Mary.
Executrix: Daughter Mary Jeffes.
Witnesses: None.

PAXSON, WILLIAM. Middle Township, Bucks Co. Yeoman.
August 23, 1709. 11/26/1709/10. C. 193.
Wife Mary. Daughter Mary wife of Thomas Walmsley and their children Elizabeth, Mary, Thomas and William.
Executor: Son William.
Witnesses: James Paxson, Thomas Watson and Jeremiah Langhorn.

SCOTT, ABRAHAM. Philadelphia. Merchant.
6/26/1709. February 3, 1709/10. C. 194.
Four first cousins in England names not given.
Executrix: Wife Hannah.
Witnesses: William Branson and John Antrobus.

COOPER, WILLIAM. Buckingham.
11/30/1709. February 17, 1709/10. C. 195.
Son Abraham. Jonathan Cooper, Hannah Cooper, Ann Pearson, Sarah Bond, Israel Cooper. Grandchildren William, Elizabeth and Henry Huddleston.
Executors: Sons Joseph and Henry.
Witnesses: Thomas Wattson, Rebecca Linton and Joseph Fell.

MARSHALL, THOMAS. Bucks Co. Stonelayer.
February 15, 1709. February 27, 1709/10. C. 196.
Mary daughter of Robert Heath. James Streater.
Executor: George Pownall.
Witnesses: Robert Heath, John Routledge, Thomas Houll and Richard Lundy, Jr.

VERBINNEN, PETER. Whitemarsh, Philadelphia. Co. Smith.
December 18, 1709. March 1, 1709/10. C. 197.
Thomas Fairman. Daughters Agnes, Michael [sic] and Hannah. Nicholas Scull.
Executrix: Wife name not given.
Overseers: Clacs Johnson of Scipak and William Johnson of Abington.
Witnesses: Thomas McCarty, Ann McCarty, Garret Seigers and Edward Farmar.

HIBBS, WILLIAM.
7/28/1708. March 5, 1709/10. C. 198.
Children Joseph, Jonathan, Jacob, William, Jeremiah, Sarah, Phebe and Hannah.
Executrix: Wife Hannah.
Overseers: Daniel Walton and William Walton.
Witnesses: Abraham Griffith and Henry English.

WILSON, ESTHER. Philadelphia. Widow.
April 17, 1710. April 25, 1710. C. 199.
Son John Bowyer and his son Benjamin and his other children whose names are not given. Son William Bowyer if he comes over here. Sons Joseph Linn and Jeremiah Elfreth. Son-in-law John Clay of Bucks Co., blacksmith, and testator's daughter Esther his wife and their children whose names are not given. Daughter Sarah wife of Willoughby Warder. Henry Elfreth of Philadelphia., shipwright, and his children whose names are not given. Jacob Janney deceased, Edward Ratchife and Solomon Warder mentioned.
Executors: Friends John Sotcher of Bucks Co., yeoman, and Henry Mallows of Philadelphia., yeoman.
Witnesses: John Hart, Lydia Warder and Richard Heath.

LANE, EDWARD. Philadelphia. Co. Yeoman.
January 4, 1709/10. April 19, 1710. C. 200.
Children James, William, Samuel, Elizabeth, Christian, Ellinor and Ann.
Executors: Wife Ann and friends James Shattick and Abraham Bickley.
Witnesses: William Howard, Johann Redwizer, Ann Catharine Redwizer and Abraham Bickley.

HOWELL, WILLIAM. Cheltenham Township, Philadelphia. Co. Yeoman.
12/20/1709. April 21, 1710. C. 202.
Daughters Margaret, Eales, Deborah, Hannah and Mary wife of John Edwards.
Executrix: Wife Mary.
Overseers: Samuel Cart, John Edwards, Daniel Thomas and Thomas Canby.
Witnesses: David Potts, Thomas Potts, Thomas Edwards, William Hugh and Daniel Thomas.

PALMER, JOHN. Philadelphia. Carter.
2/3/1710. April 25, 1710. C. 203.
Mother Elizabeth Fitzwater. Brothers Thomas and William Palmer. Cousin John Rickett of Philadelphia., locksmith.
Executor: Brother William.
Witnesses: Jacob Turner, Peter Wishart and John Cadwalader.

CARTER, JOHN. Bucks Co. Yeoman.
March 20, 1709/10. May 17, 1710. C. 204.
Children Robert, William, Mary and Martha. Kinsman William Carter of Philadelphia.
Executors: Wife Grace and friends Jeremiah Langhorne and Francis White.
Witnesses: Thomas Watson and Mary Paxson.

HEADLY, JOHN. Middletown Township, Bucks Co. Carter.
May 1, 1710. May 17, 1710. C. 205.
Son John. Sons-in-law Samuel and William Bellsford. Servant Agnes Edmunson. Daughters Lydia, Mary and Martha in England and Rebecca and Rachel Bellsford.
Executor: Son Joseph.
Witnesses: Francis White, Isaac Milner and Sarah Milner.

EVAN, DAVID. Radnor, Chester Co. Yeoman.
12/16/1709. May 17, 1710. C. 206.
Wife Mary. Other children Evan; David; Philip; John; Mary; Gwen and her sons Edward and William; Margaret and her children John and Gainor; and Sarah.
Executors: Sons Caleb and Joshua.

Overseers: Rowland Ellis and his son Rowland Ellis, Jr., Rees Thomas, Rowland Powell, Richard Ormes and John Morgan.
Witnesses: Hugh William, Humphry Ellis, William Davies and John Morgan.

COOPER, HENRY. Newtown, Bucks Co. Blacksmith.
12/6/1709. May 17, 1710. C. 209.
Children names not given.
Executors: Wife Mary and father-in-law William Buckman.
Witnesses: Robert Steaton, John Penquite and John Cutter.

TANKERSLEY, GEORGE.
May 24, 1710. June 5, 1710. C. 210.
Son Richard.
Executrix: Wife Elizabeth.
Witnesses: Thomas Peart, Timothy Stephenson and Anthony Morris.

COLE, WILLIAM. Nottingham, Chester Co.
11/31/1709/10. May 2, 1710. C. 210.
Children William and Mary. Proved at Salem, N.J.
Executrix: Wife Mary.
Witnesses: John Firth, John Paine, William Hall and Isaac Seasdorp.

POUND, ROBERT. Philadelphia. Butcher.
May 19, 1710. June 27, 1710. C. 211.
Sister Anne.
Executrix: Wife Mary.
Witnesses: William Robinson, Elisha Gatchell and Richard Heath.

GRAHAM, THOMAS. Late of Annarundell Co., Maryland. Merchant.
May 20, 1710. June 21, 1710. C. 212.
Samuel and Sarah children of William Fishbourne. Proved at Annapolis, Maryland.
Executor: William Fishbourne of Philadelphia., merchant.
Witnesses: Amos Garret, Thomas Macnamara, Evan Jones, John Michiel and Margaret Macnamara.

GOFF, MARY. Philadelphia. Widow.
July 30, 1710. August 24, 1710. C. 213.

Nuncupative will.
Executor: Edward Church of Philadelphia., cordwainer.
Witnesses: Sarah Kleinhof and Mary Sheyrd.

BROWN, JAMES. Philadelphia. Mariner.
March 8, 1709. July 8, 1710. C. 213.
Edward Church and John Smart mentioned.
Executrix: Wife Sarah.
Witnesses: Richard Heath, Richard Walker and John Bayley.

WORRILAW, SUSANNAH. Philadelphia. Widow.
February 7, 1709/10. August 1, 1710. C.214.
Nephew Joseph Pike of Barnstable, Devonshire. Niece Abigail wife of Hugh Langdon of Appledore, Devonshire. Children of son-in-law John Worrilaw. William Beak Sr. apprentice. William Till of Philadelphia., joiner. Children of Daniel Hoops of Chester Co., yeoman. Susannah daughter of Alexander Brid late of Philadelphia., mariner. Jane wife of David Breintnall. Joshua Hoops of Bucks Co., yeoman. Ralph Jackson of Philadelphia., blacksmith. The blind woman who was the wife of Moses Graseburg of Philadelphia., mariner. Levine Herberdinck and Mary his wife. Sarah wife of Daniel Flower of Philadelphia., carpenter. Servant Mary Edwards.
Executors: William Hudson of Philadelphia, tanner and Anthony Morris of Philadelphia., merchant.
Witnesses: Griffith Owen, John Forrest and Jane Bruentnall.

HEATH, ROBERT. Philadelphia. Yeoman.
1/22/1708/9. August 3, 1710. C. 215.
Wife Susannah. Daughters Susannah wife of Morris Morris and Ann wife of Richard Walln and Elizabeth, Hannah and Mary. William Dillworth and Joseph Willcox.
Executor: Son Richard.
Witnesses: William Preston, John Welsh, Richard Armitt and Ismael Bennett.

DICKINSON, WILLIAM. Plymouth Township, Philadelphia. Co.
4/20/1710. August 5, 1710. C. 217.
Children whose names are not given.
Executrix: Wife Sarah.

Overseers: John Had, John Blunston, Rowland Ellis, David Meredith, Thomas Shuts and Lumley Williams.
Witnesses: Ellis Pugh, Sr., Ellis Pugh, Jr., and William Dickison, Jr.

EVANS, THOMAS. Upper Providence, Chester Co. Carpenter.
September 10, 1710. October 3, 1710. C. 217.
Friends Thomas Powell, Sr. Elizabeth Meales and William Bockingham of Chester Co., yeoman.
Executor: Charles Hughs.
Witnesses: Thomas Powell, Jr. and Joseph Taylor.

LASSELL, THOMAS. Philadelphia. Glazier.
July 11, 1710. October 24, 1710. C. 218.
Children Thomas, James, John, Mary and Ann.
Executrix: Wife Mary.
Overseer: William Coleman of Philadelphia., carpenter.
Witnesses: Charles Sober, John Sober and John Cadwalader.

GILBERT, JOSEPH. New Buckingham, Bucks Co.
April 15, 1707. October 17, 1710. C. 219.
Children Thomas, Sarah and Mary.
Executrix: Wife Deborah.
Witnesses: James Streater, Nathaniel Bye and John Bye.

HILOART, THOMAS. Philadelphia. Joiner.
October 8, 1710. October 25, 1710. C. 220.
Sister Sarah.
Executrix: Wife Deborah. Joseph Garrett.
Overseers: Robert Pyle and Walter Martin.
Witnesses: William Monington, Richard Armitt and Francis Reynolds.

BAYNTON, PETER. Philadelphia. Chirurgeon.
June 1, 1710. October ---, 1710. C. 221.
Nephew Benjamin Baynton's son Peter. Brother-in-law John Budd. Friends Peter Lawrence, Thomas Powell, Sr. and Thomas Powell, Jr. Sisters Rebecca Budd and Sarah Moviey.
Executrix: Daughter Rebecca.
Witnesses: Rone Plumly, Abel Suder, Nathaniel Tybee and Sarah Morey.

SIDLEWORTH, EVAN. Philadelphia. Yeoman.
October 4, 1710. November 1, 1710. C. 222.
Brothers and sisters or any of their children who shall come over to this country, no names given.
Executor: Patrick Ogleby.
Witnesses: Edward Evans, Jacob Levering and Jemima Guy.

GOVE, RICHARD. Philadelphia. Joiner.
8/18/1707. November 16, 1710. C. 223.
Daughters Sarah wife of Henry Mitchell of Bucks Co., joiner, and Martha wife of Thomas Roberts, tailor, and their children whose names are not given. Solomon Cresson and David Bruntnall mentioned.
Executors: Samuel Carpenter of Philadelphia., merchant, and William Forest of Philadelphia., cordwainer.
Witnesses: David Lloyd, Evan Owen, John Shallefos (servant to Mary Fletcher) and Richard Heath.

LINTON, JOHN. Buckingham, Bucks Co.
11/1/1708. November 17, 1710. C. 224.
Son Joseph and other children whose names are not given.
Executrix: Wife Rebecca.
Witnesses: William Cooper, Jonathan Cooper and Joseph Fell.

CRESSON (REINARD), MARY. Philadelphia. Widow.
September 30, 1707. November 9, 1710. C. 225.
Children Rachel wife of Henry Sluyter, Solomon, Jacobus and Mary.
Executors: Rachael Sluyter and Solomon Cresson.
Witnesses: Francis Daniel Pastorius, Jan Doeden and Elas Eamsen.

WARREN, EDWARD. Bristol, Bucks Co. Blacksmith.
November 14, 1710. December 2, 1710. C. 226.
Son Edward.
Executrix: Wife Mary.
Witnesses: James Moon, Lemuel Oldale and Richard Webster.

ALLIN, SAMUEL. Philadelphia. Co. Cordwainer.
10/14/1699. December 5, 1710. C. 226.
Son Samuel. Grandchildren Samuel Sisom, John Parker, Samuel Parker, Richard Parker, Mary Smyth, Ann Smyth and Elizabeth

Pegg. Friends Martha Dawson, John Swift, Thomas Hort and John Baldwin.
Executrix: Daughter Priscilla Sisom.
Witnesses: John Goodsonn, Lydia Pryria and Thomas Fairman.

DUCKETT, RUTH.
5/7/1707. July 12, 1707. C. 227.
Nuncupative will. Son James' son name not given. Daughter Ruth Usher. Thomas and Sarah Usher.
Witnesses: Hannah Hill, Elizabeth Griffith, Ann Parsons and Mary Badcock.

THOMAS, JAMES. Late of Philadelphia.
4/22/1706. 9/7/1710. C. 230.
Edward Shippen and Samuel Preston of Philadelphia., merchants. Brother Gabriel Thomas. Children of brother Micah Thomas and sisters Mary Snead and Rachel Wharton names not given. Uncle James Thomas. Nieces Elizabeth, Mary and Rachel William and their brother whose name is not given. Brother-in-law Thomas Wharton. Edward and Elizabeth grandchildren of Edward Shippen, Sr. Proved in Sussex Co. on Delaware. [See supra No. 139.]
Margaret and Hannah, daughters of Samuel Preston.
Witnesses: Philip Russel, Walton Huling, Jonathan Baily and Morris Edwards.

JOBSON, MICHAEL. Philadelphia. Merchant.
October 31, 1709. February 2, 1710/11. C. 231.
Wife Mary. Sons Samuel and Michael. Grandmother Reynolds deceased. Father Samuel Jobson deceased. Samuel Jobson of London, merchant, William Frampton, Jonathan Dickinson, Thomas Barker, Hugh Cordry, John Moor, Humphry South, Nehemiah Allen, Thomas Bowman, Sabian Cole, Griffith Jones and James Wood.
Executors: John Smith and John Knowles.
Witnesses: Joseph Claypoole, Francis Knowles, Thomas King and Richard Newcombe.

LOCK, LEONARD. Philadelphia. Co.
February 2, 1709/10. February 3, 1710/11. C. 234.
Wife Dorothy. Daughter Temsy.
Executor: Son Thomas.

Witnesses: Henry Pannebakers, John Bul and Thomas How.

RICHARDS, JOSEPH. Chichester, Chester Co. Doctor of Physick.
7/6/1705. February 16, 1710/11. C. 234.
Son Joseph Richards two eldest children Susanna and Joseph. Son Nathaniel Richards' children William, Nathaniel and Elizabeth. Son-in-law Humphry Scarlott. Daughter Ann Scarlott and her eldest son name not given. Daughter Susanna Lowns and her children Joseph, James, Hannah and Susanna.
Executrix: Wife Jone.
Overseers: Philip Roman and Robert Pyle.
Witnesses: Henry Barnes and Thomas Bowater.

EMLEN, GEORGE. Philadelphia. Innkeeper.
December 17, 1710. March 8, 1710/11. C. 235.
Children George, Samuel, Caleb, Joshua, Ann, Hannah, Mary and Sarah.
Executors: Wife Hannah, brother-in-law Samuel Garret of Darby, Chester Co., and William Hudson of Philadelphia.
Witnesses: William Corker, Jr., Caleb Sharples and John Cadwalader.

BANKSON, KATHARINE. Philadelphia. Co. Widow.
January 10, 1710/11. March 12, 1710/11. C. 237.
Children Swan and (daughter) Gartary. Sisters Bridget and Barbara Boone. Swan and Martha Cock, children of deceased sister Margaret Cock. Gartery ---.
Executors: Hans Boone and Jacob Bankson.
Witnesses: Swan Swanson, Christopher Swanson and Mary Swanson.

SMITH, FRANCIS. Kennet, Chester Co. Gentleman.
April 26, 1710. May 20, 1711. C. 238.
Other children Francis, Sarah, Jane and Ann Eyre widow.
Granddaughter Anne Reese, John Martin of Chester Creek, yeoman.
Executors: Daughter Alice wife of William Vandervere and friend Jasper Yeates.
Witnesses: George Chandler, Walter Martin and William Chandler.

JAMSEN, CLAUS. Germantown.
Executor: Son Claus, sole heir.

Witnesses: Jan Dooden, Dirck Jansen and Francis Daniel Pastorius.

TOMSON, RICHARD. Marple, Chester Co.
May 7, 1711. July 18, 1711. C. 240.
Nuncupative will. Wife Hannah and children whose names are not given.
Witnesses: John Worrall, James Dickin and Martha Dickin.

BARNES, JOHN. Philadelphia. Yeoman.
8/17/1706. January 13, 1710/11. C. 240.
Wife Mary. Kinsman John Barnes. Daughter-in-law Sarah wife of William Dilwin of Philadelphia., saddler, and her children John and Elizabeth. John son of Stephen Miller. Richard Gove. Thomas Chalkley. Samuel Cart. Everhard Boulton. Thomas Canby. Robert Fletcher. Morris Movrin of Abington, yeoman. Brothers and sisters of John Barnes if they come over to this province. John Otter and Joshua Hastings mentioned.
Executors: Anthony Morris, John Goodsonn and John Webb.
Witnesses: Ellis Jones, Thomas Story and Samuel Harriott.

MILTON, ROGER. Late of Warfield, Berkshire, now at Edmund Orpwood's in Oxford Township, Philadelphia. Co.
5/5/1711. August 1, 1711. C. 243.
Nuncupative will. Father William Milton. Brothers and sisters in England whose names are not given.
Administrator: William Passmore.
Witnesses: William Passmore, Joseph Efred, Nicholas Lucken and Roger Sones.

HANSON, TIMOTHY. Frankford, Philadelphia. Co. Yeoman.
8/1/1710. September 4, 1711. C. 244.
Wife Barbara. Children Samuel, Jonathan, Mary, Barret and Elizabeth wife of Jervase Jenkins.
Executor: Son Samuel.
Witnesses: Peter Wishart, Howell Powell and John Cadwalader.

THOMAS, NATHAN. Merion. Yeoman.
2/6/1710. August 4, 1711. C. 245.

Sister Katherine Pearson. Sister Elizabeth. Cousins Thomas and Mary Pearson. Cousin John Thomas and his grandmother --- Thomas. Cousin Nathan Thomas.
Executors: Mother Margaret Thomas and brother Owen Thomas.
Witnesses: Thomas Howell and David Evan.

THOMAS, MARGARET. Merion. Widow.
April 23, 1719. ---. C. Not recorded.
Grandson John son of James Thomas and his uncle Nathan Thomas. Daughter Catharine wife of Robert Pearson. Thomas and Mary children of Robert Pearson. Grandchildren William and Hester children of son Owen Thomas. Friend Morris Llewellin.
Executor: Son Owen Thomas.
Witnesses: James John, Griffith Llewellin and Mary Llewellin.

CRISPIN, SILAS. Dublin Township. Gentleman.
May 5, 1711. August 7, 1711. C. 246.
Son Thomas. Granddaughter Sarah Loftus. Sister Rebecca Blackfan.
Executrix: Wife Mary.
Witnesses: Margaret Assheton, William Blackfan and Robert Assheton.

EDGE, JOHN. Nether Providence Township, Chester Co. Yeoman.
July 10, 1711. August 22, 1711. C. 247.
Wife Jane. Daughter Abigail Woodward and her children Edward and Abigail. Granddaughter Margaret Woodward. Granddaughter, name not given, daughter of his son John. Brother Joseph. Son-in-law Edward Woodward.
Executors: Sons Jacob and John.
Trustees: John Sharpless and James Sharpless.
Witnesses: Thomas Pearson, John Powell and John Simcock.

WRIGHT, BENJAMIN. Philadelphia. Merchant.
May 5, 1711. September 5, 1711. C. 249.
Daughter Sarah. Friend Jonathan Dickinson.
Executrix: Wife Barbara.
Witnesses: Joseph Taylor, George Calvert and Thomas Fairman.

SMITH, JOSEPH. Philadelphia. Porter.
September 5, 1710. September 6, 1711. C. 251.

Mary daughter of kinswoman Anne Mayos. Friend Anthony Morris.
Executors: Kinswoman Anne Mayos of New Bristol, Bucks County, widow, and Pentecost Teague of Philadelphia.
Witnesses: Thomas Griffith, Arthur Starr and Mary Hooper.

ATKINSON, JAMES. Philadelphia. Shopkeeper.
2/16/1711. September 6, 1711. C. 252.
Wife Hannah's daughter Sarah the wife of John Durborough. Son Thomas' children names not given. Edward Newby son of late wife whose name is not given.
Executrix: Wife Hannah.
Overseers: Ralph Jackson, Randall Spikeman and Nicholas Walln.
Witnesses: George Gray, Abel Cottey, Clement Plumsted, Katherine Parker and Israel Pemberton.

BLAYNEY, KATHERINE. Philadelphia. widow.
September 19, 1711. September 28, 1711. C. 253.
Grandchildren names not given. Friend Owen Roberts of Philadelphia, merchant.
Executor: Son-in-law John Furnis.
Witnesses: Richard Heath, David Evans and Joseph Artrobus.

WARD, RALPH. Philadelphia.
August 2, 1711. September 27, 1711. C. 254.
Son Ralph. Daughter Susanna Parham.
Executrix: Wife Margaret.
Witnesses: Daniel Ridge, Jonathan Ashton and Thomas Tresse, Jr.

ADES, RICHARD. Philadelphia County.
7/14/1711. October 1, 1711. C. 255.
Sons Thomas and John.
Executrix: Wife Elizabeth.
Witnesses: Joseph Finney, Samuel Hanson and John Cooke.

GILBERT, JOSHUA. Philadelphia. Blacksmith.
7/18/1711. October 1, 1711. C. 256.
Father John Gilbert. Servant Paul Preston.
Executrix: Wife Elizabeth.
Witnesses: John Oxley, Christopher Thompson and Richard Warder, Jr.

GREEN, JOHN. Philadelphia. Cordwainer.
September 11, 1711. October 4, 1711. C. 257.
Nuncupative will.
Administratrix: Wife Ann, sole legatee.
Witnesses: Richard Heath, Mary Grafton and Thomas Tresse.

WALTER, RICHARD. Merion Township, Philadelphia Co.
5/7/1711. October 6, 1711. C. 257.
Son Walter. Brother-in-law David Miriak. Friend Christopher Pennock. Servant James Winter.
Executor: Son William.
Overseers: John Roberts and Edward Rees.
Witnesses: William Edward, Abel Thomas and Richard Jones.

MORGAN, CADDER (CADWALADER). Merion Township, Philadelphia County.
7/10/1711. October 10, 1711. C. 259.
Brother John Morgan. Son-in-law Hugh Evan. Cadwalader second son of son-in-law Robert Evan. Sarah wife of said Robert Evan. Elizabeth daughter of son-in-law Abel Thomas. Sister-in-law Elizabeth wife of brother Lewis Morgan and her children whose names are not given.
Executors: Sons-in-law Robert Evan and Abel Thomas.
Overseers: Edward Jones, John Roberts, David Jones and Thomas Jones.
Witnesses: Robert Roberts, Moses Roberts and ... Jones.

TURNER, JOHN. Bayberry, Philadelphia County.
August 31, 1711. October 11, 1711. C. 260.
Nephew (sic) Mary (sic) Jackson. Friends Nicholas Hicks, Mary Wilson, John Pain, John Coozens, Michael Packer, Rev. John Chubb(?), Susanna Hurt, Thomas Marbe. Daniel McDaniel's sons John and James. Andrew Banctson.
Executors: Son-in-law Daniel Jackson and Jacob Hall.
Witnesses: Joseph Satterthwaite, André DeNormandie and John Hibert.

DELWYN, WILLIAM. Philadelphia.
6/12/1711. October 5, 1711. C. 264.

Wife Sarah. Son John. Friends Christopher Blackburne; John Barnes; John Woodward, laborer; John Tilly; Samuel Brookes; John Oxley of Philadelphia, carrier; Elizabeth Gibbs alias Lodger, widow; Hannah Morris, widow; Stephen Milar of Philadelphia, mariner, for his son John; Joseph Jennet.
Executors: Dr. John Goodsonn and John Webb, tailor.
Witnesses: Peter Wishart, Sarah Brigam and Thomas Botbeon.

HEATH, RICHARD. Philadelphia.
8/7/1711. October 11, 1711. C. 264.
Sisters Ann Wall, Susanna Morris, Elizabeth Livesely, Hannah Morris and Mary Heath. Cousins Ann Phipps and Thomas, John and Sephen Arnett. Friend Joseph Parker.
Executors: Brothers Richard Wall, Jr. and Morris Morris.
Witnesses: Samuel Carpenter and William Robins.

SPARKE, RICHARD. Late of Liverpool, now of Philadelphia. Mariner.
September 9, 1711. October 13, 1711. C. 265.
Mother Anne Darbyshire; brother John Sparke; sisters Margaret and Elizabeth Sparke, all of Lancashire in Great Britain. Friends Thomas Inglefield, mariner, and Dorothy Reading, nurse.
Executors: John Maccomb of Philadelphia, tailor, and Thomas Potts, tanner.
Witnesses: Giles Green, Terance Bryan and Joseph Willcox.

TILL, WILLIAM. Philadelphia. Joiner.
6/15/1711. November 3, 1711. C. 266.
Executors: Wife Anne and brother Richard Warder.
Witnesses: Thomas Story, William Benkes, Joshua Cart and Matthew Pope.

WARDER, JOHN. Philadelphia. Pipemaker.
7/28/1711. November 3, 1711. C. 267.
Wife Agnes and unborn child. Father Richard Warder. Brother Richard Warder, Jr. Sisters Anne Till and Mary Ranstead.
Executors: Wife and brother Richard Warder.
Witnesses: Sharon Coppock, Joshua Grainger and Thomas Story.

LEE (LEA), WILLIAM. Philadelphia. Merchant.
April 8, 1711. November 10, 1711. C. 268.
Daughters Prudence Sanders, widow; Sarah and Hannah. Brothers John and Joseph Lee of Yorkshire, masons, and their children whose names are not given. Friends John Hart of Bucks County, Samuel Jones of Pennapack, Thomas Martin of Chester County, Nathaniel Jenkins, Evan Thomas, Caspar Hood and Caleb Ranstead.
Executrix: Wife Joan.
Witnesses: Lionel Britton, Martin Jervis and John Cadwalader.

HUDD, JOSEPH. Upper Dublin Township, Philadelphia County.
7/2/1711. November 10, 1711. C. 270.
Sons John and Joseph. Daughter Sarah. Brother Samuel Hudd.
Executors: Wife Sarah and brothers Thomas and Jonathan Hudd.
Witnesses: John Cadwalader, the preacher (?), Thomas Hallowell and Thomas Canby.

CART, SAMUEL. Abington, Philadelphia County. Merchant.
October 8, 1711. November 3, 1711. Codicil - 8/17/1711. C. 271.
Children John, Joshua, Samuel, Joseph, Jane and Sarah. Unborn child. Kinswoman Jane Jelson.
Executors: Wife Sarah and brother John Warder and Job Goodson.
Trustees: John Warder, Job Goodson, William Fishbourn of Philadelphia, merchant, and Joseph Kirkbride of Bucks Co., yeoman.
Witnesses: Richard Taylor, Sarah Rush, Thomas Story, Henry Bennett, Anne Bennett and Lydia Warder.

BARTON, JOSEPH. Moreland, Philadelphia County.
October 3, 1711. November 16, 1711. C. 276.
Children Joseph, Thomas and Elizabeth.
Executrix: Wife Elizabeth.
Overseers: Henry Cumley and Bartholomew Longstreet.
Witnesses: Bartholomew Longstreet, Thomas Foster, Thomas Kimber and Peter Taylor.

EDWARDS, ROBERT. New Bristol, Bucks County. Cooper.
August 14, 1711. November 16, 1711.
Children John, Elizabeth and Rebecca.
Executrix: Wife Sarah.

Witnesses: Samuel Burgess, Jr., Jonathan Greave and John Rowland.

HEATHCOTE, GEORGE. Bucks County. Merchant.
November 14, 1710. November 16, 1711. C. 277.
Two grandchildren (whose names are not given), the children of John Barker in London by Testator's deceased daughter whose name is not given. Sisters Hannah Brown and Ann Lupton and their children whose names are not given, all in England. Thomas Carlton and his three brothers and sisters whose names are not given.
Executor: Cousin Caleb Heathcote of New York.
Witnesses: Willoughby Warder, Mary Blackshaw and William Bilco.

BRITTAIN, PETER. Of the West side of Brandywine, Pennsylvania. Yeoman.
11/21/1710. November 17, 1711. C. 278.
Children Elizabeth, Deborah, Thomas, Samuel and Jonathan. Unborn child.
Executrix: Wife Mary.
Witnesses: Francis Swayne, Bartholomew Coppock and Joseph Pennock.

GILBERT, JOHN. Philadelphia. Merchant.
8/8/1711. November 19, 1711. C. 280.
Daughters Sarah Elfreth, Mary Ballard and Abigail Gilbert. Grandson Joseph eldest son of son Joseph. Grandson John son of my deceased eldest son John; other children of son John whose names are not given. Grandchildren whose names are not given, the children of Henry and Sarah Eeifreth. Grandsons William and Samuel Ballard. Granddaughter Elizabeth daughter of deceased son Joshua. Mention made of Daniel England, Susanna Harward and Richard Sutton.
Executor: Son Joseph.
Witnesses: Thomas Batson, Joshua Hastinges, John Parsons and John Cadwalader.

CLEWES, JOSEPH. Macclesfield, Bucks County. Yeoman.
12/3/1709/10. November 27, 1711. C. 281.
Children Elizabeth, Rachel, John, Joseph, Thomas and George. Unborn child.

Executors: Wife Elizabeth and brother Reuben Powner (Pownall).
Witnesses: Mary Pownall, Richard Hough and Edward Kempe.

BELLIS (BELLOWS), MATTHIAS.
8/27/1711. January 2, 1711/12. C. 283.
Children William, Matthias, Joseph, Ann, Mary and Martha.
Executrix: Wife Magdalen.
Overseers: Anthony Morris and Christopher Blackburn.
Witnesses: Anthony Morris, Ellis Jones and Jane Jones.

PENROSE, BARTHOLOMEW. Philadelphia. Shipwright.
December ---, 1709. January 7, 1711/12. C. 285.
Children Dorothy, Sarah and Bartholomew. Child unborn. Brother Thomas in England. Letters testamentary granted February 17, 1713 to Toby Leech, the widow having remarried and Wm. Trent renounced.
Executrix: Wife Hester. William Trent and Toby Leech, executors, in case his wife remarries.
Witnesses: John Bowyer, Gabriel Wilkerson and John Leech.

WHITE, MARY. Philadelphia County, Widow.
6/30, 1711. January 19, 1711/12. C. 287.
Son William Antwell. Granddaughter Mary Williams and her sister Sarah Bringhams. Daughter Hannah wife of Samuel Studley and her two daughters whose names are not given.
Executor: Son-in-law Nicholas Williams.
Witnesses: Nicholas Waln, Isaac Worell and William Preston.

JENNETT, BRIDGET. Philadelphia. Widow.
November 1, 1710. January 19, 1711/12. C. 288.
Lydia Fordham and her daughters Lydia and Margaret Fordham. Daughter Hester Spencer. Daughter Sarah Parrock and her two children James and Sarah. Two daughters of daughter Hester Spencer whose names are not given.
Executor: Son-in-law James --- Parrock.
Witnesses: Francis Cooke and John Bowyer.

DAVISSON, CHRISTOPHER. Philadelphia.
January 25, 1711/12. January 30, 1711/12. C. 289.
Nuncupative will. Granddaughter Barbara Davisson.

Executor: Edwurd Church of Philadelphia, cordwainer.
Witnesses: John Price, Jone [sic] Tate and Barbara Wright.

RICHARDS, JOHN. Philadelphia. Victnaller.
November 29, 1711. January 31, 1711/12. C. 290.
Children Thomas, John, Mary and Ann. Land in Kent County.
Executrix: Wife Susannah.
Witnesses: Thomas Sison, William Hollbrooke and John Cadwalader.

STOTHORP, ANN. Philadelphia County. Widow.
6/27/1710. ---. C. 291.
Children James Dillworth, William Dillworth, Richard Dillworth and Rebecca Dillworth. Friend Joshua Fincher.
Executors: Sons William and Richard Dillworth.
Overseers: Nicholas Walln and Edman Orbwood ...?
Witnesses: William Buzby, Richard Buzby and John Buzby.

DRACOATE, RALPH. Bucks County. Yeoman.
August 26, 1710. January 3, 1711/12. C. 292.
Wife whose name is not given. Elizabeth Randall. Letters of Administration C.J.A. granted October 13, 1712 to Nicholas Randall, Philip Dracoate the son having renounced.
Executor: Son Philip.
Witnesses: Joseph Thatcher, George Willard and Nicholas Randall.

PARKE, NATHANIEL.
Rec. photostat of original will on file.

HUGHS, CHARLES.
December 9, 1711. May 8, 1712. C. 295.
Wife Rebecca. Children Francis, John, Rebecca and Ann.
Executors: Wife and Rees Ahedward.
Witnesses: Rees Ahedward and Edward Rees.

DAVID, JOHN. Great Valley, Chester County. Yeoman.
April 19, 1712. May 31, 1712. C. 296.
Brother Evan now in Wales, land in the Great Valley if he comes to Pennsylvania. Elizabeth daughter of Lewis Walker. Friends Zacheus Weaver living at Margaret Miles; Thomas Walter and David Evan. Morgan Jones.

Executor: David Evan.
Witnesses: David Morris and John Jones.

EDWARDS, ALEXANDER, SR. Montgomery, Philadelphia. County. Yeoman.
3/9/1712. December 17, 1712. C. 298.
Sons Edward, Alexander, and their children whose names are not given, and Thomas. Daughters Margaret, Martha and Bridget and the daughters (names not given) of the last two. Grandsons James James, Griffith Miles, Joseph Todd and Alexander son of son Alexander Edwards.
Executors: Wife Katherine and son-in-law Griffith Miles.
Overseers: Cadwalader ap Evans, William John, Owen ap Evan and John William, all of Gwynedd, yeomen.
Witnesses: Thomas Jones, Robert Jones and Edward George.

FINNEY, SAMUEL. Tacony. Merchant.
March 25, 1711. August 20, 1712. C. 300.
Wife - Elizabeth; her late husband Henry Trigeny, deceased. Daughters --- Redich, --- Pidgeon and Mary. Sons John, Samuel, Joseph and Charles.
Executors: Son Charles and kinsman Robert Assheton.
Witnesses: M. Phillips, Margaret Assheton and Ralph Assheton.

MILER (MILLER), ISAAC. Bristol, Bucks County. Yeoman.
6/23/1711. August 1, 1712. C. 301.
Sons Isaac and William. Son-in-law Stephen Willson.
Executrix: Wife Sarah.
Witnesses: John Routledge, Edward Miler, Edward Radclif and Joseph Kirkbride.

SHIPPEN, EDWARD, SR. Philadelphia. Merchant.
6/2/1712. August 5, 1712. Codicil - 7/10/1712. C. 303.
Wife Esther. Sons William, Edward and Joseph; the children of the two last, names not given. Wife's son Philip James. Friends Thomas Story, gentleman, and Samuel Preston, merchant, ... Son Edward estate at Hilham in Yorkshire. William Trent, John Budd and Samuel Powell mentioned.
Executors: Sons Edward and Joseph.
Witnesses: Israel Pemberton, Samuel Powell and Nehemiah Allen.

JONES, EVAN. Montgomery Township, Philadelphia County.
6/26/1712. September 17, 1712. C. 310.
Unborn child. Son John.
Executrix: Wife Lowry.
Overseers: William Edward, Cadwalader Evan, Robert Evan and Robert Roberts.
Witnesses: Thomas Evan, John Roberts and Thomas Jones.

JENKINS, WILLIAM. Abington Township, Philadelphia County. Yeoman.
12/29/1711/12. August 16, 1712. C. 311.
Grandchildren Thomas, William, Joseph, Joanna, Elizabeth, John, Benjamin and Samuel Paschall and William, Phineas, Phoebe and Sarah Jenkins. --- Thomas, merchant of Lumphy, Co. Pembroke, Wales. John Simmins of Pimchesen, Co. Pembroke. John Ball and John Barns of Chester County. Daughter Margaret Pasetwill.
Executors: Wife Elizabeth and son Stephen.
Witnesses: Thomas Canby, Morris Morris and Daniel Thomas.

COTTEY, ABEL. Philadelphia. Watchmaker.
March 14, 1709. August 16, 1712. C. 313.
Son John, if he shall return to Philadelphia. Daughter Sarah. Grandson Abel Cottey. Andrew Job.
Executrix: Wife Mary.
Overseers: Francis Cooke and Job Goodsonn.
Witnesses: James Jacob, Peter Taylor and Julian Taylor.

VAUGHAN, JOHN. Philadelphia. Carpenter.
6/23/1712. September 29, 1712. C. 314.
Joseph Ellis son of Ellis Ellis of Haverford, deceased. Evan son of said Ellis Ellis. Other sons of said Ellis Ellis whose names are not given. Hugh Morgan of Radner, Chester County. The now youngest son of Morris Smith of Passyunk. Daniel youngest son of Richard ... If any of the testator's relations come over from Great Britain within seven years, the nearest of kin is to have the land bought from John Thomas.
Executors: Friends Samuel Preston of Philadelphia and Henry Lawrence of Haverford.
Witnesses: Thomas Stapleford, Mary Cote and John Cadwalader.

KENISON, JAMES. Philadelphia. Sadler.
August 26, 1712. September 30, 1712. C. 316.
Wife Susanna. Rebecca Corker, Joshua Fincher. William Fillpot.
Executors: Friends William Corker and Henry Lewis.
Witnesses: Thomas Potts, Thomas Jenkins and Joshua Fincher.

HARWOOD, JOSEPH. Philadelphia. Mariner.
September 6, 1712. October 6, 1712. C. 317.
Son Joseph. Henry Sprogle.
Executrix: Wife Alice.
Witnesses: Theodorus Lord, John Henry Sprogle and John Williamson.

JONES, GRIFFITH. Philadelphia. Merchant.
October 4, 1712. October 27, 1712. C. 318.
Wife Elizabeth. Sons-in-law Peter Livewell and Septimus (son of Patrick Robinson, deceased) Robinson. Joseph and Ann Willcox and their daughters Sarah and Ann. William Chancellor and Rebecca his wife. Sarah Loe and her sister Mary of West New Jersey. Granddaughters Elizabeth and Ann Jones. Son Joseph and his wife Margaret and their children whose names are not given. Grandchildren of sister Jone in Ireland. Children of Joseph Willcox whose names are not given. Widow Barker.
Executor: Son Joseph.
Witnesses: Hugh Graham, Samuel Powell and William Jones.

JOHN, WILLIAM. Gwynedd, Philadelphia County.
August 11, 1712. November 1, 1712. C. 321.
Daughters Gainor, Ellin and Katherine. Sons-in-law William Lewis and David Llywellin. John High. Ellis David, Evan Robert, Edward Folk.
Executors: Wife Jane and son John.
Witnesses: Robert Jones, Edwin Foulke, Thomas Jones, Robert Jones (another of that name) and Evan Griffith.

CRAPP, JOHN. Philadelphia County.
October 18, 1712. November 15, 1712. C. 323.
Daughter Mary, other children whose names are not given and unborn child.
Executrix: Wife Susanna.

Witnesses: [Rev.] Evan Evans, [Rev.] John Humphreys, Jonathan Ashton and John Budd.

ASSON, THOMAS. Oxford Township, Philadelphia Co. Bricklayer.
September 23, 1712. November 18, 1712. C. 323.
Children William, John, Mercy and Mary.
Executrix: Wife Mary, with the assistance of David Goffinge and John Van Laer.
Witnesses: Henry Mallows, Annie Andra and Solomon Hall.

SWANSON, SWAN. Philadelphia County. Yeoman.
July 30, 1712. December 19, 1712. Codicil - August 18/19, 1712. C. 325.
Brothers Peter and John Swanson. Sisters Katherine wife of James Lacony of West New Jersey, yeoman, and India Swanson. John son of Jacob Coolin of West New Jersey.
Executors: Wife Mary and John Stilton, yeoman.
Witnesses: John Lawrence and Andrew Sandel. Codicil - India Swanson and Mary Swanson.

COOKE, MARGARET. Philadelphia. Widow of Arthur Cooke.
10/23/1712. January 24, 1712/13. C. 326.
Sons Joseph and Benjamin. Daughter Sarah. Granddaughters Margaret Morris, Mary Cooke and Katherine Vaughan. John Cadwalader.
Executor: Son John.
Witnesses: Hugh Cordry, Richard Wood and Deborah Cordry.

RICKETTS, JOHN. Phila. Locksmith.
9/6/1712. December 20, 1712. C. 327.
Sister Elizabeth Jackson. Uncle Thomas Palmer. John Brooks.
Executor: Uncle Wm. Palmer.
Witnesses: Elizabeth Mifflin, John Furker and Ralph Jackson.

WEST, JOHN. Late of Bristoll in Great Britain and now of Philadelphia. Mariner.
December 2, 1712. January 2, 1712/13. Codicil - Of even date and 2nd, December 13, 1712. C. 329.

Daughters Mary, Martha and Elizabeth. Codicil - Brother William West, sister Mary Bromage, and Henry Little, gentleman, all of or near Bristol.
Executors: William Winston, gentleman and --- Baily, clerk of St. James Parish, Bristol, and John Eyres, of Philadelphia, baker.
Witnesses: Henry Munday, George Mifflin, John Cadwalader, William Smith and William Jacob.

PARSONS, ANN. City of Philadelphia, widow of John Parsons, carpenter.
April 5, 1705. August 26, 1710. C331.
Only daughter of my sister Susannah in Great Britain. Thomas Parsons. My brother Parsons his son by his second wife. My husband's sister's daughter Mary. --- (?) Wadington, sister of Fras. Mary. My sister in law Mary Parsons. William Sylor, my husband's sister's son. John Tylor. William Alloway, son of William Alloway. Friend Elizabeth Griffith, Friend Margaret Paul. --- daughter Ann ---. Friend John Salbel(?) and wife Agnes ---. Thomas Story --- Richard Scill---. Elizabeth Griffith, Susannah Gaill---?, Israel Preston and Samuel Carpenter.
Witnesses: Israel Pemberton, Ralph Cross.

FLEMING, PATRICK. Philadelphia. Retailer.
---. ---. C. ---.
Daughter Anne. Sister-in-law Mary Sims.
Executrix: Wife Christian.
Witnesses: Thomas Pryor, John Jones and Owen Hughes.

BARTRAM, WILLIAM. Darbey, Chester Co.
October 18, 1710. January 17, 1712. C. 335.
Wife, unnamed.
Son: John and James.
Executors: Benjamin Chambers, William Smith his uncle, father-in-law and Joseph Harvey.
Witnesses: John Maris, Jonathan Hood and William Smith.

GRINN//TCH, SAMUEL. Philadelphia County. Mason.
January 13, 1712/13. January 5, 1712/13. C. 336.
Original will missing.
Administratrix: unknown

Witnesses: William Marshall and Mary Groom.

BOON, ANN. Widow of Andrew Boon.
January 8, 1712/13. August 21/27, 1712/13. C. 337.
Daughter: Katherine.
Executors: not named.
Witnesses: Judith Joakam, who declared the decedent had three daughters, Andrew Boon, Moses Jonksor(?), James Boon.

TIBBEN, HENRY. Germantown, Philadelphia County. Husbandman.
March 23, 1712/13. April 4, 1713. C. 338.
Children Thomas, Peter, Johannes and Gertrude.
Executrix: Wife Sibilla.
Witnesses: Johanne Reienstor, William Freygers and Claus Brown.

RICHARDSON, JOHN. Kent County on Delaware. Yeoman.
March 18, 1712. March 25, 1712/13. C. 339.
John Hirons.
Executor: William Hirons.
Witnesses: Gilbert Falconar, Joseph Lushir and Thomas Wilson.

POOL, WILLIAM. Philadelphia. Blockmaker.
March 7, 1712/13. March 25, 1712/13. C. 239.
Elizabeth, Mary and Rebecca daughters of son Nathaniel Pool.
Estate in St. Michael's Parish, Bristol, England now in the hand of the testator's mother Sara Pool.
Executor: Nathaniel Pool.
Witnesses: Ann Rudd, Ann Clay and Thomas Tresse, Jr.

WARD, WILLIAM. mariner.
April 2, 1713. April 9, 1713. C. 341.
Abigail Stanton and her son Daniel. Sisters Elizabeth and Jane Ward.
Executor: Cousin Joshua Cockfield.
Witnesses: John Kearsey, Richard Warner and John Whitpaine.

CHADS, FRANCIS. Birmingham, Chester County. Yeoman.
Jan 15, 1712. April 27, 1713. C. 342.
Children Sarah, Grace, Betty, Ann, John and Francis.

Executrix: Wife Grace.
Witnesses: Edward Bennet, Sarah Bennett and John Pack.

SPENCER, JAMES. Philadelphia. Mariner.
April 6, 1712. May 1, 1713. C. 343.
Daughters Mary, Jane and Hannah. Brother Samuel.
Executrix: Wife Mary.
Witnesses: Johannes Nys, Joseph Henchman and Milcah Andrews.

THOMAS, JOHN. Philadelphia.
February 10, 1712/13. May 2, 1713. C. 344.
Daughter Given relict of Micah Thomas and her five children whose names are not given.
Executors: Wife Sarah, William Trent and Benjamin Morgan.
Witnesses: Evan Evan, clerk, John Humphrys, clerk, and Edward Glover.

QUARY, ROBERT. Philadelphia. Gentleman.
December 23, 1706. May 11, 1713. C. 345.
Sarah Elliott. Mrs. Margaret Tench. Thomas Tresse. Daniel Graham of Queens County, Ireland.
Executrix: Wife Sara.
Witnesses: James Logan, Josiah Rolfe, John Moore and Thomas Tresse, Jr.

HADDON, SAMEUL.
3/14/1713. May 15, 1713. C. 347.
Administrator: Swan Rambo, heir.
Witnesses: Lawrence Boore and Mary Boore, his wife.

BARROW, THOMAS. Newton in Cartmail, Lancaster, blacksmith.
May 15, 1713. July 22, 1713. C. 347.
Father George Barrow of the above place. Nathan Gibson, Sarah Fallowfield. Thomas Barnes. James Willson.
Executors: Peter Fearon and David Willson.
Witnesses: John Davies and Thomas Barnes.

MALLOW, HENRY. Oxford Town, Philadelphia County. Yeoman.
June 19, 1713. July 3, 1713. C. 349.

Children Henry, Thomas, Tamason, Margery and Mary all in Great Britain.
Executrix: Wife Sarah.
Overseers: Clemens Plumsted and Richard Walker.
Witnesses: Thomas Graves, John Keble and Solomon Hall.

VANDERSLUYSE, REYNIER. Philadelphia. Baker.
July 3, 1713. July 13, 1713. C. 350.
Children Arnold, Henry, Johannes, Anthony, Anna and Elencha.
Executrix: Wife Anna.
Witnesses: Lodowick Christian Sproye, John Cadwalader and --- Gunthers?

SANDERS, EDWARD. Philadelphia.
March 26, 1712/13. August 6, 1713. C. 351.
Mary Mayos. Abraham Drarihous. Elizabeth Hooper. Sarah Woolstone. Ann Woods.
Executors: William Drarihous and Jonathan Woolstone; the latter to receive the proceeds of what the testators takes with him to Barbados.
Witnesses: John Lovegrove and Andrew Sim.

ARROWSMITH, SARAH. Widow of John Arrowsmith, late of Philadelphia.
February 17, 1709/10. September 14, 1713. C. 352.
Executor: Son John Newman.
Witnesses: Clement Plumsted, F. Nevill and Noah Lawrence, Jr.

HAMMOND, HANNAH. Wife of John Hammond, of St. Panerus near Chichester, Sussex, England, needlemaker.
1/3/1707/8. September ---, 1713. C. 353.
Jonathan Shell of Rumboldsweek, Sussex, England, yeoman. William Walter of Chichester, England, merchant tailor. Stephen Stapler of Philadelphia, butcher. John Sotcher of Pennsbury, Bucks County, yeoman. Hannah and Rebecca daughters of Isaac Hammond of Chichester, needlemaker. Elizabeth Roberts of Philadelphia, tailoress. Hannah wife Thomas Kendall. Thomas Withersham. Susanna Cadman. John Fagg. Rebecca daughter of James Steel of Philadelphia, carpenter. Daniel of said John Hammond.
Executors: Stephen Stapler and John Sotcher.

Witnesses: Anthony Morgan, Thomas Story and Richard Newcombe.

REECE, THOMAS. Haverford, Chester County. Yeoman.
7/7/1713. October 10, 1713. C. 356.
Other children Sarah, Daniel, Mary, David, Isaac, Philip, Miriam, Thomas and John. Sister Margaret Reece of Pembrokeshire. David Lewis mentioned.
Executor: Son Samuel.
Trustees, guardians and overseers: Rowland Ellis, Reece Thomas, David Morris, Henry Lewis and Rowland Powel.
Witnesses: Rowland Ellis, Henry Lewis, Rowland Powell and David Morris.

PIDGEON, JOSEPH. Philadelphia. Merchant.
March 10, 1710/11. October 27, 1713. Codicil - November 17, 1711. C. 357.
Children Joseph, Mary, Rebecca and Ann. John Bird, Sarah Brown, Edward Church, William Carter, Francis Rawle, Thomas Sisom, Lewis Dewes, Peter Rambo, Jr., Swen Rambo.
Administratrix: Wife Elizabeth, c.t.a.
Witnesses: William Fisher, Stephen Bazelee and Robert Gerard.
Bondsmen: Robert Asheton, Esq., and Samuel Monkton, apothecary.

MILES, RICHARD. Radnor Township, Chester County. Yeoman.
August 29, 1713. December 23, 1713. C. 361 and 366.
Niece Sarah daughter of David Miles. Children Richard, James, Evan, John, Jane, Sarah, Hannah and Abigail. Grandson Edward Powell. Nephew Mirick Davies. Morris Jones mentioned.
Executors: Wife Sarah and son-in-law Joseph Powell.
Guardians: Brother-in-law William Davies and father-in-law of testator daughter John Powell.
Witnesses: Thomas Thomas, Ruth Miles and William Meredith.

JACOB, ROBERT. St. Michael's, Barbados. Vinter.
September 2, 1707. November 9, 1713 - Barbados. C. ---.
Being about to depart from the island. On March 24, 1713/14 Anthony who had married Sarah Jacobs, the widow, joined with her in executing a power of attorney to collect debts to John Conly of St. Michael's who was about to visit New York.
Executors: Wife Sarah, William Read and William Charnley.

Witnesses: Joseph Swaine, Thomas Taylor and Francis Delaet.

ATKINSON, HANNAH.
November 28, 1713. January 7, 1713/14. C. 367.
Daughter Grace wife of Edward Pleadwell. Daughter Sarah wife of John Durborow. Grandsons Joseph and John Durborow. Cousin Clement Plumsted trustee for daughter Hannah. John Day former husband of testatrix.
Executors: Sons-in-law Edward Pleadwell and John Durborow.
Witnesses: William Burge, J. Eyer, Thomas Wilson and Henry Haynes.

REDMAN, JOHN. Philadelphia. Bricklayer.
January 28, 1713/14. March 1, 1713/14. C. 370.
Daughter Mary wife of William Ryall. Daughter-in-law Jane widow of deceased son John Redman and her children Joseph and Sarah Redman. Son Thomas Redman's children John and Martha.
Executors: Wife Susannah and sons Thomas and Joseph.
Witnesses: William Corker, Jr., John Cadwalader and Edward Warner.

MEALES, SAMUEL. Philadelphia. Cooper.
4/2/1713. March 5, 1713/14. C. 371.
Intending a voyage to Great Britain. Katherine widow of Thomas Burden of Philadelphia., yeoman. Son Samuel. Daughter Elizabeth Baldwin.
Executors: David Brintnall, merchant, and Thomas Griffith of Philadelphia., cordwainer.
Witnesses: Elizabeth Wainwright, Samuel Wainwright, Charles Brockden and John Sober.

KOITE (KITE), JAMES. Blockley, Philadelphia County.
7/21/17--. March 24, 1713/14. C. 372.
Son Abraham. Daughter Grissell Lewis. Grandson Mordecai Lewis. John Simonds and his wife and children; John Warner; Isaac Warner and Emmanuel Walker are mentioned.
Executors: Wife Martha and son James.
Witnesses: John Warner, Ann Warner.

DU CASTELL, EDMOND.

April 4,1702. March 25, 1713/14. C. 373.
Intending voyage. Brother Abraham Boom. Eve daughter of John and Mary Doeden. Brothers and sisters names not given.
Executrix: Wife Christian.
Witnesses: Thos. Hobbard and Richard Armitt.

PHILLIPS, LEWIS. Newcastle County. Carpenter.
October 29, 1714. November 3, 1715 - at Newcastle. C. 374.
About going to England. Jacob Sorency. Elizabeth Price; Anne Price.
Executor: Friend David Price of Newcastle.
Witnesses: Ann Thomas, John Paine and Elizabeth Paine.

LICKFOLD, WILLIAM. Horsham, Sussex, England. Yeoman.
February 28, 1711/12. April 8, 1715 - London. C. 376.
Kinsman James Eade of Horsham, gentleman, property at Horley, Surrey, in the tenure of Katherine Stedwell widow, Sussex, in the tenure of John Linvill. Kinsmen Thomas, Robert, William and Henry Eade, Abraham Upfold, John and William Billinghurst, James Yates and his daughter Elizabeth, William Harding, Benjamin Trigg, Richard Smith and his five children whose names are not given. Kinswomen Sarah Bennet, Jane Loenden, Widow ---rock late of Ifield, Joan Snelling, Elizabeth White, Ann Hurat, Jane Wheeler, Hannah Billinghurst, Joan Purlacy widow and her maiden daughter name not given, Ann Hampton, Mary Yates, Martha Fallows and her seven children whose names are not given, Jane Upfold of Bishop's Sterford, Hertfordshire, spinster and Joan Naswell widow, her sister. Friends Aaron Albright, John Linvill and Thomas Humphry. Isaac Norris mentioned.
Executors: James Eade and Jane Upfold.
Overseers: Nathaniel Owen, Richard Hayton, William Wrugg and William Walker.
Witnesses: Richard Thistlewait, George Chalkley and Edward West.

FROGG, JOHN. Philadelphia. Merchant.
August 17, 1706. March 30, 1717. C. 378.
Going for a voyage.
Executrix: Wife Mary.
Witnesses: Samuel Peres, Hugh Graham, Thomas Atkins.

BARKER, THOMAS. London. Wine cooper.

April 9, 1710. April 20, 1710 - London.
Executrix: Wife Martha.
Witnesses: John Aldred, Martha Tomkins and John Smith.

GEE, JOHN. London. Merchant. Son of Joshua.
October 20, 1720 - New York. November 15, 1720. C. 380.
Brother Joshua Gee. Sister Sarah Gee.
Executor: John Spratt of New York.
Witnesses: William Vullette, N. M. Cook, John Rolland and Aide Peyster, Jr.

CARPENTER, SAMUEL, the elder. Philadelphia. Merchant.
2/6/1714. April 15, 1714. D. 1.
Son Samuel and Hannah his wife and son John and Ann his wife. Isaac Norris and Richard Hill, both of Philadelphia, merchants. Brother Joshua Carpenter and George Painter mentioned. Son William Fishbourn and Hannah his wife. On his wife's decease (Hannah) sons Samuel and John Carpenter and William Fishbourn and Hannah, his wife, to be the Executors.
Executrix: Wife Hannah.
Coadjutors: Brothers Joshua Carpenter, Samuel Preston and friends Isaac Norris and Richard Hill, Caleb Pusey of Chester County.
Witnesses: Richard Anthony, George Painter, Charles Brockden.

STANTON, ABIGAIL. Philadelphia. Widow.
May 10, 1714. May 31, 1714. D. 3.
Son Daniel, but should he die to the three children (whose names are not given), her sister whose name is not given and brother Thomas Spicer.
Executors: Brother-in-law Daniel Cooper and friend Elias Hogg.
Witnesses: Thomas Chalkley, Christian Broadgate, Joshua Lawrence.

TRESSE, THOMAS. Philadelphia. Merchant.
April 30, 1714. June 1, 1714. D. 3.
Sister Margaret Tench; cousins Joshua and Thomas Tresse. Hugh and Margaret Tresse the children of cousin Thomas Tresse; sister Elizabeth Bate in Great Britain and her two sons John and William Mawmell; brother Hugh Tresse and his children, Charles, Hugh and Sarah Tresse who are now in Great Britain; uncle William Mallett, now in Philadelphia; to friend John Hart, of Bucks County, a Baptist

minister; Samuel Jones and Abel Morgan both Baptist ministers; friend James Poulter of Philadelphia, wheelwright; Edward Church of Philadelphia, a Baptist deacon.
Executor: Cousin Joshua Tresse.
Witnesses: John Williamson, Sarah Quary, Elizabeth Pidgeon, Mary Andrews.

MIFFLIN, JOHN. The Northern Liberty of Philadelphia. Yeoman.
September 10, 1713. July 11, 1714. D. 4.
Children: Edward, George, John, Patience, Elizabeth, Jane, Samuel, Jonathan. Philip Kearney, widow Fonderslayse mentioned.
Executrix: Wife Elizabeth.
Witnesses: David Evans, Thomas Potts, John Cadwalader.

THORNTON, JOHN, JUNIOR. Late of Hemell Hempsted, Hertfordshire, now of Philadelphia. Merchant.
November 26, 1712. June 15, 1714. D. 5.
Friend Jonathan Sell; friend Andrew Heden; sister Elizabeth Thornton of Hemell Hempsted, spinster. Charles Brockden held an estate in West New Jersey.
Executors: Friends Thomas Chalkley and Charles Brockden, both of Philadelphia, gentlemen.
Witnesses: Peter Stretch, William Monington, Edward Smont, Francis Knowles.

GODFREY, THOMAS. Bristol Township, Philadelphia County. Malster.
6/10/1714. August 23, 1714. D. 5.
Children, Mary Row and Anne Beck. Grandson Thomas Godfrey, Junior.
Executrix: Wife Luce.
Witnesses: Samuel Richardson, John Lucken, George Boone, Mary Luken.

PRATT, JOHN. Abbington Township, Philadelphia County. Yeoman.
September 14, 1714. October 1, 1714. D. 6.
Children: Abraham, Thomas, Alexander, John, Jeremiah, Ester, and Sarah.
Executrix: Wife Ester.
Witnesses: Edmond Reagh, Mary Page, Henry Stirke.

BOYDEN, JAMES. Philadelphia. Mariner.
August 18, 1711. October 15, 1714. D. 6.
Children: Daniel, James, Mary, John and Sarah. Signed at Antigua, West Jersey.
Executors: Wife Meriam and George Fitzwater of Philadelphia, merchant.
Witnesses: Richard Daniell, William Pauling, Peter Laricount, Richard Tregeny, Jeffery Burth, Phillip Johns.

HARPER, JOHN. Philadelphia. Mariner.
September 30, 1713. November 6, 1714. D. 7.
Son John. Brother Josiah Harper.
Executrix: Wife Deborah.
Witnesses: Samuel Hudson, James Tucker, John Sorber.

CHAVE, BENJAMIN. Late of Port Royal in Jamaica. Tailor.
September 27, 1714. November 6, 1714. D. 8.
Now at sea in the Sloop Mary Anne, Samuel Jacob, master, bound for Philadelphia. Brother Thomas Chave of the Parish of Bishopshall near Taunton in Somersetshire. William Myers of Curacoa mentioned. Signed on board the Sloop Mary Anne.
Executor: Thomas Hurst of Philadelphia.
Witnesses: J. Watkins, Joshua Cockfield, Samuel Jacob, David Lindsay, James Warren and Francis Gibson.

IRONMONGER, JOHN. Hilltown, Philadelphia County. Yeoman.
3/31/1703. November 8, 1714. D. 8.
Eldest brother William Ironmonger of Hemington, Leicestershire, England. Brother Thomas Iremonger in England. Sisters Ann and Margaret. Wife's sisters, Hester wife of Robert Wallis, Hannah wife of Daniel Howell, Susannah wife of Jacob May and Rachell Latan.
Executors: Wife Sarah and John Hood, Senior of Darby, Chester County.
Witnesses: Ann Hood, John Hallowell and Sarah Hermon.

CARVER, JOHN. Bylery, Philadelphia County. Malster.
2/26/1713. November 8, 1714. D. 9.
Sons James, John and Richard. Daughter Mary Knight.
Executors: Wife Mary and son John.
Witnesses: John Dunkan, Joseph Gilbert and George Dunkan.

BAILY, JOHN. Philadelphia. Mariner.
October 23, 1714. November 10, 1714. D. 10.
Wife, deceased, name is not given. Sister Elizabeth Waterford of Bristol in England. Sister Sarah Huer late of Lawfords Gale, Gloucestershire. Mr. Phillips, the minister of Philadelphia; Mrs. Mary French of New Castle; Dorothy Hogsflesh of this place.
Executors: John Porterfield, Josiah Rolfe and Clement Plumstead, all of Philadelphia, merchants.
Witnesses: Richard Asmitt, George Gray, Junior, and Charles Brockden.

SIDEBOTHOM, THOMAS. Willistown, Chester County.
October 28, 1714. November 16, 1714. D. 11.
To our daughters Alice, Mary and Elizabeth and to his step daughter Ann Pruddie [sic] daughter of his lately deceased wife (whose name is not given) by her former husband Joseph Pryddre [sic]. Nuncupative will.
Executors: Daniel Williamson of Newtown, and Thomas Edwards of Easttown, both of Chester County.
Witnesses: Walter Davies and David Davies.

LLOYD, ROBERT. Merion Township, Philadelphia County.
April 30, 1714. November 16, 1714. D. 12.
Children, David, Robert, Rees, Richard, Hannah, Gwen, Sarah and Gainor. Edward Thomas and Owen Roberts mentioned. Brother Thomas Lloyd.
Executrix: Wife Loury.
Trustees: Robert Jones, Richard Jones, Thomas Lloyd, Junior, friends Robert Evan, Rowland Ellis and Robert Jones of Merion.
Witnesses: Edward Fowlke, William Robits and Thomas Albir.

DU CASTLE, CHRISTIAN. Philadelphia. Widow.
September 27, 1714. November 23, 1714. D. 13.
Children: Samuel, Edmund, Christian.
Executors: Sister Weintie Collett and friend Edward Church, both of Philadelphia.
Witnesses: Ann Budd, William Kinersly, Mary Chase.

COOKE, FRANCIS. Philadelphia.

June 2, 1705. November 26, 1714. D. 14.
Executrix: Wife Mary.
Witnesses: David Lloyd, Richard Heath, John Crapp, Pentecost Teague.

WILLIAMS, ROGER. Philadelphia. Carpenter.
November 3, 1714. December 6, 1714. D. 14.
Executor: Jeoffrey Pollard of Philadelphia, gentleman.
Witnesses: Thomas Caess, Sarah Morris and John Cadwalader.

BENIT, HENRY. Abington Township, Philadelphia County. Husbandman.
8/25/1714. December ---, 1714. D. 15.
Children's names not given.
Executrix: Wife Anne.
Overseers: Thomas Canby, Morris Morris and Richard Martin, all of Philadelphia County, yeoman.
Witnesses: William Rontleg and John Roberts.

SAY, WILLIAM. Philadelphia. Shopkeeper.
August 3, 1713. November 22, 1714. D. 15.
Eldest son William, the other children's names not given.
Executrix: Wife Mary.
Advisor: Friend Francis Cooke.
Witnesses: Francis Cooke, John Herris and George Coats.

ARETS, LENART. Germantown, Philadelphia County. Weaver.
December 1, 1714. December 17, 1714. D. 16.
Executors: Eldest daughter Catherine wife of Thomas Jones, daughter Margaret Arets, and youngest daughter Elizabeth Ann Arets.
Overseers: Denis Kunders and Reiner Tysen.
Witnesses: John Lucken, --- Looff, Daniel Pastorius, Griffith Jones.

WILLIAM, DAVID. White Marsh Township, Philadelphia County. Yeoman.
9/27/1714. December 18, 1714. D. 17.
Sons, Isaac and Joseph, daughters Phebe, Ester Denis.
Executor: Son Rees.
Witnesses: Thomas Colley, George Ransberey and Lumley Williams.

FAIRMAN, THOMAS. Philadelphia.
7/27/1711. December 22, 1714. D. 17.
Sons Thomas (now in the army of the Duke of Marlborow) and Benjamin. Daughters Ruth wife of Nicholas Heglin, Abigail wife of Jeremy Hopton.
Executrix: Wife Elizabeth.
Advisor: David Powel of Philadelphia; John Smart; Thomas Millard; Peter Virbin; Mattotsen; William Palmer.
Witnesses: John Stary, Thomas Williams, William Cotes and Neailes Loykens.

THOMAS, GABRIEL. Philadelphia. Yeoman.
December ---, 1714. December 22, 1714. D. 18.
Elizabeth the eldest and Mary and Grace the youngest daughters of his sister Mary Snead. Nuncupative will.
Executrix: Sister Mary Snead.
Witnesses: John Cadwalader of Philadelphia, gentleman, and John Warder of Philadelphia, hatter.

SHIPPEN, EDWARD. Philadelphia.
December 8, 1714. January 10, 1714. D. 19.
Wife Francina, daughter Margaret Shippen. Brother Joseph Shippen. Rev. Francis Phillips, Senior, Rev. Mar. Jannie. Sisters-in-law, Hariana and Augustina Vanderheyden. Held estate in Hillkow, Yorkshire and in Boston, New England.
Executors: Clement Plumstead and Charles Read.
Trustees: Brother Joseph Shippen, Benjamin Vining and Samuel Carpenter, son of Samuel Carpenter.
Guardian to daughters: Charles Read or if he die to friend Benjamin Vining.
Witnesses: W. Hamilton, John Kearsley, Sarah Rolfe, Elizabeth Lamb.

HARRISON, MARY. Philadelphia. Widow.
August 26, 1714. December 24, 1714. D. 20.
Daughters Sarah and Mary Harrison and son Daniel Harrison.
Executors: Eldest son Joseph and son John.
Witnesses: William Harry, Mary Furnis and John Cadwalader.

DAWES, EDWARD. Plymouth, Philadelphia County. Yeoman.

December 13, 1714. December 27, 1714. D. 20.
Wife Sarah. Children - Edward, John, Mary, Abraham, Benjamin, Sarah, Elizabeth, David and Hannah.
Executors: Brother Abraham Dawes and brother-in-law John Cadwalader, both of Philadelphia County.
Trustees: Brother-in-law John Roades and Isaac Shoemaker, both of Philadelphia County.
Witnesses: John Hanson and Phillip Ames.

BOON, WILLIAM. Boon's Island, Philadelphia County. Yeoman.
September 24, 1714. December 27, 1714. D. 21.
Children William, Anika and Gumbo.
Executrix: Wife Margaret.
Overseers: Brother Hance Boon and brother-in-law Andrew Jones.
Witnesses: Andrew Boon, Jr., Christopher Vardaman, Jr. and John Blumston, Jr.

FORREST, WILLIAM. Philadelphia. Cordwainer.
8/30/1715. January 15, 1714. Codicil - 10/11/1712. D. 22.
Sisters Ann White and Mary Hotkins, their children's names not given. Richard Townsend, Edmund Lovett and Sarah Wilmor mentioned. Codicil - Sister Ann White, Mary Hotkins, their children's names not given.
Executors: Wife Joan, Isaac Norris of Philadelphia, merchant, and William Hudson of Philadelphia, tanner.
Witnesses: Thomas Story, Anthony Morris, Anthony Morris, Jr. and Josh Lawrence.
Witnesses to Codicil: Thomas Story, Francis Knowles and Thomas Griffith.

TIBBIE, THOMAS. Philadelphia. Carpenter.
10/6/1714. January 6, 1714. D. 22.
Executrix: Wife Ann.
Trustee: Friend William Coleman of Philadelphia, carpenter.
Witnesses: James Tucker, Emanuel Walker and John Cadwalader.

FISHER, JOSEPH. Dublin Township, Philadelphia County.
December 12, 1711. January 21, 1714. D. 24.
Wife's name not given. Son Joseph's eldest son [if he should have one - name not given] and his eldest daughter Isabell Fisher. Sister's

(name not given) daughter Mary Archer. Sister's (name not given) daughter Martha Bell.
Executor: Son Joseph, sole devisee.
Witnesses: Daniel Doris, John Swift and Edward Farmar.

GRAY, JEREMIAH. Philadelphia. Baker.
January 7, 1714/15. January 29, 1714. D. 24.
Wife Joannah. Children Jeremiah and Martha.
Executors: Brother William Gray and friend William Hudson of Philadelphia, tanner.
Witnesses: Justinian Fox, George Emlen and Charles Brockden.

EDWARD, WILLIAM. Blockley Township, Philadelphia County.
December 29, 1714. January 29, 1714. D. 25.
Son Edward, daughter Mary, daughter Elizabeth wife of Thomas Lloyd, daughter Katherine, daughter Sarah, daughter Ellen. Merion Meeting.
Executrix: Wife Jane.
Overseers: Sons Edward William, Thomas Lawrence, Henry Lawrence and Thomas Lloyd and friends David Jones and Thomas Jones.
Witnesses: James Hinton, Jenkin David and Abel Thomas.

MASON, RICHARD. Dublin Township, Philadelphia County. Yeoman.
November 30, 1714. February 2, 1714. D. 25.
Children - Thomas, Joseph, Benjamin, Abraham Mason and daughters - Mary, Sarah, Hannah, Elizabeth and Susannah Mason.
Executrix: Wife Abigail.
Witnesses: William Buzby, Robert Mason and Henry Stirke.

HAYWOOD, JOHN. Philadelphia. Cordwainer.
11/17/1707/8. February 3, 1714. Codicil - December 30, 1714. D. 26.
Children Rebecca Haywood and Elizabeth, second daughter, child unborn. Thomas Marle, a lot called Whitehart. Abraham Carpenter and Mary Beavan, widow, mentioned. Absalom Petitt. Codicil - Overseer cousin Anthony Morris, Jr. of Philadelphia instead of cousin Thomas Story.
Executrix: Wife Mary.
Witnesses: Thomas Story, Francis Richardson and John Piggott.

Overseer: Cousin Thomas Story.
Witnesses to Codicil: Joseph Shippen, Charles Brockden and Ruth Emley.

DAVIS, WILLIAM. Whippan, Philadelphia County.
10/24/1714. February 10, 1714. D. 27.
Children: William, Mary, Elizabeth, Barbara, Sina, David and John.
Executrix: Wife Mary.
Trustees: Henry Lewis of Haverford and Lumley Williams of Plymouth.
Witnesses: Robert Naylor, Johanna Redwizer, David Harry and William Coulston.

JAMES, EDWARD. Philadelphia. Bricklayer.
November 27,1714. February 15, 1714. D. 28.
Eldest son William, daughters: Sarah, Anne, Alice.
Executrix: Wife Ann.
Witnesses: Nehemiah Allen, Joseph Tuckett and John Cadwalader.

OLDMAN, THOMAS. Philadelphia. Carpenter.
11/15/1714. February 21, 1714. D. 29.
Eldest son Thomas, daughter Elizabeth, wife of Paul Preston and their children Elizabeth Gilbert and Ann Preston; son Joseph, daughter Sarah, Hester, Mary, son Joseph and daughter Ann. John Hart is mentioned.
Executrix: Wife Elizabeth.
Advisors: Friends Christopher Blackburne of Philadelphia, tailor, and Henry Clifton of Philadelphia, weaver.
Witnesses: Joseph Yard, Edmund Woolly and Charles Brockden.

BINGHAM, JAMES. Philadelphia. Yeoman.
December 16, 1714. January 10, 1714/15. D. 30.
Daughter Ann wife of John Heap of Philadelphia, shipwright. Son James and daughters Mary Elizabeth and Hannah. Sister Margaret. Friend Joseph Appleton of Philadelphia, cooper. He owned a tenement in Philadelphia in High St. and an estate in Eversham Township, in Burlington County, New Jersey. Daniel Cumsant, Thomas Smith, tenants, mentioned.
Executrix: Wife Ann.
Witnesses: Phillip Roman, John Price and Charles Brockden.

BETTLE, JOHN. Philadelphia. Carpenter.
2/18/1715. April 28, 1715. D. 31.
Wife's name not given. Eldest son John, daughter Sarah Crawford and daughter Hannah Bettle, the youngest children, William, Samuel and Josiah Bettle. Friend Elizabeth Swift of Philadelphia, widow. Joseph Taylor of Philadelphia, cordwainer.
Executors: Friends Samuel Preston and Clement Plumsted, both of Philadelphia, merchants.
Witnesses: William Betredy, Anthony Ward, Thomas Peters and Charles Brockden.

HOLTON, ARTHUR. Philadelphia. Baker.
April 30, 1715. May 30, 1715. D. 32.
Only daughter Mary Holton. Sisters Sarah, Mary and Ann living near Sarum Wilthsire, their children's names not given. Cousin Hannah Guest; John Gordson, Anthony Morris, Senior. John Nys, Silon Smith and John Carpenter, merchant, mentioned as his tenants in Philadelphia. He had a bolting house on the south side of the alley previously called Carpenter's Alley between Front and Second Streets in Philadelphia.
Executrix: Wife Elizabeth.
Advisors: William Mornington and Anthony Morris, Junior.
Witnesses: Anthony Harbley, Peter Stretch, Edward Scull and Caspar Kleinhoff.

BOWEN, JOHN. Whittland Township, Chester County, Pennsylvania.
April 10, 1715. May 17, 1715. D. 33.
Wife's name not given. Daughter Anne Bowen.
Executors: Sons Evan and John.
Witnesses: Thomas Davids, Rees Prichar, Theophilus Thomas and David Daviss.

DAVIES, WILLIAM. The Manor of Mount Joy, Philadelphia County.
---. July 30, 1715. D. 34.
Children: William, Benjamin, David, Dorithey, Gwenllian, Mary, Katherine, Sarah and Priscilla.
Executrix: Wife Gwenllian.
Overseers: Friends Rees Thomas, Thomas Thomas, Rowland Ellis and Rowland Ellis, Junior.

Witnesses: Rowland Ellis, Richard Iddings and Rees Thomas.

NEWMAN, JOHN. Philadelphia. Saddler.
July 9, 1715. August 10, 1715. D. 35.
Son John. Mention is made of his mother Sarah Arowsmith, deceased.
Executrix: Wife Margaret.
Witnesses: John Bowne, Thomas Coates, Lionell Brittin and Joseph Willcox.

FULWEILER, HANS JACOB. Chester County, Pennsylvania. Husbandman.
June 1, 1715. June 27, 1715. D. 36.
Executrix: Wife Barbara.
Witnesses: John Pott, William Evance and Johannes Rietter.

GREEN, WILLIAM. Philadelphia.
October 27, 1714. September 2, 1715. D. 36.
Executrix: Sister Elizabeth, wife of John Sharp of West New Jersey.
Witnesses: Caleb Jacob, John Knight, Ennion Williams.

NICHOLS, JOSHUA. Philadelphia. Merchant.
10/24/1715. ---. D. 36.
John Ashton and John Hughes of George's Creek. Phillip Bennit of Montgottsfield in Gloucestershire.
Executors: Hester Nichols, of New York, widow, and her children Thomas and Mary Nicholas (i.e., Thomas and Mary).
Witnesses: John Warren and William Mason.

SCRASE, RICHARD. Late of the County of Sussex in Great Britain, now of Pennsylvania.
September 1, 1715. September 17, 1715. D. 37.
Uncle Walter Scrase and Charles Scrase of Blackington County of Sussex, Great Britain. Sister Anne, wife of John Houlder; sister Elizabeth, wife of Jonas Revett; sister Susanah, wife of James Lusford. Kinsmen Dennis and Solomon Rockford.
Executor: James Steel of Philadelphia.
Witnesses: Thomas Shute and Thomas Hood.

PUGH, RICHARD. Montgomery Township, Philadelphia County.
September 23, 1715. October 8, 1715. D. 37.
Children: Robert, John, Katherine, Elizabeth, Ann, Margaret and Jane.
Executrix: Wife Margaret.
Overseers: Friends John Humphrey, Oliver Bevan, Cadwallader Evan and Robert Jones.
Witnesses: William Morgan and William Roberts.

FLEET, THOMAS. Late of Hampshire, England, now residing in Philadelphia. Shipwright.
November 30, 1714. October 12, 1715. D. 38.
Executor: William Harries, late of Hampshire, England, now of Philadelphia, shipwright.
Witnesses: Jane Bitting, Sarah Fisher and John Cadwalader.

MOORE, RICHARD. Radnor Township, Chester County, Pennsylvania.
---. October 16, 1715. D. 38.
Wife Phebe, son John, and daughter whose names are not given.
Nuncupative will declared in the hearing of Stephen Evans, david Harry, Rees Thomas.
Trustees: "his father David Meredith's brother John Moore," cousin John Moore and cousin David Jones.

JANNEY, RANDOLPH. Philadelphia. Merchant.
December 1, 1715. December 8, 1715. D. 39.
Wife's name not given. Father William Janney of Mawley, Cheshire, England. Brother Thomas Janney, sister Mary, wife of George Pawley, their children: Deborah, Mary, Sarah and Thomas Pawley. Sister-in-law Agness, wife of Samuel Stretch. Mother-in-law Sarah Righton; kinswoman Sarah, Thomas, William, Mercy and Joseph all the children of Thomas and Sebilla Masters. Hannah Salloway; Thomas Welch of Congerton, Cheshire, England. William Wild of Barnet, Hartfordshire, England; friend Griffith Owen. Kinswoman Miriam Boyden; cousin Abel Janney and whose children's names are not given. For the poor of the Quakers of the Philadelphia Monthly Meeting.
Executors: Thomas Chalkley and James Steel.
Witnesses: Paul Preston, Jeremiah Elfreth and Samuel Edmundson.

CROSWHITT, JOHN. Philadelphia County. Joyner.
January 2, 1715/16. January 21, 1715. D. 40.
Children, William, Thomas and Jane Croswhitt and Anne Fleming.
Nuncupative will.
Executrix: Wife Christian.
Witnesses: William Bowell, Samuel Richardson and John Cadwalader.

LEWIS, DAVID. Haverford, Chester County, Pennsylvania. Yeoman.
1/24/1714/15. January 28, 1715. D. 40.
Children Joseph Susannah, Hannah, James and Sarah Lewis.
Executrix: Wife Katherine.
Trustees: Lewis David of Darby, Richard Hayes, Henry Laurance, Daniel Lawrance and Henry Lewis, all of Haverford Township.
Witnesses: Lewis David, Henry Lewis, Richard Hayes and Henry laurance.

MURDOCH, JOHN. Philadelphia. Mariner.
January 30, 1715. February 4, 1715. D. 40.
Wife Elizabeth. Brother Zacharias Murdoch. He had an interest in the brigantine "Ann and Elizabeth."
Executor: Friend George McCall of Philadelphia, merchant.
Witnesses: Alexander Mill, H. Graham and Hugh Lowdon.

ROBERTS, MOSES. Merion, Pennsylvania.
12/16/1715/16. February 28, 1715. D. 41.
Brother Aaron Roberts, brother Evan Roberts, brother Ellis Roberts, Gainor Roberts. Sisters: Rachel, Jane and Mary Roberts. Nieces: Katherine and Rachel Roberts; Margaret Edwards, Eliza. Roberts; Sarah Dickinson; Jane daughter of Abel Thomas; John Kelley; Thomas Bowen; John Roberts and his daughter Elizabeth; Robert Roberts.
Executors: Ellis Roberts, his brother, and friend Robert Roberts.
Witnesses: John Roberts and David George.

WILLIAMS, EVAN. Skipack, Philadelphia County. Yeoman.
August 28, 1715. March 3, 1715. D. 42.
Wife Dorothy. children: Ann, Elizabeth, Lewis and David Williams.
Executors: Friends Richard Jones and Thomas Kenworthy.
Witnesses: Daniel Dismal, Thomas Wilt and Thomas Lock.

YELDALL (VELDALL), ROBERT. Philadelphia. Cooper.
January 16, 1715. March 5, 1715. D. 42.
Wife Jane. Children: Anthony, John and William. Brother Anthony Yeldall's children, Edward and Frances "living in Chanell Row near King Street in Westminster in ye house of Richard Perries called ye Blue Poste in London." John Mall, John Comb, Valentine Bird, John Ireson, William Lee are all mentioned.
Executors: Wife Jane and son Anthony.
Assistant to Executors: William Moning of Philadelphia, merchant.
Witnesses: Thomas Shoemaker, John Breinbnall and Joshua Lawrence.

WEBB, JOHN. Philadelphia.
6/21/1711. March 15, 1715. D. 44.
Wife Anne. Daughter Susanna and her husband William Monington. Kinsman Joseph Webb and son of Hannah Lea of Chester County; sister Sarah wife of Nathaniel Perrin; sisters Mary and Rachel Webb and brother Daniel Webb who is in Great Britain. Thomas and John Redman, Robert Burrow, Reinier Jansen, John Gentry, Robert Adams are all mentioned.
Executor: William Monington.
Witnesses: Henry Cliffton, Hugh Dusborow, Samuel Taylor and Joseph Webb.

HOMER, WILLIAM. Philadelphia County.
9/3/1714. March 17, 1715. D. 45.
Children: eldest son William and two others whose names are not given.
Executrix: Wife Elizabeth.
Witnesses: William Carver, Alexander Mode and Everard Bolton.

BARTLESON, EUSEBIUS. Whitemarsh Township, Philadelphia County.
January 8, 1715. March 19, 1715. D. 45.
Wife's name not given. Children: Bartle, Henry, Katharine, Mary, Peter and John.
Executors: Friends Edward Farmar and Derrick Johnston.
Witnesses: Isack Dilbeck, John Ridwitzer and Caspar Stool.

WILLIAMS, LUMLEY. Plymouth Township, Philadelphia County. Yeoman.
11/25/1714/15. March 31, 1716. D. 46.
Step-children: Benjamin, Joshua, Phebe, Sarah, Jonathan and Ruth Dickinson.
Executrix: Wife Sarah.
Trustees: David Meredith, Ellis Pugh, Thomas Pugh, Rowland Ellis, Junior.
Witnesses: Robert Naylor, John Redwitzer and Thomas Coaldy.

HAMER, JAMES. Olicoah, Philadelphia County. Weaver.
12/25/1715. April 11, 1716. D. ---.
Wife Margaret. Children: James, Adam, Mary, Sarah, Deborah and Margaret. Margaret is married but her surname is not given.
Executor: Son james.
Overseers: Lewis Walker and Joseph Richardson.
Witnesses: Thomas Johnes, Robert Evans, Joseph Richardson and Thomas Reese.

BOUDE, GRIMSTON. Philadelphia. Innkeeper.
February 3, 1715. April 3, 1716. D. 47.
Children: Joseph, Samuel, John, Thomas, Henrietta.
Executrix: Wife Mary.
Witnesses: Mary Appleton, Peter Gibson and Rachel Turoies.

SPARKES, RICHARD. Philadelphia. Carpenter.
January 14, 1714/15. April 30, 1716. D. 48.
No children named.
Executrix: Wife Joan.
Witnesses: Nicholas Ashmead, Thomas Rutter, Junior and John Cadwalader.

MURREY, HUMPHREY. Cheltenham Township, Philadelphia County. Yeoman.
September 25, 1715. May 7, 1716. D. 49.
Wife's name not given. Brother Leonard Murrey. Cousin John Murrey. Richard Buctler. John Cadwalader of Abbeton. Daniel Yously. William Hermer. Mary Kimball. Jane Laurence. His two daughters-in-law, names not given. James Sykes and Sarah Hader mentioned. He held an estate in West Jersey.

Executors: Son Richard and grandsons Humphrey and Thomas Murrey.
Witnesses; David Davies, John Harris and Nicholas Hicks.

CASPER, JOHN. Oxford Township, Pennsylvania. Yeoman.
February 26, 1714/15. May 4, 1716. D. 50.
Children: John, Josiah, Ralph, Joseph, Mary, Elizabeth and Charles.
Executrix: Wife Ann.
Witnesses: Robert Thomas and Charles Finney.

BOLTON, EVERARD, JUNIOR. Cheltenham Township, Philadelphia County. Glover.
12/23/1715/16. May 8, 1716. D. 50.
Children: Elizabeth, Prisilla, Samuel and Mary.
Executrix: Wife Mary.
Trustees: His father Everard Bolton, Morris Morris and Robert Fletcher, yeoman, all of this Province.
Witnesses: Robert Eastburn, Samuel Bolton and Henry Stirke.

YARD, JOSEPH. Philadelphia. Bricklayer.
May 16, 1716. July 6, 1716. D. 51.
Children: Joseph and five younger sons whose names are not given.
Executrix: Wife Mary.
Witnesses: William Bissell, John Lloyd and John Cadwalader.

SMITH, SARAH. Philadelphia. Widow.
7/8/1715. July 6, 1716. D. 52.
Daughters: Dorothy Empson and Grace Thompson. Granddaughters: Mary Empson, Sarah Thompson and Ann and Dorothy Smith. He held an estate in Chester, Pennsylvania.
Executor: Son-in-law Richard Empson.
Witnesses: William Lingard, John Cadwalader and Martha Cadwalader.

HUGHES, ELLIS. East Town, Chester County.
1/11/1715/16. July 13, 1716. D. 53.
John Lewis and Rees, who are in Great Britain. Friend William John Adams; friend Bridget Ellis; friend Elizabeth Ellis; Rachel Ellis; Landlady, Lydia Ellis. Thomas Godfrey and Issac Tho. mentioned.
Executor: Friend John Ellis.

Overseers: Benjamin Humphrey and Newland (Rowland) Ellis, Junior.
Witnesses: Newland (Rowland) Ellis and Thomas Ellis.

DOUGLASS, JOHN. Philadelphia. Gentleman.
October 3, 1715. August 4, 1716. D. 53.
Daughter Mary Douglass. Brother Rev. Mr. William Grey and sister Mary Basden. He held an estate in Charleston, South Carolina.
Executrix: Wife Sarah.
Witnesses: William Laurence, Daniel Jones and Ralph Asheton.

TYSON, CORNELIUS. Germantownship, Philadelphia County. Weaver.
April 6, 1716. July 27, 1716. D. 54.
Wife Margaret and youngest son Peter. Children: eldest son Matthias, Barbara wife of Matthias Cunrade, Alitic wife of John Cunrade, Williaminte wife of Paul Engle, Fanniske wife of Laurentz Henrick.
Executrix: Wife Margaret.
Witnesses: William Strepers, Herman Grothausen and Fr. Daniel Pastorius.

TEYSER, DIRCK, JUNIOR. Manahattwana, Philadelphia County. Cordwainer.
April 16,1 714. August 6, 1716. D. 54.
Brother Peter.
Executrix: Wife Deborah.
Witnesses: John Henry Sprogell, Arnold Custer and Matthaus Crantzman.

CHEETAM, JOHN. Philadelphia. Tailor.
1/16/1715/16. August 9, 1716. Codicil - June 28, 1716. D. 55.
Wife Anne. Children: Eldest daughter Hannah, John, Mary, Joseph.
Codicil - Giving certain power to Executors.
Executors: Wife and Anthony Morris, Junior.
Witnesses: David Breintnall, Solomon Cresson, Joan Forrest, Jacob Shoemaker, William Mason and Joan Forrest.

WORRALL, PETER. Bucks County, Pennsylvania. Wheelwright.
6/3/1694. September 8, 1716. D. ---.

Luke Brindley of Bucks County is mentioned.
Executrix: Wife Mary.
Witnesses: William Gabitas, Joseph Paull and Phinehas Pemberton.

GRAVES, THOMAS. Oxford Township, Philadelphia County. Yeoman.
Mary 14, 1715. September 21, 1716. D. 57.
Wife's name not given. Daughter Susannah, wife of Robert Bateman of Willingall, Spain, Essex County, England, weaver.
Executor: Henry Hower of Philadelphia, barber.
Witnesses: Alexander Asbuthnott, Robert Gordon and Charles Brockden.

MIFFLIN, JOHN, SENIOR. Blockley Township, Philadelphia County. Yeoman.
10/5/1715. September 22, 1716. D. 57.
Wife Elnor.
Executrix: Elizabeth, daughter-in-law, wife of John Mifflin, Junior.
Witnesses: Thomas Shute, Jacob Qubri and John Mifflin, Junior.

ROBERTS, ELLIS. Gwynedd, Philadelphia County. Labourer.
August 18, 1716. October 1, 1716. D. 58.
Father Robert Ellis. Sister Catherine and her son John. Churches spoken of at Philadelphia, Oxford and Radnor. Mr. Tolbet, the priest at Philadelphia for service at his burial. Uncle Robert David of Merion; Uncle Edward Rees of Merion; Humphrey Bate; Ellis Pugh; Evan Ellis; Edward Thomas of Merion; Rowland Hugh; Thomas Foulk; Cadder Evan Pugh; Thomas David; Hugh Griffith; Evan Roberts; Robert Humphrey's wife whose name is not given; John Humphrey; Ellis Lewis; Humphrey Jones; Elizabeth Pugh; Gaynor Row; Hugh Jones.
Executors: Friends Ellis Pugh and Evan Ellis.
Witnesses: Edward Foulke, Ellis Hughe and Hugh Foulke.

PHIPPS, JOSEPH. Abington Township, Philadelphia County. Yeoman.
2/1/1709. October 13, 1716. D. 59.
Wife Sarah. Children: Joseph, Isaiah and John.
Executor: John.

Overseers: Friends Samuel Cart and Thomas Canby of Abington Township.
Witnesses: Henry Bennett, Morris Morris, Matthis Tissen and William Powell.

WRIGHT, JOSEPH. Dublin Township, Philadelphia County. Yeoman.
September 5, 1716. October 13, 1716. D. 60.
Children Martha, William, Joseph, Elizabeth and Jane Wright.
Executrix: Wife Jane.
Witnesses: Anthony Yerkes, Abraham Richards and Henry Stirke.

CLUBB, JOHN. Oxford. Clerk.
December 14, 1715. November 9, 1716. D. 60.
Son Richard. Nuncupative will.
Executrix: Wife Isabella.
Witnesses: John Talbot and Charles Sober.

BURSON, GEORGE. Gilbert's Manor, Philadelphia County. Yeoman.
November 26, 1715. November 13, 1716. D. 61.
Wife Hannah. Children: Ann, Mary, William, George, James and Joseph.
Executors: Two eldest sons James and Joseph Burson.
Witnesses: Joseph Richardson, Andres Crormer, Joseph Wells and Elizabeth Richardson.

CLEST, MARTHA. Oxford, Philadelphia County, Pennsylvania.
October 5, 1716. November 17, 1716. D. 62.
Sister Elizabeth Fry and Mary Wobber, who seem to be living in England. James son of Joseph Paull, Junior. Sarah Cart; Margaret Paull; Elizabeth Paull; Jane Paull; Ann Knowles; Ann Powell; Liddy Wawder; Joanna Kelly. Nephews: George Browne and John Wobber, who are living in England.
Executor: Job Goodson.
Witnesses: Thomas Canby and John Willmerton.

TENCH, MARGARET. Philadelphia. Widow.
March 20, 1714/15. November 18, 1716. D. 62.

Samuel Monckton of Philadelphia, practitioner in physick, John Smith of Philadelphia, gentleman.
Executrix: Friend Sarah Quarry of Philadelphia, widow, and at her death to the children (names not given) of my brothers and sisters.
Witnesses: Mice Vandervere, Edith Ward and John Swift.

BILTON, SAMUEL. Philadelphia County, living on the Schuylkill River, where there was a ferry.
November 6, 1716. December 4, 1716. D. 63.
Benjamin Chambers. Nephew Jackson and Elizabeth his wife.
Executrix: Wife Sarah.
Witnesses: Andrew Sandel, Junior, William Powell and Jane Byfield.

BUZBY, WILLIAM. Oxford Township, Philadelphia County. Yeoman.
October 17, 1716. December 5, 1716. D. 64.
Daughter Elizabeth wife of Roger Shalley. Edward Orpwood, John Harper, dec'd., Qisanaaman's Creek, John Shallcrose Tackony, Miriam Seary,John Worrall, Edward Shippen, dec'd., Thomas Fairman mentioned.
Executors: Wife Sarah and son John.
Advisor: Brother Robert Buzby.
Witnesses: John Worrell, Andrew Frazar and Charles Brockden.

TOMLINSON, RICHARD. Oxford, Philadelphia County. Yeoman.
3/15/1716. January 4, 1716. D. 65.
Children: Richard, William, Joseph, James, John, Mary, Elizabeth and Sarah Tomlinson.
Executrix: Wife Sarah.
Trustees: John Shallcross and Joseph Paull, Junior.
Witnesses: John Brown, Richard Worell, Junior and Thomas Canby.

CHANDLER, JOHN. Philadelphia. Yeoman.
September 8, 1716. January 12, 1716. D. 65.
Daughter Mary. Brother Richard Chandler's children (names not given) of Surrey County, England, wheelwright.
Executrix: Wife Elizabeth.
Witnesses: Joshua Carpenter, Jonathan Ashton and John Cadwalader.

FISHER, JOHN. Springfield, Philadelphia County. Yeoman.
December 8, 1716. January 30, 1716. D. 66.
Wife Catharine. Children: John, Joseph, Mary (who is the wife of Richard Regan) and Sarah Fisher. Nicholas Scull mentioned.
Executors: Wife Catharine and friend William Harmer.
Witnesses: Allen Foster, Junior, Mary Foster and Nicholas Scull.

APPLETON, JOSIAH. Philadelphia. Cooper.
July 28, 1716. February 10, 1716/17. D. 67.
Eldest daughter Mary and other children whose names are not given.
Executrix: Wife Mary.
Witnesses: James Smith, Sarah Collingwood and John Cadwalader.

FURNIS, THOMAS. Philadelphia. Carter.
September 16, 1716. February 10, 1716/17. D. 67.
Executrix: Daughter Mary Furnis.
Witnesses: Samuel Shoords, Daniel Harrison and Joseph Harrison.

CHEETAM, ANNE. Philadelphia. Widow.
6/13/1716. March 1, 1716/17. D. 68.
Four children names not given.
Executors: William Hudson of Philadelphia, tanner, and Anthony Morris, Junior of Philadelphia, brewer.
Witnesses: Samuel Hudson, John Breintnall and John Cadwalader.

COLLET, RICHARD. Byberry Township, Philadelphia County. Yeoman.
March 18, 1716. April 1, 1717. D. 68.
Wife Elizabeth. Daughters Rachel and Mary.
Executor: Only son John.
Witnesses: John Webster, James Rush and Henry Stirke.

HUNT, JAMES. Kingsess, Philadelphia County. Yeoman.
1/29/1717. April 3, 1717. D. 69.
Wife Sarah. Daughter Mary wife of Abraham Marshall; daughter Anne Blumston and her children, Sarah, Hannah, and Mary; Elizabeth, son James' daughter; and their children, Samuel, Eliza, John, James, Abraham and Hannah; grandson James Bartram.
Executor: Son James.
Witnesses: Benjamin Bonsall, Enoch Bonsall and Obadiah Bonsall.

RAMBO, JOHN. Passyunck, Philadelphia County. Yeoman.
November 23, 1716. April 19. 1717. D. 71.
Daughter Mary. Brother Andrew. Sisters names not given. William Powell, of Philadelphia, cooper and Andrew Supplee of Philadelphia mentioned.
Executrix: Wife Christian.
Overseer and Trustee: Brother Andrew.
Witnesses: Andrew Landel, Peter Evans and George Yard.

NAYLOR, ROBERT. Plymouth Township, Philadelphia County. Yeoman.
April 20, 1717. May 17, 1717. D. 71.
Wife's name not given. Daughter Mary Boulton; daughter-in-law Mary, widow of son John Naylor, deceased; grandson John Naylor, daughter Elenor Webster. Nuncupative will.
Executors: Son Joseph and daughter Priscilla.
Witnesses: Nicholas Scull and John Nicholas Knight.

WARNER, JOHN. Blockley Township, Philadelphia County. Yeoman.
September 17, 1716. May 20, 1717. D. 72.
Wife's name not given. Children: John, daughter Margaret Rodes, Mary Warner, William, Isaac, Esther, Sarah, Jane, Joseph, Swan.
Executors: Swan, John and Mary Warner.
Witnesses: Martha Corksha, Catharine Chandler and Edward Warner.

SHEPERD, SAMUEL. Philadelphia. Joyner.
June 9, 1707. May 30, 1717. D. 73.
Brother James. William Shepard of Barbados. Sister-in-law Mary, wife of James Allen of Bridlington of West New Jersey.
Executor: Friend James Shattick of Philadelphia County, yeoman.
Witnesses: Anthony Taylor, Josiah Appleton and Justinian Fox.

BOYDEN, MERIAM. Philadelphia. Widow.
10/12/1716. June 1, 1717. D. 73.
Children: Daniel, James, Mary, John and Sarah Boyden.
Executors: Brother-in-law Daniel Radley and friend George Fitzwater.
Advisors: Friend James Logan and Gilbert Falconer.

Witnesses: Thomas Cannon, John Henmarch and Margaret Jones.

WILSON, JOHN. Boston, Massachusetts. Mariner.
October 12, 1714. July 15, 1717. D. 74.
Executrix: Wife Mary.
Witnesses: Bartholomew Carthew and Gyles Green.

WRIGHT, BARBARA. Philadelphia. Widow of Benjamin, lately deceased.
July 14, 1715. July 22, 1717. D. 75.
Daughter Sarah Wright. Sister Ann Peppiatt of London, England. Deceased husband Benjamin Wright's sister (name not given) living in the Province of Barbados. William and Clement Plumstead, Junior sons of Clement Plumstead. Friend Mary Dickinson of Philadelphia.
Executors: Friends Clement Plumstead and Israel Pemberton of Philadelphia, merchants.
Witnesses: Constance Lowdon, Ruth Emiley and Charles Brockden.

COCKFIELD, JOSHUA. Philadelphia. Merchant.
March 14, 1716. August 12, 1717. D. 76.
Daughter Hannah Cockfield. Sloop Mary, John King, Commander, Jamaica. Aunt Alice Herring; his father who is living and whose name is not given. William Ward. Brothers Zachariah and Thomas Cockfield; Zachariah Herring. [Original missing.]
Executrix: Wife Elizabeth.
Trustee: Father-in-law William Hudson.
Witnesses: John Whitpain and Maurice Lisle.

ELLIS, RACHEL. Haverford, Chester County.
8/9/1716. August 19, 1717. D. 76.
Sisters: Elizabeth, Bridget, Rebeka. Mother's name not given.
Cousins Rowland Ellis, Elizabeth Ellis and Edward Rees.
Executor: Brother Evan Ellis, and at his death, to brother William Ellis.
Witnesses: Edward Rees and Rowland Ellis.

PEARSALL, EDWARD. Radnor Township, Chester County. Tailor.
June 26, 1717. August 28, 1717. D. 77.
Wife Dorothy, child unborn; brother Richard Pearsall. Servant Richard Hughes mentioned.

Executors: Wife and brother Richard.
Witnesses: Hugh William, James Pugh, and Merick Davies.

PAULL, JOSEPH. Oxford, Philadelphia County. Yeoman.
4/---/1717. September 3, 1717. D. 78.
Daughter Ann, wife of John Knowles, their children Sarah, Elizabeth, Ann, Margaret, and Hannah Knowles; son Henry, son John and his children Joseph, Jonathan and John Paull; son James; son Joseph,who is to assist his mother in her executorship, and his children James and Elizabeth Paull.
Executrix: Wife Margaret.
Witnesses: Hugh Willcocks, Elenor Ostsber (Webster) and Thomas Canby.

MIRICK, WILLIAM. Blockley Township, Philadelphia County. Yeoman.
July 20, 1717. September 6, 1717. D. 79.
Wife Mary, son William, daughter Hannah.
Executors: Brothers Roger and David Mirick.
Witnesses: Thomas Lewis and Thomas William.

KäSTNER, PAUL. Germantown, Philadelphia County. Weaver.
August 31, 1717. September 11, 1717. D. 79.
Wife Mary, children: Christina, Samuel, Jacob and George. Elizabeth Pettinger's daughter Betty; daughter Mary. Friends Samuel Gulden, Caspar Leutebecher and Johannes Hildbrand. He held an estate at Strasburg, Chester County, Pennsylvania.
Witnesses: Jan Dooden, Paul Engel, Senior and Francis Daniel Pastorius.

PRESTON, WILLIAM. Frankford, Philadelphia County.
5/29/1714. October 9, 1717. D. 80.
Wife Ann. Children: Amor, Able, Paul, Priscilla and Sarah.
Executors: Wife and son Paul.
Witnesses: Thomas Canby and Morris Morris.

GILLING, DAVID. Philadelphia. Blacksmith.
December 4, 1716. October 22, 1717. D. 81.

Children: eldest son Robert, now in Ireland, Francis, Thomas, David and Joshua. At the death of their mother Francis and Thomas are to be executors.
Executrix: Wife Catherine.
Trustees: Friends Jedediah Andrews, John Van Laer and Timothy Stevenson.
Witnesses: John Van Laer, John Kearsley and Peter Evans.

WILSON, THOMAS. Philadelphia, late of London. Gentleman.
August 19, 1717. October 22, 1717. D. 82.
Executors: Friends Robert Asheton and Charles Read, both of Philadelphia, to be assisted by friends Dr. John Kearsley and Charles Rogers.
Witnesses: Evan Evans, D. D., John Talbot and John Nichols.

ENGLAND, THOMAS. Philadelphia. Merchant.
December 10, 1709. October 26, 1717. D. 83.
Daughter Sarah England.
Executrix: Wife Hanna.
Witnesses: Yeates Conwill, Elizabeth Hill and James Steel.

BOULDING, WILLIAM. Philadelphia. Tailor.
6/25/1708. November 13, 1717. Codicil - 6/29/1708. D. 83.
Wife Elizabeth, two children whose names are not given. In the event of their death, Robert Felham of Whittlesey, Isle of Ely, Cambridgeshire, England, husbandman. He held an estate in Chester County.
Executors: Wife and friend Abraham Bickley of Philadelphia, merchant.
Witnesses: William Southbe, John Palmer and John Cadwalader.
Witnesses to Codicil: William Southbe, Thomas Bradford and John Cadwalader.

SNOW, JEREMIAH. Philadelphia. Mariner.
October 18, 1717. November 14, 1717. D. 85.
Executrix: Wife Mary.
Witnesses: Jedediah Andrews, Charles Brockden and William Strutt.

ANDREWS, MATTHEW. Late of St. Peter's Parish, Isle of Antigua, now of Philadelphia.

7/6/1717. November 14, 1717. D. 85.
Wife's name not given. Children: Edmund and Elizabeth.
Executors: Henry Hodge, Thomas Chalkley, both of Philadelphia, merchants, John Lightfoot, Richard and Archibald Cochran of the Isle of Antigua, merchants.
Witnesses: Isaac Marryott, Mary Thorp and John Cadwalader.

STREIPERS, WILLIAM. Sommer-housen in the Germantownship, Philadelphia County.
October 18, 1717. November 15, 1717. D. 86.
Children: Peter Jansen, Leonard, John, Catherine, assistants to Executor. Friends John Lucken and Dennis Kunders.
Executrix: Wife Mary.
Witnesses: Herman Grothause, Abraham Thinnen(?) and Francis Daniel Pastorius.

QUARY, SARAH. Philadelphia. Widow.
December 18, 1716. December 28, 1717. D. 87.
Husband's nephew Richard Andrews of Cork, Ireland. Niece Jane Hornes of Bristol, England. Cousins Samuel Monkton and Susannah his wife; John Moore of Philadelphia and Rebecca his wife and their son John; Mary wife of Peter Evans; Rev. Jon Talbot; Grace Parsons, Philadelphia, widow. Sisters Susannah Stone, Jane Walton and Ann Bayly. The brothers and sisters of Margaret Tench (names not given).
Executors: Samuel Monkton and John Moore.
Witnesses: Elizabeth Ware, David Loyd, Edward Glover and Alice Tuthull.

FISHER, JOSEPH. Dublin Township, Philadelphia County.
October 23, 1717. December 2, 1717. D. 89.
Children: Isabel, Mary and Martha. Nuncupative will.
Executrix: Wife Mary and brother Edward Farmer, assistant.
Witnesses: John Swift and Edward Farmer.

THOMAS, DAVID. Philadelphia. Husbandman.
7/23/1717. January 3, 1717. D. 89.
Mistress Mary Badroth. Friends Joseph Everard and Abraham Carliell.
Witnesses: Joseph Cross, Samuel Powell and Thomas Griffith.

OWEN, GRIFFITH. Philadelphia. Physician.
January 3, 1717. January 6, 1717. D. 90.
Wife Sarah. Sarah (wife of Jacob Jonathan Coppock) and Ann (wife of John Whitpaine). Son-in-law William Sanders and daughter-in-law Mary (wife of Samuel Marriot).
Executors: Children Edward, Griffith and John.
Witnesses: Robert Roberts, George Shirro and Thomas Jones.

JANSEN, CUNRAD. Germantown, Philadelphia County. Weaver.
December 20, 1717. January 14, 1717. D. 91.
Wife Fenken, names of children not given.
Executors: Jan. Hend and Dirk Jensen.
Witnesses: Isaac Van Sintern, Herman Thunen and Samuel Pastorius.

TAYLOR, BERNARD. Philadelphia.
May 16, 1716. February 17, 1717. D. 92.
Executrix: Wife Susannah.
Witnesses: Benjamin Peters, Joseph Ankrobus and Grizell Wilson.

PARKER, MOSES. Philadelphia. Joyner.
June 27, 1717. March 1, 1717. D. 92.
Wife Mary (of England).
Executor: Charles Rogers of Philadelphia, merchant.
Witnesses: John and Ann Knowles and John Cadwalader.

HOWELL, PHILLIP.
October 31, 1717. February 8, 1717. D. 93.
Names of children not given. Cousin Jacob Howell, Edward Goodwin.
Executrix: Wife Ann.
Witnesses: Abraham Lake, Phillio Milward and Richard Dobson.

STEVENS, ANTHONY. Philadelphia. Cordwainer.
December 12, 1717. March 18, 1717. D. 94.
Children: William and Mary of Bath, England. Hugh, son of Thomas and Elizabeth Tresse.
Executrix: Wife Alice.
Witnesses: John Austin, Charles Spurway and Thomas Tresse.

FORDHAM, BENJAMIN. Annapolis, Maryland. Gentleman.

August 11, 1716. April 24, 1718. D. 94.
Children: Richard, Sarah, Benjamin, John, Joseph, James, Margaret and Lydia.
Executor: James Parrok, Philadelphia, shipwright.
Witnesses: Edward Roberts, Edward Jones and John Cadwalader.

POUND, JOHN. New Castle County, Pennsylvania. Mariner.
April 29, 1718. May 14, 1718. D. 95.
Wife Lowry. Children: Samuel, John, Jacob, Isaac, Andrew, Abraham, Alice and William.
Executor: Son John.
Trustee: Edmond Arrowsmith.
Witnesses: Susannah Fleming, Margaret Richardson and John Cadwalader.

QUERK, JANE. Philadelphia. Widow.
May 8, 1718. May 26, 1718. D. 96.
Joshua Carpenter of Philadelphia, gentleman, Enoch Story. Sarah his wife and their children Patience and Robert; Sarah (wife of Matthew Robinson, turner) and their son David; Elizabeth (daughter of David Powell, surveyor.)
Executors: Enoch Story and Mathew Robinson.
Witnesses: David Harry, Joseph Trotter, John Cadwalader.

DAVIDS, MEREDITH. Gwynedd, Philadelphia County.
2/11/1718. June 21, 1718. D. 96.
Children: David, John, Elizabeth, Mary and Sarah.
Executrix: Wife Gwen.
Overseers: Cadwalader Evan, Robert and John Jones.
Witnesses: Evan Griffith and Cadwallader Morris.

WARREN, JACOB. Philadelphia. Mariner.
June 9, 1718. July 7, 1718. D. 98.
Children: William and Isaac.
Executrix: Wife Mary.
Trustees and Overseers: John Warder (hatter) and Anthony Morris, Junior (brewer).
Witnesses: John Widdifield, Jacob Usher and William Strutt.

PREAS, RICHARD. Philadelphia.

May 7, 1718. August 2, 1718. D. 98.
Executrix: Wife Susannah.
Witnesses: Thomas Stapleford and John Cadwallader.

CLEMSON, JAMES. Philadelphia.
July 12, 1718. August 5, 1718. D. 98.
Wife Joan. Children: John, James, Thomas and Sophia.
Executors: Henry Pearce and son-in-law Henry Guest.
Witnesses: James Lloyd and Mary Harris.

THOMAS, DAVID. Philadelphia County. Yeoman.
June 29, 1717. August 6, 1718. D. 99.
Wife Mary. Children: Thomas, Richard, David, Samson David, John David, Catherine, Anne (Evans), Gwen and Mary.
Executors: Sons John and Samson and William Evans.
Witnesses: Griffith and William Jones.

WHARTON, THOMAS. Philadelphia. Tailor.
February 11, 1714. September 4, 1718. D. 100.
Children: Richard, Mary, James, Joseph, Thomas, Rachel and John.
Executrix: Wife Rachel.
Trustees: John Warder (hatter) and William Henderson (tanner) of Philadelphia.
Witnesses: Thomas Okley, George Plumley and Joseph Lawrence.

MOORE, GEORGE. Philadelphia. Mariner.
December 15, 1715. September 18, 1718. D. 100.
Executor: James Portens, devisee.
Witnesses: Thomas Ferris and John Cadwallader.

PASCHALL, THOMAS. Philadelphia. Pewterer.
September 12, 1716. September 18, 1718. D. 101.
Children: Thomas and Mary. Grandchildren's names (twenty-one) not given.
Executors: Henery Flower, Henery Badrock, Benjamin Paschall.
Witnesses: Hugh Graham, Edward Foy and Henry Stevens.

BURTON, ANTHONY. Philadelphia. Mariner.
June 28, 1718. October 3, 1718. D. 102.

Mother Ann Risdon, Aunt Elizabeth Hannus. Brother George Risdon.
Executrix: Wife Love.
Witnesses: Nathaniel Griffiths, Joseph Antrobus, Abraham Lining and Elizabeth Griffith.

WHITPAINE, JOHN. Philadelphia. Merchant.
October 28, 1718. October 28, 1718. D. 102.
Children: Zachariah and Sarah. Grandfather Richard Whitpaine.
Executrix: Wife Ann.
Witnesses: Samuel Carpenter, Nathaniel Griffith and Maurice Lisle.

MAY, JACOB. Philadelphia. Inn-holder.
September 11, 1718. October 18, 1718. D. 103.
Son Moses.
Executrix: Wife Mary.
Trustees: Pentecost Teague of Philadelphia (merchant).
Witnesses: Edmund Davis, Samuel Richardson and John Cadwallader.

HANNIS, ANDREW. Philadelphia.
September 15, 1718. November 11, 1718. D. 104.
Wife Dorithy. Children: John, Andrew and William and Margaret (Kirk). Grand-child Mary.
Executors: Sons John, Andrew and William.
Witnesses: Daniel Jones and Peter Cox.

THOMAS, JOHN. Passyunk, Philadelphia County. Yeoman.
June 14, 1718. December 10, 1718. Codicil - October 3, 1718. D. 105.
Wife Patience. Children Evan, Catherine, William and Mary.
Executor: Son Evan.
Trustees: Edward Roberts and John Cadwalader.
Witnesses: David Evans, John and Edward Jones, Evan Evans, Peter Evans.

LONGACRE, ANDREW. Kingsess, Philadelphia County.
October 10, 1718. December 10, 1718. D. 107.
Executors: Wife Maudlen and son Andrew.
Children: Peter, Andrew, Gabrell, Ellen.

Witnesses: John Yocum, William Everson and Samuel Plunston.

GOUGH, WILLIAM. Late of Cork, Ireland, now of Philadelphia. Mariner.
December 9, 1718. December 10, 1718. D. 107.
Son John.
Executrix: Wife Jane of estate in Ireland.
Executors: Benjamin Vining and Charles Read of Philadelphia, merchants.
Witnesses: Jeremiah Finch, John Betenson, Ann Pearson and Anne Gough.

OTTERSON, OTTER. Bristol, Bucks County, Pennsylvania. Tailor.
February 4, 1718. March 4, 1718. D. 108.
Elizabeth (daughter of Clause Johnson), Mary daughter of William Watson; Jeremiah Langhorn of Middleton.
Executor: Jeremiah Langhorn.
Witnesses: Stoffel Van Land and David Wilson.

WHITESIDE, JOHN. Late of Great Britain, now of Philadelphia. Merchant.
December 10, 1718. December 27, 1718. D. 109.
William Howell and Jeremiah Brown (attorney-at-law) of the Island of Nevis.
Executor: Edward Mankin.
Witnesses: Edward Roberts, John Evans and John Cadwalader.

POWELL, MARY. Philadelphia. Widow.
September 13, 1718. December 13, 1718. D. 110.
Grand-children Rachel and Jane Morgan and their parents Judith and Abel Morgan, gentleman; John Jones cousin of said Abel; Elizabeth (wife of William Thomas, weaver); Samuel Jones and Thomas Griffith (Baptist teachers); William Hennisley (weaver); Thomas Thomas son of William Thomas (cooper).
Executor: Abel Morgan.
Trustees: Abel Morgan, David Powell (surveyor), Thomas Potts, Senior and Junior (tanners), William Betredge (glazier), James Bollen, gentleman, and Thomas Bibb (tanner).
Overseers: Griffith Miles and William Thomas.
Witnesses: Mary and Nicholas Dowdney and John Cadwalader.

HIBERD, JOHN. Biberry, Philadelphia County. Husbandman.
June 21, 1718. January 29, 1718. D. 111.
Executor: Friend James Rush of Biberry, devisee.
Witnesses: Daniel Jackson and Josiah Hart.

ANDREWS, ELIZABETH. Philadelphia. Widow.
October 4, 1718. January 7, 1718. D. 112.
Cousin Robert Vaughan of North Wales in trust for sister Ellin Owen; two daughters of said sister, names not given; cousins Robert, Hugh, Thomas, Elizabeth and Grace, children of sister Gwen; Edward, Margaret and Mary, children of sister Mably Rees; niece Jane Maries; step-son Simon Andrews; his wife and son Thomas; Elizabeth, daughter of cousin Thomas Jones; Anne, daughter of cousin Robert Jones; Thomas, son of cousin John Cadwalader, also the daughters of said John, Mary and Rebecca; Jane, daughter of Anthony Moore Smith; Margaret Nicholas; Martha, daughter of Rebeccah Cadwalader.
Executor: Rees Prees.
Trustees: Cousin Robert Jones and John Cadwalader.
Witnesses: Abraham Cox, Gwen Morgan and John Cadwalader.

RAKESTRAW, WILLIAM. Philadelphia. Malster.
December 29, 1718. February 2, 1718. D. 113.
Wife Elizabeth. Children: John, Grace (Zane), Elizabeth, Sarah, Ann, Mary, William and Thomas. Grand-son Joseph Rakestraw. Son-in-law Nathaniel Zane.
Executors: William and Thomas.
Trustees: William Hudson, William Tidmarsh and Thomas Chalkley.
Witnesses: Tobias Nilee, William Hatcher and John Cadwalader.

UPFOLD, JANE. Late of Great Britain, now of Philadelphia. Spinster.
---. February 4, 1718. D. 115.
Cousin Joan, widow of John Belacey; cousin Ann Hempton; brother Abraham (all of England) Rebecca and William Blackfan; Joan Humphreys of Philadelphia; Sarah Owen of Philadelphia; Elizabeth wife of Alderman Samuel Richardson of Philadelphia; Charles Brockden, gentleman; Ann Oxly; William Ragg, merchant; Nathaniel Owen of England, merchant and Frances his wife; Francis Knowles, shop-keeper; Ann wife of John Jones of Philadelphia, cordwainer; Dr.

Edward Owen of Philadelphia; sister Joan, wife of George Pierce of England; cousin William Haswell. Nuncupative will.
Executors: Abraham Buckley and William Fishbourn, merchants.
Witnesses: Charles Brockden, Sarah Owen, Catherine Kent, Elizabeth wife of Thomas Howell, Jane Curwaine and Edward Owen.

PUGH, ELLIS. Philadelphia. Mason.
November 29, 1718. March 16, 1718. D. 116.
Sons Thomas, Job and Ellis. Son-in-law Ellis Roberts; grand-daughters Katherine and Mary Meridith; Sinah Pugh; grand-son Ellis Pugh; daughter Ellin Davids. Wife's name not given.
Executor: Son Job.
Overseers: Son-in-law Meredith Davids, David Meredith, John Moore and Robert Jones.
Witnesses: John Moore, Wan Griffith, Cadwallader Jones and Robert Jones.

PARKER, JOHN. Philadelphia. Skinner.
May 6, 1717. April 6, 1719. D. 117.
Nuncupative will.
Executrix: Wife Mary.
Witnesses: Jane Bing and Joshua Lawrence.

TREGENY, BRIAN. Philadelphia. Merchant.
February 14, 1718. April 22, 1719. D. 118.
Brother Charles Finney and George Fitzwater. Testator's mother Elizabeth, wife of Edward Evans of Philadelphia, joiner. Cousin Mary Lord, daughter of sister Mary; sister Elizabeth, wife of Charles Finney; cousin Henrietta Tregony, daughter of brother Henry; Sarah, wife of Samuel Blunstone; Priscilla, wife of John Vanlan, Junior of Philadelphia, merchant; Mary, wife of George Fitzwater of Philadelphia, merchant.
Executors: Charles Finney and George Fitzwater.
Witnesses: Charles Brockden, William Strutt and Mary Weaver.

WALLTON, DANIEL. Bibery, Philadelphia County. Husbandman.
2/29/1718. April 25, 1719. D. 119.
Children: Samuel, Daniel (wife Elizabeth), Joshua, Joseph, Benjamin and Nathan.

Executrix: Wife Mary.
Witnesses: Josias Hill, John Browne, John Clifton and Henry Clifton.

FOX, BENJAMIN. Late of Bermuda, now of Philadelphia. Mariner.
April 28, 1719. May 1, 1719. D. 121.
Shadlock Rivers, mariner, and Samuel Wainwright of Philadelphia, tailor. Testator's mother, Jane Fox.
Witnesses: Charles Brockden, William Strutt and Elizabeth Dennis.

BASS, JOHN. Philadelphia. Carpenter.
April 14, 1719. May 1, 1719. D. 121.
Father Jacobus Bass. Brothers: John Noble, William and Joseph Harrison and sister Susannah Harrison.
Executors: Step-father Joseph Harrison and Catherine his wife.
Witnesses: Herbert Corrie, Benjamin Oram and John Cadwalader.

DAVIS, PETER. Horsam, Philadelphia County. Yeoman.
2/22/1719. May 16, 1719. D. 122.
Daughter Margaret.
Executors: Wife Rebecca and brother-in-law William Mitchner.
Witnesses: Thomas Palmer, Richard Kenderdine and Evan Lloyd.

ADAMS, ROBERT. Oxford Township, Philadelphia County. Yeoman.
July 27, 1717. June 6, 1719. Codicil - May 19, 1719. D. 123.
Sister Mary Coats and her son Robert; nieces Elizabeth and Anne Adams; nephews William, Richard and Robert Adams.
Executor: Son Robert. Codicil - Brother Walter and his wife Elizabeth are made co-executors.
Witnesses: William Jones, Anne Jones, John Smith, Joseph Hawley and Josiah Harper.

RICHARDSON, SAMUEL. Philadelphia. Gentleman.
4/6/1719. June 13, 1719. D. 125.
Wife Elizabeth. Children: Joseph, daughter Ann Cartlidge, wife of Edward Lane, daughter Mary m. Wm. Hudson and daughter Eliz. m. Abraham Bickley. Grand-children William, Samuel, James, Eleanor, Elizabeth and Anne (issue of daughter Ann by Edward Lane) and three children of said Ann by Edmund Cartlidge (names not given); Ambrey, Edward, Richard, William, Eleanor, Barbara and Elizabeth (children of said Joseph and Elizabeth Richardson); Samuel, William,

John, Mary, Elizabeth, Susannah, Hannah and Rachel children of son-in-law William Hudson, tanner, (name of wife not given). Great grand-daughter Hannah child of Joshua Cockfield.
Executors: William and Samuel Hudson.
Witnesses: Abraham Bickley, John Ogden and John Cadwalader.

MILES, GRIFFITH. Bristol, Philadelphia County. Yeoman.
March 28, 1719. June 13, 1719. D. 126.
Children: Griffith, Samuel, John and Esther (names of other daughters not given)
Executors: Wife Bridget and son Griffith.
Overseers: Mirick Davies and Joseph Todd.
Witnesses: Samuel Jones and Thomas Turner.

THOMAS, WILLIAM. Philadelphia. Weaver.
January 12, 1718. June 22, 1719. D. 128.
Wife Elizabeth. Children: Edward Rees and Samson. Abel Morgan of Philadelphia.
Executors: Edward Church and John Holme.
Witnesses: Humphrey Bates, Abraham Watkins and John Cadwalader.

TEAGUE, PENTECOST. Philadelphia. Merchant.
June 15, 1719. July 4, 1719. D. 129.
Father William Teague of the town of Marazion, England; friend David Richards; friend Israel Pemberton of Philadelphia. Kinsman Pentecost Teague; cousin Constance, wife of William Dunstain, Executrix.
Executrix: Wife Elizabeth.
Witnesses: Robert Ashton, David Lloyd and Joshua Lawrence.

PRIGG, RICHARD. Philadelphia. Innholder.
August 18, 1719. September 29, 1719. D. 130.
Son William, daughter Anne.
Executrix: Wife Catherine.
Witnesses: Paul Wilmerton, John Goheen and John Cadwalader.

COATS, THOMAS. Philadelphia. Merchant.
September 18, 1719. September 30, 1719. D. 131.

Children: Enoch, Samuel, Elizabeth, Sarah and Mary. Rowland Powel, Haverford, Chester County, miller.
Executors: Wife Bulah, son Enoch and daughter Elizabeth.
Trustees: George Fitzwater, Israel Pemberton and Samuel Levis, Junior. William Palmer and wife (not named), Widows Prigg, Smith and Clubb mentioned.
Witnesses: William Lawrence, Owen Roberts, Edward Roberts and Josiah Lawrence.

POTTS, THOMAS. Bristol Township, Philadelphia County.
3/6/1719. October 3, 1719. D. 133.
Brother-in-law (of wife's) Samuel Bowne of Fleshing, Long Island, husbandman, Joseph Latham of New York, shipwright named. Son Thomas.
Executrix: Wife Judith.
Witnesses: Griffith Jones, Samuel Pastorius and Francis Daniel Pastorius.

ROBERTS, WILLIAM. Blockly, Philadelphia County. Husbandman.
September 8, 1707. October 12, 1719. D. 134.
Sons John and William.
Executrix: Wife Affy.
Witnesses: Henry Lewis, John Thomas and John Hughes.

KELLEY, WILLIAM. Philadelphia. Shopkeeper.
January 14, 1716/17. October 19, 1719. D. 135.
Son William. William Kelley son of brother (not named). Children of Job Harvey of Derby, Chester County (not named), Clement Plumsted and Job Harvey also named Executors renounced.
Executrix: Wife Johanna.
Witnesses: Edward Pilkinton, William Biddle, Junior, and Daniel Durborow.

CLELAND, JAMES. Philadelphia. Merchant.
October 15, 1719. October 19, 1719. D. 136.
Mother Margaret Cleland. Thomas Withers or Thomas Harrison of Barbados, Colonel John Moody, late governor of Placentia mentioned.
Executors: Brother William and Thomas Harper of Barbadoes, merchant.
Executor for Pennsylvania: George McCall, Philadelphia, merchant.

Witnesses: H. Graham and William Assheton.

NENSS, JOHN. Germantown. Weaver.
September 25, 1719. October 29, 1719. D. 138.
Children Cornelius, Matthis, William, Gertrude, Alitje, Wÿnard. Wife Elizabeth.
Executors: John Cunrads, Roxbury Township, shoemaker, and John Lucken, Bristol Township, weaver.
Witnesses: Jan Leusen, Isack van Sintern and Hermann Thunen.

WORELL, RICHARD. Dublin Township, Philadelphia County. Yeoman.
June 11, 1718. October 31, 1719. D. 139.
Wife Rachel. Daughter Rachel Bennet. Benjamin Duffield and Ishmael Bennet are mentioned.
Executor: Son Richard.
Witnesses: John Worell, Jonathan Livezey and Henry Stirke.

MOORE, JOHN. Blockley Township. Blacksmith.
September 21, 1719. November 4, 1719. D. 140.
Wife Jane. Mother not named. Sister Mary Pound. Children: Richard, James, John, Mordecai, Jane, Rose, Margaret, Mary, and Martha.
Executors: Wife Jane and son James.
Trustees: Friends David Thomas, Robert Jones and Edward Williams.
Witnesses: David Jones, Sarah Cuerton, Edward Williams and Robert Jones.

MARTIN, AUDRE. Abington Township, Philadelphia County. Weaver.
October 24, 1719. November 9, 1719. D. 141.
Martin Jansen son of brother not named at Creifield, Germany.
Executors: Friend William Jansen, Abington Township, weaver, and Dirck Jansen, Germantown, weaver.
Witnesses: George Bewly, Lewis Roberts and Paull Hendrick.

MüLLER, GEORGE. Somerhausen.
September 21, 1719. November 18, 1719. D. 142.

Wife Anna-Sibilla, daughter of Wiegard Levering. Children whose names are not given.
Executor or Guardian: Herman Grothausen.
Witnesses: Abraham Tunese, Johann Rebenstock and Johann Adolf Grotthaüsen.

LEADER, ISAAC. Philadelphia. Mariner.
November 7, 1710. January 1, 1719. D. 14.
Estate in Great Britain and elsewhere.
Executrix: Wife Sarah.
Witnesses: Richard Heath and Joshua Lawrence.

EVERETT, JOSEPH. Philadelphia. Maltster.
January 7, 1719. January 12, 1719. D. 143.
Brothers and sisters in Great Britain (names not given). Samuel Brooks, laborer.
Executors: Friends Jacob Usher and John Knowles, carpenters.
Witnesses: William Corker, Junior, James Davis and William Strutt.

PASTORIUS, FRANCIS DANIEL. Germantown, Philadelphia County. Yeoman.
December 26, 1719. January 13, 1719. D. 144.
Sons John Samuel and Henry.
Executrix: Wife Anne, and after her decease the two sons.
Witnesses: Dirck Jansen, Cunrad Cunrade and George Bringhurst.

ROBESON, ANDREW. Emity Township, Philadelphia County.
---, 1719/20. February 27, 1719/20 and March 7, 1719/20. D. 145.
Roxborrow Township is also mentioned. Sons Andrew, Israel (and his three children names not given), son Jonathan, David, Thomas, Samuel, Peter. Daughters: Elinor, Mary and Margaret. John Owan mentioned. Neversink mentioned as being the land given to son Peter.
Executors: Sons Andrew, Israel and Jonathan.
Witnesses: John Farker and John Cammell.

PERES, SAMUEL. Philadelphia. Merchant.
May 12, 1719. February 29, 1719/20. D. 146.
Executrix: Wife Mary Magdalena.
Witnesses: William Robins, William Allen and John Turner.

JONES, DAVID. Bristol Township, Philadelphia County. Yeoman.
January 24, 1719. March 5, 1719/20. D. 147.
Daughter Anne.
Executrix: Wife Jane.
Trustees: Father-in-law Humphrey Bate and John Meriddith.
Witnesses: Jacob Leech, John Potts and Thomas Leech.

KREY, JOHN. Philadelphia County. Yeoman.
February 17, 1719/20. March 18, 1719/20. D. 148.
Wife Sytge. Children: Deborah, Susannah, Catherine, Maria, John, William, Peter and Jacob. Letters were granted, only to wife Sytge and Isaac Opdegraf.
Executors: Wife Sytge, John Henry Sprogell, Dirk Opdegraf and Jacob Sensenig.
Witnesses: Henry Kassell, William Dewees and Isaac Opdegraf.

LAMBERT, HANNAH. Philadelphia. Spinster.
December 7, 1719. March 25, 1720. D. 149.
Sister Elizabeth wife of Nile Grant, their son Thomas and daughters Elizabeth and Hannah. Kinswoman Hannah daughter of Thomas Kitchin.
Executor: Cousin John Lambert.
Witnesses: John Browne and George Mifflin.

TAYLOR, JOSEPH. Philadelphia. Brewer.
March 12, 1719/20. March 26, 1720. Codicil - March 17, 1719/20. D. 150.
Daughter Hannah. Richard and Humphrey Morrey and Joseph Shippen mentioned.
Executors: Wife Sarah and friend Peter Stretch, Philadelphia, watchmaker.
Trustees: Father John Fisher and Peter Stretch.
Witnesses: David Hughes, Ralph Oliver, Charles Brockden, Nehemiah Allen, Charles Osborne and Anthony Hartley.

PARSONS, HUGH. Philadelphia. Tailor.
1/2/1719. April 5, 1720. D. 152.
Cousin John Young of Wrexall, Somerset County, Great Britain, yeoman, and Grace his wife; also their children John, Anne, Mary and Dorothy. Cousin John Parsons, ibidem, yeoman and Dorothy his wife,

also their children Elizabeth, Anne, Mary, Dorothy, Grace and Eleanor. Uncle Richard Parsons of Bristol, England, cordwainer, and his four children, names not given, Deborah Greene, John Shalcross, Oxford Township, Philadelphia County, yeoman, and his wife Hannah. Abraham and John Hooper.
Executors: Mary --house, John Evans, John Knowles, Israel Pemberton and John Warder.
Witnesses: Joseph Hawley and John Willmerton.

BROOKE, JAMES. Lymerik Township, Philadelphia County.
March 9, 1719/20. April 15, 1720. D. 153.
Children: Jonathan, James, Samuel, David, Sarah and Elizabeth. Brother Matthew. Mr. Edward Farmar mentioned. Father John Brooke mentioned.
Executor: Son Jonathan.
Witnesses: Jacob Peterson, William Woodle and David Hay.

MATHIAS, EDWARD. Trer Duffryn Township, Chester County.
April 29, 1720. May 4, 1720. D. 155.
Brothers - Thomas and Lewis. John Griffith, Jr. and his wife Catherine. Edward Richard and Richard Rowland, Senior, mentioned.
Executor: Henry David.
Witnesses: Morgan David, David Jones and Robert Roger.

HUGHS, EDWARD. Eastown, Chester County.
December 11, 1716. May 14, 1720. D. 155.
Wife Mary. Children: Evan, Morgan, Margaret, Mary, Sarah, Elinor and Catherine. Grand-children Mary, David, Elizabeth, children of John David and Catherine (Hughs) David.
Executors: Son Evan and friend William Davies of Radnor, gentlemen.
Tutors and Guardians: Brother Morgan Hughs. Brother-in-law Philip David and friend Thomas Edwards.
Witnesses: Hugh Howell, David Thomas and Thomas Edwards.

COOMBE, MOSES. Pestauk upon Susquehanna. Yeoman.
February 4, 1719/20. May 16 and August 15, 1720. D. 157.
John son of John Coombe, deceased, and nephew to said Moses receives land at Cannasuka on Susquehanna. Martha, daughter of

said John Coombe and niece to said Moses. Father John Coombe. Sister Mary.
Executors: John Warder and Peter Bezallion.
Witnesses: Antony Sadowskj, Mounce Jones and John Jones.

LEWIS, THOMAS. Amity, Philadelphia County. Shoemaker.
February 21, 1719/20. May 17, 1720. D. 158.
Son John.
Executrix: Wife Charity.
Witnesses: Walter Cambell, Robert Stackhoos, Antony Sadowskj and John ---.

BLACK, WILLIAM. Posion, Philadelphia County. Laborer.
February 11, 1719. May 18, 1720. D. 158.
Executrix: Wife Helean.
Witnesses: John Black and Robert Black.

TRESSE, SARAH. Philadelphia. Spinster.
April 21, 1720. June 4, 1720. D. 159.
Father Hugh Tresse. Brothers Thomas, Joshua and Hugh (deceased). Sister Mary, Philadelphia, widow of said Hugh, and their children James, Charles and Hugh. Uncle Thomas Tresse and Aunt Margaret Tench mentioned.
Executor: Friend David Abbot of Philadelphia, mariner, (belonging to a snow under command of Owen Meredith).
Witnesses: Nicholas Cron, William Coxsens and Charles Osborne.

MANKIN, EDWARD. Philadelphia. Merchant.
May 4, 1720. June 15, 1720. D. 159.
Daughters Catherine and Ann.
Executrix: Wife Margaret.
Witnesses: Gabriel Wilkinson, Thomas Tresse and John Cadwalader.

EVAN, ANN. Lymerick, Philadelphia County.
April 4, 1720. June 18, 1720. D. 160.
Sons: Owen, George, David and William. Daughter Elizabeth.
Executors: William and Owen.
Witnesses: John Davis, Thomas Addis and David Hey.

BROOKE, MATTHEW. Lymmerick, Philadelphia County. Yeoman.

April 1, 1720. June 18, 1720. D. 161.
Wife Ann. Children not named.
Executors: William Evans, John Davis and Owen Evans.
Witnesses: John Roades, Hendrick Peters and David Hey.

MC WILLIAMS, JOHN. Philadelphia. Merchant.
December 16, 1719. July 18, 1720. D. 162.
Real estate in Maryland and elsewhere. Nephew Thomas McWilliams, surgeon in Potomac, ibidem. Children of Thomas Edgar in Dumfrees, and of William McWilliams, Junior, son of William McWilliams, now or late of Greenhead in the parish of Corlevorack. James Hind of Dumifrees by Agnes Edgar.
Executrix: wife Rose.
Witnesses: William Allen, William Assheton and Joseph Turner.

SAVAGE, SAMUEL. Mahanatania, Philadelphia County. Yeoman.
September 25, 1719. July 19, 1720. D. 163.
Children Thomas, Samuel, Joseph, John, Ruth, Rebecca. Brother John Savage, father-in-law Thomas Rutter and Jonathan Davis of Hopewell in Hunterdown County, East Jersey.
Executrix: Wife Anna.
Witnesses: Peter Rutter, Job Noble and David Hey.

JENNINGS, JOHN. Philadelphia. Mariner.
August 8, 1719. June 29, 1720. D. 164.
Executrix: Wife Ann.
Witnesses: John Scutt and John Leech.

ROBERT, ROGER. Radnor Township.
July 5, 1720. August 16, 1720. D. 166.
Sons Robert, John and Owen. Daughter Jane. Grand-sons Roger Robert, Roger Pugh. Step-daughters Katherine and Rachel.
Executrix: Wife Mary.
Witnesses: Robert Jones, Rees Thomas, William Thomas and Robert Evan.

JONES, GRIFFITH. Skypack, Pennsylvania. Yeoman.
July 21, 1720. August 23, 1720. D. 165.

Wife Sarah, who can settle upon and improve land bought of Anthony Morris upon Matchin. Children John, Ann and Mary. Sons-in-law Daniel and John Morris.
Executrix: Wife Sarah.
Witnesses: Andrew Cornish and John Colcott.

BROWNE, JOHN. Philadelphia. Tallow-chandler.
September 6, 1720. September 23, 1720. D. 165.
Brother Thomas of Bucks County and his wife Mary and their children George, Thomas, Mary, John, Alexander, Elizabeth, Joseph and Esther.
Friend John Dow, collar-maker.
Executors: Wife Elizabeth and Thomas Chalkley.
Witnesses: John Warder, Rice Peters and Joshua Lawrence.

WAITE, JOSEPH. Philadelphia. Bricklayer.
November 9, 1718. August 29, 1720. D. 166.
Provision made for a child unborn, though not certain of wife's pregnancy.
Executrix: Wife Martha.
Witnesses: Theophilus Spurrier, Samuel Robins, Thomas Nickson and Thomas Pryor.

MASSY, SAMUEL. Philadelphia. Tallow-chandler.
6/15/1720. September 26, 1720. D. 167.
Children: Sarah, Daniel, Wight, Elizabeth and Mary. Land in Baltimore and Kent Counties, Maryland, called Delph and Delphs and Bright Helmston, also a tract bought of Thomas Brocklesby.
Executrix: Wife Sarah.
Overseer: Friend Ennion Williams.
Witnesses: George Robinson, Junior, Vallintine Robinson and Catherine Robinson.

MARL, THOMAS. Bristol Township, Philadelphia County. Carpenter.
6/30/1720. October 1, 1720. D. 168.
Mother Margaret Marl. Sisters Ann, Elizabeth, Hannah, Mary, Susanna, Esther, Rachael and Catherine. Brother John. Catherine and Rachael daughters of brother-in-law Isaac Williams.
Executor: Father Thomas.

Witnesses: Ann Whartlebee, Thomas Shaughnessey and Samuel Pastorius.

EVERNDON, NATHANIEL. Wicacoe, Philadelphia County. Cordwainer.
October 9, 1719. October 26, 1720. D. 169.
Daughters Mary and Martha and nephew John Smith. William son of Joshua Kenelby, Dorset County, Maryland, yeoman.
Executor: John Johnson, ibidem, yeoman.
Witnesses: Christopher Swanson, William Sanders and Joseph Fox.

LE PIERRE, JOHN. Philadelphia. Surgeon.
August 11, 1720. October 1, 1720. D. 170.
Executors: Frances wife of Nicholas Niarr of Philadelphia, baker, and Katherine their daughter.
Witnesses: John Songhurst, Charles Osborne, John Dupuy and Mark Dalmast.

FREKE, JOHN. Late of Barbadoes, now of Philadelphia. Merchant.
August 25, 1720. October 10, 1720. D. 170.
Executor: Thomas Polegreen for Pennsylvania, and other Executors in Barbadoes.
Witnesses: William Assheton and Charles Rogers.

MONCKTON, SAMUEL. Philadelphia. Apothecary.
August 27, 1720. October 4, 1720. D. 171.
Wife Rachael. Sister Sarah. Wife deceased. Brothers and sisters not named.
Executors: Father-in-law Robert Assheton and brother Philip Monckton.
Overseer: James Tuthill.
Witnesses: Elizabeth Tresse, Mary Martin and Susannah Harwood.

BIBB, THOMAS. Philadelphia. Tanner.
October 3, 1720. October 11, 1720. D. 172.
William Hudson, Philadelphia, tanner. Daughters: Ruth, Mary and son Thomas.
Executrix: Wife Rebecca.
Witnesses: George Emlen, Charles Brockden and Joseph Fox.

JONES, WILLIAM. Philadelphia. Vintner.
June 30, 1720. October 19, 1720. D. 172.
Son William. Daughter Joane wife of John Jones.
Executrix: Wife Ann.
Witnesses: Henry Smyth and John Smith.

GATCHELL, JEREMIAH. Philadelphia. Wheelwright.
August 6, 1720. October 22, 1720. D. 173.
Daughter Sarah. Son Jeremiah and other children not named.
Executrix: Wife Catherine.
Witnesses: John Martindell, Mary Campion and John Cadwalader.

WHEELER, ANDREW. Moyamensing, Philadelphia County. Yeoman.
March 7, 1719. March 26, 1720. D. 174.
Wife Anna Maria. Children: Ann, Mary, Andrew, John and Samuel. Jacob Bankson and Edward Carleton mentioned.
Executor: Benjamin Bankson, Philadelphia, yeoman.
Witnesses: Maurice Lisle, Maurice Justice, Rowland Rice and Joseph Lawrence.

PRICE, PHILIP. Merion Township, Philadelphia County. Yeoman.
December 11, 1719. November 22, 1720. D. 175.
Daughter Sarah Lewis. Grand-children Isaac Price; Samuel, Daniel, Sarah, Mary, David, Isaac, Philip, Miriam and John the children of Thomas Rees late of Haverford. Also the grand-children, the children of John Lewis, New Castle, Delaware County as follows: Elizabeth Stout, Philip, Stephen, Josiah, Sarah, Mary and Ann Lewis. Joan, wife of Hugh David, Lettice wife of Samuel Rees, Rebecca wife of Thomas Rees.
Executrix: Wife Margaret.
Overseers: Rees Thomas, Morris Lewellin and Robert Jones.
Witnesses: Rees Thomas, Owen Roberts and Richard Thomas.

OWEN, THOMAS. Whitland Township, Chester County. Yeoman.
August 17, 1720. November 24, 1720. Codicil - October 9, 1720. D. 176.
Wife Elizabeth. Children: Richard, Owen, Samuel, Thomas, John, Mary, Elinor (and her three children not named) and Katherine. John Marty and David Jones mentioned.

Executor: Son Richard.
Witnesses: Alexander Owen, Thomas John, Thomas Edwards and Thomas Hubbert.

RICHARD, ROWLAND. Tredyfrun, Chester County.
4/13/1720. December 7, 1720. D. 178.
Sons Rowland, Isaac and John. Daughters Elizabeth, Gainor, Sarah, Ruth, Margaret and her children John and Mary. Grand-daughter Jane Longworthy. David Powell and John Cadwallader mentioned.
Executors: Wife Katherine with sons John and Samuel.
Overseers: Father-in-law Hugh Jones and friends Hugh, William, Hary, David and Robert Jones.
Witnesses: Hugh Jones, Hugh William and Robert Jones.

WIDDIFIELD, JOHN. Philadelphia. Joiner.
January 10, 1720. January 31, 1721. D. 179.
Son John (estate in Newcastle upon Tyne, England and in Philadelphia). Sisters Dorothea --- of Newcastle and Mary Lange near Durham, England. George Calvert, shopkeeper. Children: Elizabeth, Mary, Ann, child unborn, Hannah, Sarah.
Executors: Wife Mary and Joshua Lawrence.
Witnesses: Christopher Blackburn, Ebenezer Large and William Lawrence.

WAITE, MARTHA. Philadelphia. Widow.
November 1, 1720. February 9, 1720. D. 180.
Daughter Phoebe. Niece Martha Blackshaw. Children: Jonathan, George, Johanna.
Executors: Joseph Kirkbride, Bucks County and daughter Johanna Biles.
Witnesses: Samuel Robins, Thomas Redman and William Corker, Junior.
Footnote: Originial reads Children: Jonathan, George and Joanna Biles. Martha Blackshaw married first George Biles and had above children. He died 1708. She then married Joseph Waite between 1718-1720. (see pa. 407.) M. C. Woods, Jan 4, 1923.

CLAY, ROBERT. Philadelphia. Mariner.
April 10, 1711. February 11, 1720/1. D. 181.
Father Robert Clay of Sheifield in Yorkshire.

Executors: Wife Ann.
Witnesses: William Poole, Robert Lidderdail and John Fisher.

SHEPHARD, SAMUEL. Philadelphia. Yeoman.
February 14, 1720. March 20, 1720/1. D. 182.
Wife Ann (provision made for child unborn, though not sure of wife's pregnancy). Cousins John son of John Church and Rebecca and Solace the two youngest daughters of Edward Church.
Executors: Edward and John Church.
Witnesses: John Kearsley and John Cadwalader.

KOLLOCK, JACOB-LEWIS. Sussex on Delaware. Merchant.
December 30, 1720. March 14, 1720/1. D. 184.
Original missing. Children: Jacob, Simon, Cornelius, Hester, Jane and her husband William Trons, Hannah, Magdalen. The seven children are also named Executors. Roger Traines mentioned.
Administratrix: Wife Mary.
Witnesses: Samuel Davis, Junior, Preser'rd Coggeshall and Timothy Coe.

JONES, SARAH. Sheepack, Pennsylvania.
December 25, 1720. April 7, 1721. D. 185.
Widow of Griffith Jones, deceased. Children: Ann, John and Mary. Sons-in-law Israel, Daniel and John Morris.
Executor: Friend Griffith Jones.
Witnesses: James Shattick and Thomas Lock.

DAVID, ELLIS. Goshen Township, Chester County.
August 1, 1719. April 12, 1721. D. 186.
Daughter Katherine [Haines], step-daughter Margaret. Wife not named.
Executors: Son David, daughter Donse [David] and son-in-law Isaac Haines.
Overseers: Son-in-law Hugh Evans, cousin David Jones, and friends William Lewis and Robert Jones.
Witnesses: David George and George George.

CUNDIT, WILLIAM. Lower Dublin, Philadelphia County.
November 21, 1719. December 31, 1720. D. 186.

Children: Mary, Rebecca, Ann, Leonard and John. (Probate clause wanting.)
Executor: Son John.
Witnesses: Thomas Rush, Andrew Bankson and Jonathan Hibbs.

ROBERTS, JOHN. Merion, Philadelphia County. Wheelwright.
2/22/1721. May 17, 1721. D. 187. Codicil - 2/22/1721.
Aunt Ann and cousin Robert Roberts. Sister Rebecca. Testator provides for an unborn child though he does not pronounce his wife pregnant. Codicil of same date with same witnesses.
Executrix: Wife Hannah.
Overseers: Brothers Matthew and Joseph and step-father Hugh Evans and Robert Jones.
Witnesses: John Vaughan, Owen Roberts and Robert Jones.

DAVIS, EDMUND. Philadelphia. Pewterer.
September 16, 1715. May 20, 1721. D. 189.
Jacob May, his wife Mary and son Moses. Brother Henry Davis of Trelick Grange in Monmouthshire, South Wales, and Mary his wife.
Executors: Owen Roberts and Thomas Tresse.
Witnesses: Thomas Denton, Matthew Burchfield and Samuel Johnson.

WYNNE, JONATHAN. Blockley Township, Philadelphia County. Yeoman.
January 29, 1719. May 17, 1721. D. 190.
Children: Thomas, John (land in Chester County), Jonathan (land ibidem), Hannah, Mary, Sydney, Martha, Elizabeth.
Executrix: Wife Sarah.
Overseers: Brothers-in-law Edward Jones and Daniel Humphrey, or in case of their decease John Cadwalader and Jonathan Jones.
Witnesses: Rowland Ellis, Thomas Jones and Edward Jones, Junior.

LINDERMAN, JOHN. Roxbury Township, Philadelphia County. Husbandman.
October 25, 1720. June 5, 1721. D. 191.
Children: John, Henry, Abraham, William, Christian, Samuel, Hannah, Rachel, Elizabeth, Zachariah. Daughter Elizabeth Powel (?).
Executrix: Wife Catherine.
Witnesses: Elizabeth Meals, Samuel Pastorius and William Dewees.

NILE, TOBIAS. Philadelphia. Shipwright.
June 8, 1721. June 27, 1721. D. 192.
Sons Edward, Tobias. Andrew Robinson and his wife Magdalen mentioned.
Executrix: Wife Jane.
Witnesses: Richard Cooke, William Rakestraw and James Hide.

PARSONS, THOMAS. Oxford Township, Philadelphia County. Millwright.
September 2, 1717. June 17, 1721. D. 193.
Wife Mary. Son Joseph, daughter Sarah. The executors receive land in Salem County, West New Jersey bought of Hannah Salter. Friend William Stockdale of Bucks County to advise and assist. William Stanley, Robert Parsons and Michael Atkins mentioned.
Executors: Sons Thomas and James.
Witnesses: Swen Warner, William Strutt, Charles Osborne and Charles Brockden.

HUGHES, EDWARD. Philadelphia. Potter.
June 18, 1721. June 30, 1721. D. 194.
Children Mary Sely, Edward Hughes.
Executors: Wife Ann and son-in-law Isaac Sely.
Witnesses: Richard Redman, Samuel Hastings and Thomas Tresse.

WALKER, JOHN. Gloucester County, New Jersey. Yeoman.
5/18/1707. July 15, 1721. D. 195.
Brother Richard Walker; his son William who receives estate in Gisbrough in Cleveland in Yorkshire; also a younger son and two daughters not named. The four children of sister Ann Postgate (not named). The three children of sister Sarah Hunt (not named).
Executrix: Wife Sarah.
Witnesses: Thomas Carlile, John Kay and John Kay, Junior.

STAGG, JOHN. Late of Melshire, Wilts County (Wiltsshire?) near Marlbourer, Great Britain. Yeoman.
July 7, 1721. July 17, 1721. D. 196.
Mother Mary Stagg, Wilts County, widow. Brother Joseph and sister Mary, spinster of Eastin, ibidem. William Romain, testator's partner mentioned.
Executor: Thomas Case of Philadelphia, cordwainer.

Witnesses: William Creed and Richard Morgan.

HOOD, JOHN. Darby, Chester County. Yeoman.
October 23, 1719. September 30, 1721. D. 197.
Grandson John, eldest son of son John, deceased, and his brother Abraham. The heirs of son Joseph mentioned. Grandchildren not named. Thomas Werth, attorney for the heirs of Matthew Gratton. John Blumston, Swan Swanson.
Executors: Sons Samuel, Thomas and Jonathan.
Witnesses: Samuel Kenard, Samuel Bethell and Deborah Hood.

MORRIS, ANTHONY, SENIOR. Philadelphia. Merchant.
July 10, 1721. November 2, 1721. D. 199. Codicil - 6/18 & 31, 1721.
Wife Elizabeth, former wife Mary. Children by wife Elizabeth, Sarah, Luke, Hannah, Isaac, Israel. Also sons James, William and Anthony, Brewer, who with Israel Pemberton is Executor. Daughter Elizabeth Lewis. Grandson Anthony son of son Anthony and other grandchildren not named. John Roads of Whitemarsh, William Gray, Rachael Reiner, Mary Codington, Luke Watson (son Isaac's Mother's brother) mentioned. Lands in Philadelphia and Chester County.
Witnesses: Caspar Wüster, Joshua Lawrence, Isaac Brown, John Wilson, George Sheed and Elizabeth Hill.

BRITTIN, LIONEL. Philadelphia. Merchant.
November 12, 1721. January 20, 1721. D. 203.
Date correct. Sons-in-law Philip and Michael Kearney. Daughter Rebecca Kearney. Granddaughters Johanna Kearney, Elizabeth. Henry Hodge mentioned.
Executrix: Wife Elizabeth.
Witnesses: Elizabeth Chandler, James Bingham and Peter Evans.

HERBENDICK, LEVINE. Philadelphia. Weaver.
October 24, 1721. January 1, 1721/2. D. 205.
Brother-in-law Anthony Loof of Germantown, weaver.
Executors: Friends William Hudson and Thomas Griffith of Philadelphia.
Witnesses: Caspar Hoodt, Samuel Hudson and Samuel Ogden.

OTTEY, JOHN. Kingessing, Philadelphia County.
January 5, 1721. December 17, 1721/2. D. 205.

Mother Ann Ottey, brothers: Thomas, Philip, Richard and Christopher.
Executor: Brother Philip.
Witnesses: Justa Justis, John Morton and Benjamin Cliffe.

LAICON, NEELES. Northern Liberties, Philadelphia County. Yeoman.
December 3, 1721. January 17, 1721/2. D. 206.
Daughters: Mary, Christian, Ann, Elizabeth, Susanna and Bridget.
Estate on Redcliffe Creek, New Castle County to be sold.
Executors: Wife not named, and John Rambo.
Witnesses: Francis Rawle, Elizabeth Williams and Edward Hartsfield or his wife.

ELLIS, BENJAMIN. Kent County, Maryland. Carpenter.
October 26, 1721. February 1, 1721 (date correct). D. 207.
Sister Joan, wife of William Burroughs. Daughter Ann. Not the original.
Executor: Brother William of the said county, carpenter.
Witnesses: George Mifflin, Joseph Taher and Charles Osborne.

BIRD, ANN. Philadelphia. Widow of Andrew Bird, late of Philadelphia, brazier, deceased.
September 12, 1720. February 14, 1721/2. D. 207.
Grand-daughter Mary King daughter of daughter Elizabeth.
Children: Andrew, George, John, Rachael, (Elizabeth), Grace and Ann.
Executrix: Daughter Elizabeth.
Witnesses: Joseph Shippen, William Ireson and Joshua Lawrence.

JUSTEA, JUSTEA. Kingsessing, Philadelphia County. Yeoman.
February 7, 1721/2. February 17, 1721. D. 208.
Children: John, Mounts, Justea, Andrew, Charles, Morten, Ellin Morton, Mary Justea. John eldest son of brother Charles Justea and his brothers Frederic and Joseph and sisters Elizabeth, Ann and Mary. Signed Justa Justis.
Executors: Sons Andrew and Charles.
Witnesses: Jones Jones, Charles Yocum and Edward Smout.

KIRK, SAMUEL. Darby, Chester County. Mason.

December 26, 1721. February 21, 1721. D. 209.
Intended wife Rachael Elis. Brother and sisters not named.
Executor: Brother John.
Witnesses: John Warner and John Lewis.

YOCUM, MOUNTS. Kingsessing, Philadelphia County.
February 12, 1721/2. February 24, 1721. D. 300.
Wife Margaret. Sister Mary Morgin. Mounts son of brother Peter Yocum, brothers Andrew, Charles and Swan. The Swedes Church.
Executors: Brother Andrew and Andrew Boone.
Witnesses: Isaac Lidman (?), Andrew Yeouring and Edward Smout.

HUMPHREY, CHARLES. Moreland, Philadelphia County.
Husbandman.
February 11, 1721/2. March 10, 1721/2. D. 301.
Wife Uriah. Sons, Thomas and Charles, daughter Hannah.
Trustees and Administrators: Henry Comly and Thomas Gill.
Witnesses: Richard Marple, Evan Stephens and Silas Watts.

PAUL, JOHN. Abington, Philadelphia County. Yeoman.
February 9, 1721/2. March 10, 1721. D. 303.
Wife Mary. Children: Joseph, Jonathan, John, Mary, Thomas and child unborn.
Executors and Overseers: Brother Joseph and brother-in-law Thomas Livezey, though wife Mary is named.
Witnesses: Edmond McVeagh, Henry Paull and John Simcock.

WALN, NICHOLAS. Northern Liberties, Philadelphia. Yeoman.
11/30/1721/2. March 19, 1721/2. D. 304.
Children: Nicholas, William, Jane, Hannah, Mary, Sarah and Elizabeth.
Executors: Wife Jane and son Richard.
Witnesses: Evan Price and John Simcock.

WALN, NICHOLAS. Son of Nicholas Waln, late of the Northern Liberties of Philadelphia, yeoman, deceased.
12/6/1721/2. March 19, 1721. D. 305.
Brothers William and Richard. Sisters not named. Friend Hannah Maris.
Executors: Mother Jane and brother Richard.

Witnesses: George Emlen, John Prigg and Isaac Cooper.

STEPHENS, HENRY. Philadelphia. Mariner.
March 21, 1714/5. April 5, 1722. D. 307.
Executrix: Wife Martha.
Witnesses: George Moore and Samuel Johnson.

ROBERTS, OWEN. Gwynedd, Philadelphia County. Yeoman.
1/25/1719. April 16, 1722. D. 308.
Son Robert, daughter Lydia Mendenhall.
Executrix: Wife Mary.
Overseers: John Hugh and John Humphrey.
Witnesses: Thomas Foulke and John Evans.

VAN LAER, JOHN. Philadelphia County. Baker.
July 3, 1720. April 16, 1722. D. 309.
Children not named.
Executrix: Wife Mary.
Trustees and Overseers: James Tuthill and Joseph Redman, merchants.
Witnesses: Thomas Read, Henry Flower, Junior and Peter Evans.

DAVIS, JOHN. Philadelphia. Tailor.
December 7, 1720. April 19, 1722. D. 310.
Daughters Mary, Elizabeth and Anne. Anthony Hartley, vintner, and Jonathan Cockshaw, weaver, are also named executors but they did not qualify.
Executrix: Wife Mary.
Witnesses: John Roberts, Mary Cadwalader and John Cadwalader.

STEPHENS, JOHN. Radnor, Chester County. Bachelor.
2/1/1721. May 1, 1722. D. 311.
Sister Phoebe James, Mary, Stephen and Sarah children of brother-in-law Henry Houlston. Niece Mary daughter of Thomas More of Marple. John son of David Morris. Thomas, Philip and John children of Thomas Parry. Brother Stephen Evans. Nephew John son of sister Phoebe. Brother David Stephens named.
Executors: Brothers Stephen Evans and Evan Stephen.
Witnesses: John Jones, David Harry, Robert Jones and Thomas Griffiths.

PASTORIUS, JOHN SAMUEL. Germantown. Weaver.
2/29/1722. May 2, 1722. D. 312.
Two children not named. Daniel and John. Nuncupative will.
Executors: Wife Hannah Lukin and Anthony Clinckin.
Witnesses: Dirk Jansen, Thomas Potts and John Jarrott.

THOMAS, EVAN. Philadelphia County. Yeoman.
February 3, 1721. May 22, 1722. D. 313.
Brother Edward Thomas and his four children (not named). Wife's cousins John and Rebecca children of Job Bate, deceased.
Executors: Wife Sarah and Thomas Bullock of Philadelphia, innkeeper.
Witnesses: Samuel Johnson, Thomas Cawley and Peter Evans.

MAJOR, ELIN. Late of London, now of Philadelphia. Widow.
April 18, 1722. May 18, 1722. D. 314.
Ann Steward his daughter mentioned.
Executor: James Steward of Philadelphia, tailor, receiving property in Brumpton Lane parish of Kensington, London, which was willed to testatrix by her father Edward Stark and also any legacy left to testatrix by her mother Elin Stark.
Witnesses: Thomas Perrey, Henry Jones, Walter Gruffyth, Junior and Edward Crossthwaite.

HOOPER, STEPHEN. Philadelphia.
December 2, 1721. June 4, 1722. D. 315.
Wife Elizabeth.
Executor: Son Stephen.
Executor in Trust: Friend Daniel Pegg.
Witnesses: Thomas Robins and Charles Spurway.

THOMAS, PETER. Willistown, Chester County. Yeoman.
December 29, 1719. July 3, 1722. D. 316.
Wife Sarah. Sons: Peter, Jacob and Joseph.
Executor: Son Peter.
Witnesses: John Hood, Jonathan Hood and Samuel Bethell.

DICKINSON, JONATHAN. Philadelphia. Merchant.
May 8, 1722. June 21, 1722. D. 317.

Sons Joseph, John, Jonathan (and Hannah wife of the latter). Brother Caleb Dickinson. Daughters Hannah and Mary. Barbara Wright and William Dellworth mentioned.
Executors and Trustees for Pennsylvania: Isaac Norris, James Logan, George Claypoole of Philadelphia, merchants.
Executors for Jamaica: Brothers-in-law Isaac and Jonathan Gale, where they reside and where testator has two estates named Barton and Pepper.
Witnesses: Benjamin Vining, H. Graham, Hugh Cordry and Bartholomew Cordry.

GILLINGHAM, YEAMANS. Oxon Township, Philadelphia County.
May 9, 1722. July 21, 1722. D. 324.
Sons James and John. Sons-in-law Henry Paul and James Willson also named executors, but they renounced.
Executrix: Wife Mary.
Witnesses: Paul Wilmerton, James Parsons and Nathaniel Holton, Junior.

CARPENTER, JOSHUA. Philadelphia. Brewer.
August 27, 1720. August 2, 1722. Codicil - July 23, 1722. D. 325.
Daughter Sarah Story, her husband Enoch, son Robert and daughter Patience. Sisters Mary Hogsflesh and Damaris Hunt near London. Cousin Ann Busfill and her children William, Mary, Mercy and Joshua. Cousins Abraham and Thomas Mitchell.
Executrix: Wife Elizabeth.
Witnesses: Peter Evans, Philip Monckton, Thomas Nevell, Elizabeth Henmarsh and Mary Butler.

GEE, JOHN. Son of Joshua Gee. Merchant in London.
October 26, 1720 - New York. November 15, 1720. D. 327.
Original will missing. Brother Joshua and sister Sarah Gee. This will is a copy from the original in the New York office which was proved before William Burnet, Esq. November 15, 1720. The certification is dated August 2, 1722.
Executor: John Spratt.
Witnesses: Is. Vallitte, Hibbs Cook, John Rolland and A. D. Pleyster, Junior.

STILBY (STILLY), JOHN. Myomensing (sic) Philadelphia County. Yeoman.
April 24, 1722. September 1, 1722. D. 327.
Wife Garthro. Children: William, John, Peter, Morton, Sarah, Christian and three other (names not given) or five unmarried daughters.
Executors: Brother-in-law John Skooton and sons William and John. The former deceased leaving the two latter executors.
Witnesses: Garrett Garrett, Morton Garrett and John Cadwalader.

BLACKBURN, CHRISTOPHER. Philadelphia. Tailor.
7/11/1722. September 29, 1722. D. 329.
Daughter Rebecca.
Executrix: Wife Rachael.
Witnesses: Thomas Nickson, Ralph Jackson and John Cadwalader.

REDMAN, JOSEPH. Philadelphia. Merchant.
August 7, 1722. September 24, 1722. D. 330.
Children: Joseph, John, Susanna Assheton who receives estate in the parish of St. Sidewell's, Exeter, England (bought of Samuel Borden. Daughter Rebecca McComb. Sister Mary Real. Father John. John Richardson of Christeen, New Castle County upon Delaware, merchant, and Thomas Lawrence of Philadelphia, merchant, to advise and to assist. Henry Evans, George Fitzwater, George Claypoole, William Assheton, Lionel Brittain and brother-in-law Robert Assheton mentioned. [A sister Sarah is named in a note appended to the will. (John Budd affirmed that testator declared the codicil or indorsement void. It is only in this indorsement that sister Sarah's name is mentioned.)]
Executrix: Wife Sarah.
Witnesses: Charles Brockden, John Beere, Isaac Porter and Joseph Richardson.

WORRELL, PETER. Philadelphia. Glover and tanner.
September 25, 1722. October 5, 1722. D. 332.
Vestry of Christ Church, Philadelphia. Godson, James Duchee. Brother John Worrell. Nephew Peter Worrell. Thomas Bibbs mentioned.
Executrix: Wife Susanna.
Witnesses: Anthony Ducher and Caspar Kleinchoff.

EDWARDS, MOSES. Willistown, Chester County. Weaver.
October 15, 1722. November 17, 1722. D. 333.
Wife receives estate here and in Great Britain.
Executrix: Wife Ann.
Witnesses: Griffith Jones and David Evan.

BADCOCK, ALEXANDER. Philadelphia. Cordwainer.
August 15, 1722. November 30, 1722. D. 334.
Daughter Elizabeth.
Executrix: Wife Mary.
Overseer: John Durborow.
Witnesses: Hugh Durborow, James Bingham and Joseph Bankson.

GRAVES, WILLIAM. Philadelphia. Merchant.
November 29, 1722. December 10, 1722. D. 335.
Housekeeper, Grace Whitaker of St. George's Creek County of Newcastle on Delaware. Spinster daughters Ann, Mary (their whereabouts is not named). Edward Forrest late of Kingstreet, London, whalebone seller.
Executor: John Leacock, merchant.
Witnesses: Sarah Read, Deborah Read and Frances Read.

PAINTER, GEORGE. Philadelphia. Cooper.
December 21, 1722. January 1, 1722/3 ? D. 336.
Cousins Peregrine Weston, cooper, and Edward Weston, bricklayer. Nephew George son of testator's sister Deborah Shires, deceased. Brother Edward Roberts and his children Hugh, Jane and Susanna by his wife Susanna sister of testator, deceased. Daughter Susanna. William Peart mentioned.
Executors and Trustees: Brother John Smith, Marlborough Township, Chester County, yeoman and friend Israel Pemberton, Philadelphia, merchant.
Witnesses: Charles Brockden, gentleman, George Calvert, shopkeeper, and Jonathan Cockshaw, weaver.

WORELL, RICHARD. Dublin Township, Philadelphia County. Yeoman.
November 4, 1722. January 5, 1722. D. 339.
Children: Richard, Samuel and Robert, Hannah, Susanna.
Executrix: Wife Hannah.

Overseers: Brother-in-law Mourris Morris and Thomas Livezey.
Witnesses: Daniel Davis, Margaret House and John Simcock.

BULLARD, RICHARD. Philadelphia. Mariner.
April 16, 1722. January 7, 1722. D. 341.
Executrix: Elizabeth Jones.
Witnesses: James Steward, Thomas Perrey and Richard Thomas.

SUTTON, JOHN. Frankford, Philadelphia County. Tailor.
January 6, 1722. January 19, 1722. D. 341.
Children: Luke, John, Thomas, William, Oswin, Mary and Elizabeth.
Executrix: Wife Parnell.
Witnesses: Joseph Hawley and William Hall.

KIMBER, THOMAS. Ciscel County, Province of Maryland. Yeoman.
December 20, 1722. January 23, 1722. D. 343.
Son Thomas, daughter Mary. Roger Laramore and Garret Otterson mentioned. Pons Creek, Ciscel County mentioned.
Executors: Sons John and James.
Witnesses: Robert Mason, Richard Marple and John Simcock.

ELKENTON, THOMAS. Philadelphia. Sawyer.
January 7, 1722/3. February 25, 1722. D. 345.
Executrix: Friend Martha Way.
Witnesses: Mor Howell, Zachariah Butcher, James Wood and William Biddle, Junior.

MORGAN, ABEL. Lower Dublin Township, Philadelphia County. Yeoman.
December 15, 1722. March 15, 1722. D. 345.
Daughter Jane and other children not named.
Executrix: Wife Judith.
Witnesses: John Meredith, Peter Chamberlin and John Hart.

JUSTEA, SWAN. Kingsess, Philadelphia County. Yeoman.
April 19, 1722. March 9, 1722/23. D. 347.
(No mention made of James Hunt in the qualification. Wife Catherine sole Executrix). Children: Peter, Swan, Britts Roads, Judith and Ann. Brother Mouns Justea.
Executors: Wife Catherine and son James Hunt.

Witnesses: Joseph Boyce, Andrew Yocum and Samuel Blunston.

BRADFORD, THOMAS. Philadelphia. Carpenter.
6/30/1721. February 2, 1722. D. 349.
Daughter Rebecca wife of William Coleman, carpenter. Daughter Rachael Bradford (estate in Bucks County, also in New Bristol, ibidem). Grandsons: William, Junior and Thomas Coleman. Grand-daughter Elizabeth, wife of Daniel England, Junior and her children Thomas and Elizabeth. Grand-daughters Ann and Sarah Coleman. James Coates, William Burge and Joan Forrest mentioned.
Executors: Israel Pemberton, merchant, and Samuel Powell, carpenter.
Witnesses: Richard Webster, Edward Owen and John Cadwalader.

SHOEMAKER, JACOB, SENIOR. Philadelphia. Turner.
9/22/1722. February 13, 1722. D. 351.
Sons Jacob, George and Thomas. Son-in-law John Breintnall and his children David and Mary.
Executrix: Wife Margaret.
Witnesses: Evan Jones, Catharine Chandler and John Cadwalader.

SMITH, JOHN. Philadelphia. Wheelwright.
February 24, 1721. June 5, 1722. D. 352.
Son John.
Executrix: Wife Alice.
Witnesses: John Price, William Bantoft and John Durbrow.

KNIGHT, JOHN NICHOLAS. Whitemarsh Township, Philadelphia County. Yeoman.
December 28, 1722. January 28, 1722. D. 353.
Children's names not given.
Executrix: Wife Margaret.
Witnesses: Adam Herman and John Shiers.

MAYFIELD, JOHN. Philadelphia.
March 15, 1722/23. March 25, 1723. D. 354.
Father Richard, Kildare County, Freland receives house in Philadelphia, or if he is not alive, property to go to testator's brother (not named). The Baptist Meeting. The family of Joanna Parker of Philadelphia (no other names given).

Executors: Solomon Cresson and Edward Warner.
Witnesses: Thomas Hartt, John Nicholas and Nicholas Rogers.

LOWDON, HUGH. Philadelphia. Merchant.
1/21/1722. May 6, 1723. D. 355.
Also to the two latter Executors with Charles Brockden, gentleman, in trust Robert Grace, grandson of wife Constance. Thomas Gamble, son of sister Helen, apprentice to Thomas Stapleford, joiner, and William Gamble his brother. Peter Wishart, tallow-chandler, Richard Ormes, Radnor Township, Chester County, Rowland Ellis, Senior, Katherine Burthen, widow, Mary sometime wife of Thomas Davis, Sarah wife of William Herne. Dennis Cunrad and Issac and Peter Shoemaker of Germantown. Richard Townsend. John Bird, Robert Hinds; John Gregory (from whom testator bought estate in Bellingsport, Gloucester County, West New Jersey.) Sarah Hall and Clement Plumsted (from whom estate in Salem County, ibidem). John Blimston, John Townsend, brother of Richard aforesaid.
Executors: Wife Constance, friends Hugh Graham, practitioner of physic and Charles Read, merchant.
Witnesses: John Jones, Richard Redman, William Fisher, Jr., Charles Brockden and Ruth Burden.

VINSON, WILLIAM. Mariner.
February 4, 1722/23. June 5, 1723. D. 358.
Martha Copper, Robert Davis, William Warren, Oliver Golfrey mentioned. Letters Testament to Robert Davis.
Witnesses: Manby Vale, Thomas Gibson, Robert Clements and Thomas Esworthy.

HILSABECK, JOHN.
October 13, 1722. June 10, 1723. D. 359.
Daughters: Anna-Margaret Knight and Elizabeth Gulden.
Executrix: Wife Anna Margaret.
Witnesses: John Henry Kirsten and Abraham Ishman.

LANGDALE, JOSIAH. Late of Bridlington Key, Yorkshire.
2/14/1723. June 28, 1723. D. 359.
Joseph Bond, Hannah Carpenter relict of Samuel Carpenter, deceased, mentioned. Will signed on board the ship London Hope

laying at anchor in the Downes near Deale in Great Britain, where he died. Proved at Philadelphia.
Executrix: Wife Margaret (daughter of William and Isabel Burton, yeoman, late of Yorkshire, deceased).
Witnesses: John Annis, Senior, Commander of the Ship London Hope, Sarah Dinsdale, John Estaugh and Isaiah Cardel.

TRUMP, MICHAEL. Upper Dublin Township, Philadelphia County. Yeoman.
November 25, 1719. July 20, 1723. D. 360.
Children: Caspar (the eldest), Michael, Johannes and Catherine.
Executors: Wife Mary Elizabeth, Abraham leFever and John Cunrade of Upper Deblin, yeomen.
Witnesses: Philip Christian Zimermann, Samuel Pastorius and Francis Daniel Pastorius.

GOADBY, JOHN. Citizen of London, now of Philadelphia. Clothworker.
July 8, 1723. August 5, 1723. D. 361.
Brother Samuel Goadby, Moorfield, London.
Executors: William Burge and Andrew Simmow, both now or late of Philadelphia.
Witnesses: Johannis Nye, John Noble and Joshua Maddox.

LEWIS, THOMAS. Mountgomery, Philadelphia County. Husbandman.
12/19, 1722/23. August 6, 1723. D. 362.
Son Richard and his son Thomas, son George. Grand-children: Thomas (aforesaid), Edward, Mary and Elizabeth. Thomas Story and Ann his wife. Letters Testamentary to Richard Lewis.
Witnesses: John Robert, John Sagant.

WILLIAMS, HENRY. Blocklay Township, Philadelphia County. Yeoman.
July 15, 1723. July 24, 1723. D. 363.
Wife Margaret. Sons David, William and John.
Executor: Son John.
Witnesses: Richard Lewis, Elizabeth Lewis, George Morgan and William Davies.

CLUBB, ISABELLA. Philadelphia. Widow.
June 17, 1723. August 1, 1723. D. 364.
Son Richard. Sisters Catherine, Jane, Margaret and Sybella.
Susanna Harwood, widow, Katherine Gatchell, Widow Andrews, Mary Prigg, Widow Markham, Nurse Shaw, Widow Morgan, Old Everet, Mrs. Lock, Peter Evans, Servant Catherine Dickinson. (This will contains a clause showing that Peter Evans qualified as executor before Samuel Bushill, but nothing said about the other one.)
Executors: John Kearsly and Peter Evans.
Witnesses: John Cadwalader and Edward Roberts.

SCUTT, JOHN. Philadelphia. Mariner.
July 27, 1723. September 5, 1723. D. 365.
Executrix: Wife Sarah.
Witnesses: Jedidiah Andrews, Rebecca Spofford and Sarah Meyrick.

THOMAS, JOHN THOMAS. Merion Township, Philadelphia County. Yeoman.
May 25, 1721. September 16, 1723. D. 366.
Margaret wife of James Mortimer. Nephews: Thomas Edwards, Morris Thomas, John Thomas.
Executor: Cousin Benjamin Humphrey of Merion.
Witnesses: Henry Lewis, Jenkin David Lewellin and Evan David.

LEWIS, DAVID. Haverford Township.
September 9, 1723. September 23, 1723. D. 366.
Children: James, Edmund, Amos, Enoch, Elizabeth, Ellen and Ann.
The Quaker Meeting at Haverford. Brethren Lewis, Evan, William Lewis and Robert Jones to assist.
Executors: Wife Ann and eldest son William.
Witnesses: Richard Hayes, John Parry and John Jones.

ROSE, AQUILA. Philadelphia. Printer.
August 19, 1723. September 23, 1723. D. 367.
Son Joseph.
Executors: Wife Mary and friend John Copson of Philadelphia, merchant.
Witnesses: James Milner, Charles Brockden, Charles Osborne and John Zenger.

PUGH, THOMAS. Philadelphia County. Mason.
3/3/1723. October 1, 1723. D. 368.
Brother Job Pugh also named being absent. Sons: Jesse and Roger.
Executrix: Wife Jane.
Trustees and Executors: Robert Jones of Merion, Meredith Davis, Roberts Roger, Job Pugh and Ellis Roberts.
Witnesses: John Roger, Thomas Ellis, Ellis Roberts and Meredith David.

WILMERTON, JOHN. Oxford Township, Philadelphia County. Yeoman.
September 1, 1723. October 11, 1723. D. 368.
Wife Frances. Children: Hannah, John and Paul. Brother Paul Wilmerton. Katherine Brown and Pallace Brown the sisters and Sydney and John Brown the brother of wife Frances. Nicholas Buzby and John Wells mentioned. (The last named executor renounced.)
Executors: Wife Frances, brother-in-law John Shallcross of Oxford Township, yeoman, and Joseph Paul, ibidem.
Witnesses: John Knowles, John Brown, James Milner and Charles Osborne.

LENOIR, ISAAC. Philadelphia. Glazier.
October 8, 1723. October 23, 1723. D. 369.
Father-in-law Hugh Cordry of Philadelphia, pulleymaker and his son Bartholomew to advise and assist.
Executrix: Wife Mary.
Witnesses: Edward Owen, John Soughurst and Charles Osborne.

MC COMB, JOHN, JUNIOR. Philadelphia. Merchant.
July 22, 1723. October 23, 1723. D. 370.
Child unborn to receive estate in America also that in England devised to testator by his father-in-law Joseph Redman, deceased. Cousin Edward Williams, Junior, his brother John Williams and Margaret Williams, aunt of testator. Cousin Susanna Assheton Junior. Matthew Ranton mentioned.
Executrix: Wife Rebecca.
Overseers and Guardians: Father John McComb, and friend Alexander Wooddrop.

Witnesses: Ad. Hamilton, Esther Shippen, Sarah Warren and William Chancellor.

HOGHERMOOTE, ADAM. Germantown, Philadelphia County. Weaver.
October 18, 1723. October 26, 1723. D. 371.
Wife Catherina. Children: Mathies, Samuel, Barbara.
Executors: Peter Shoemaker and Derick Jonson.
Witnesses: George Warner, Johannes Leen and Griffith Jones.

EDWARD, JOHN. Upper Merion, Philadelphia County. Laborer.
September 11, 1723. October 30, 1723. D. 372.
Cousins: Mary, wife of Thomas Reess, Blandina wife of Jonathan Miller, friends Jenkin David of Radnor, Richard Bevan. Mother Grace Morgan and sisters Jane and Margaret Edwards in Wales.
Executor: John David.
Witnesses: Hugh Hughes, Jenkin David and John German.

FROGBY, HENRY. Philadelphia. Joiner.
October 12, 1722. December 3, 1723. D. 373.
Brothers: Thomas, Jacob, Arthur, Richard and Joseph. Apprentice Abraham. Minister and church wardens of Christ Church to advise and assist.
Executrix: Wife Margaret.
Witnesses: William Graves, Elizabeth Heumarsh and Charles Osborne.

MONCKTON, PHILIP. Philadelphia, Pennsylvania. Apothecary.
December 3, 1723. December 9, 1723. D. 374.
Brothers Dr. Charles and Alexander Monckton of Great Britain, sister Sarah Monckton of the City of London, spinster. Letters granted to latter Executrix.
Executrixes: Cousin Sarah Mark of Philadelphia, with said Sarah Monckton.
Overseers: James Tuthill, Thomas Tresse.
Witnesses: Edward Owen, Richard Parker and Anne Jones.

MARRIOT, ISAAC. Philadelphia. Carpenter.
September 15, 1723. December 10, 1723. D. 375.
Brother Harris Marriot of London, pewterer.

Executrix: Wife Jane.
Witnesses: Joseph Taylor, Rice Peters and Charles Osborne.

EVAN, OWEN. Gwynedd.
10/4/1723. December 20, 1723. D. 375.
Children: John, Cadwallader, Evan, Robert, Thomas, Elizabeth, Mary, Jane deceased. Grandsons Owen son of son Robert and Owen son of son Thomas.
Executrix: Wife Elizabeth.
Overseers: Brothers Robert and Cadwalader, sons Evan and Robert and cousins Evan son of Thomas Evan and his brother Owen Evans.
Witnesses: Thomas Evans, Hugh Jones and Owen Evans.

MALLOWS, SARAH. Oxford Township, Philadelphia County. Widow.
December 16, 1723. December 27, 1723. D. 376.
Kinsman Solomon Hall, his children John and Sarah (cousins of testatrix) and cousin Elizabeth his wife. Cousin Peter Taylor, his wife Sarah and son John. Cousins Jacob, Mary and Elizabeth, children of cousin Jacob Hall, deceased. God-daughter Sarah Weyman. Money left towards the purchasing of a settlement for a minister that shall belong to Oxford church.
Executor: Kinsman Joseph Hall.
Witnesses: Charles Finney, John Comins and Robert Lee.

JOHN, GRIFFITH. Tredyfryn, Chester County. Yeoman.
February 6, 1722. January 7, 1723. D. 378.
Wife Elizabeth. Grand-daughter Christian David. Daughters Mary, Martha and their children not named, Prichet, wife of Lewelin David and her children not named.
Executor: Son David John.
Witnesses: Griffith John, John George and William Davis.

HILL, JOSIAS. Byberry, Philadelphia County. Roper.
November 6, 1723. January 8, 1723. D. 379.
Abel Hinkson and his daughter Elizabeth. Mary widow of Daniel Walton, deceased, also his sons Benjamin, Nathan and Daniel; Jane daughter of son Daniel; Mary daughter of Daniel, Senior. Daughter Hannah. The Byberry Meeting. Nathaniel Watmore.
Executor: Joshua Walton of Byberry Township, yeoman.

Witnesses: Joseph Walton, Benjamin Walton and James Paine.

MASTERS, THOMAS. Philadelphia. Merchant.
December 4, 1723. January 16, 1723. D. 380.
Mother Sarah Righton. Cousin Richard Tysen. Daughters Mercy, Sarah Buckley. Grandson Thomas Buckley and the rest of his mother's children (not named). John Stacey, Benjamin Fairman, George Coates, Joseph Pidgeon, William Sharlow, Jacob Kollack, Samuel Buckley, Samuel Hassell and Ann his wife; John Estaugh attorney of Elizabeth and Catherine Collins and John Wightman mentioned.
Executors: Sons Thomas, William, estate in Bermuda.
Witnesses: Charles Read, John Hyatt and Charles Brockden.

REES, ABRAHAM EDWARD. Whitemarsh Township, Philadelphia County. Husbandman.
September 5, 1723. February 12, 1723. D. 384.
Eldest son Edward, son Thomas and daughters Alice, Ellen and Elizabeth.
Executor: Son Robert.
Overseers: David Jones of Blockley and Joseph Robert of Merion.
Witnesses: John Hutchin and Rowland Ellis.

STORY, ENOCH. Philadelphia. Gentleman.
July 25, 1722. January 22, 1723. D. 385.
Eldest son Robert, youngest son Enoch, daughter Patience.
Executrix: Wife Sarah.
Witnesses: Thomas James, Edward Fretwell and Joseph Antrobus.

WOOD, ANN. Philadelphia. Widow.
October 7, 1723. February 24, 1723. D. 386.
Thomas the son and Hannah wife of said Henry Hodge. Daughter Ann Bolton. Grand-children Thomas and Slater Clay; Robert and Ann Bolton.
Executors and Trustees: Son John Curtis and friends Henry Hodge and Charles Read, Philadelphia, shopkeepers.
Witnesses: Philip Monckton, Charles Brockden and Mary Andrews.

HATFEILD, GEORGE. Philadelphia. Freeholder.
7/6/1722. March 20, 1723. D. 388.

7/6/1722. March 20, 1723. D. 388.
Children: Susannah, Talbert, Jane and son George Hatfield.
Executrix: Wife Jane.
Witnesses: William Holbrooke, John Savage and Henry Clifton.

RAMBO, GUNNAR. Matson, Philadelphia County.
January 4, 1723/4. March 20, 1723/4. D. 388.
Eldest son John. Sons Peter, Mounce, Andrew, Gabriel, Elias.
Grand-daughter Catherine Holston.
Executor: Son Elias.
Witnesses: Edward Farmar, Joseph Gray, Peter Yokam and Lovell Jackson.

JONES, JOHN. Philadelphia. Merchant.
July 4, 1721. January 17, 1722. D. 390.
Original will missing. Wife Joan, property in the dominion of Wales or elsewhere in Great Britain.
Executrix: Wife Joan.
Trustees: John Lloyd of Ragat and Robert Pierce of Cesn---.
Witnesses: John Cadwallader, Edward Roberts and Peter Evans.

LEAK, THOMAS. Late of Jamaica, on board the Brigantine Hope.
March 3, 1723/4. April 7, 1724. D. 391.
James Story, Joseph Hammerton, George Spafford (mate), Zephaniah Holwell (passenger), Brinolders DeHaes (Master). Nuncupative will.
Executrix: Daughter Elizabeth in London.
Witnesses: Brinolders DeHaes, George Spafford and Zephaniah Holwell.

JACOB, CALEB. Philadelphia. Merchant.
1/13/1720. April 4, 1724. D. 391.
Friend Mary Widdifield of Philadelphia, widow, brother Richard of Limerick, Ireland and his son Isaac. Sister Joan Dickinson of Waterford, ibidem, and her daughter Mary.
Executors: Edward Roberts, John Knight and John Cadwalader.
Witnesses: William Lawrence, Joseph Antrobus and Elizabeth Walton.

HARPER, ANN. Philadelphia County. Widow.
June 2, 1719. April 20, 1724. D. 393.

Executrix: Daughter Elizabeth.
Witnesses: Richard Horsley and Peter Evans.

LOFTUS, LEESON. Philadelphia. Boulter.
October 19, 1721. May 18, 1724. D. 393.
Daughter Sarah Hannis and her husband Andrew, daughter Anne. Son Thomas.
Executrix: Wife Ann.
Overseers: Friends George Fitzwater, Andrew Robinson and Thomas Tresse.
Witnesses: Samuel Baker and Richard Redman.

LLOYD, PATIENCE. Philadelphia. Widow.
August 14, 1720. June 30, 1724. D. 394.
Grand-daughters Deborah Moor, Patience Story. Testatrix also directs that her body be buried by the side of her husband, Thomas Lloyd.
Executor: Son-in-law Richard Hill; son Enoch Story also thereto named being deceased.
Witnesses: John Weaver and Charles Osborne.

BAYLEY, JAMES. Philadelphia. Mariner.
September 27, 1722. July 28, 1724. D. 395.
Executrix: Wife Sarah.
Witnesses: Joseph Claypoole, Thomas Chase and John Cadwalader.

JAMES, PHILLIP. Philadelphia. Sadler.
October 15, 1723. August 3, 1724. D. 396.
Son of Phillip James of said city, cooper, deceased, about to take a voyage to Great Britain. Sister Sarah Beaumont in Great Britain.
Executrix: Mother Esther Shippen.
Witnesses: Samuel Powell, W. Chancellor and Mathew Phillips.

HUMPHREY, JOAN. Philadelphia.
6/2/1724. August 7, 1724. D. 397.
Friends Ann and Mary Cross, Elizabeth Powell. Maid Elizabeth Burnsted, Nehemiah Allen, Senior.
Executrix: Hannah Knowles.
Witnesses: Mary Dwaryhons, Elizabeth Hooper, Deborah Powell and Frances Knowles.

ROBERTS, JOHN. Merion Township, Philadelphia County.
7/3/1722. August 31, 1724. D. 397.
Brother Richard and his daughter Margaret. Niece Margaret daughter of testator's sister Ann. Poor of the Monthly Quaker Meeting. Owen Roberts mentioned.
Executors: Son Robert and daughter Elizabeth.
Overseers: Robert Jones, Robert Evans and Thomas Jones.
Witnesses: Edward George, Gainor Jones and Thomas Jones.

READ, JOHN. Philadelphia.
August 31, 1724. September 4, 1724. D. 398.
George Plumly, cutler, and Edward Warner, carpenter, thereto named having renounced. Children: John, Deborah, Frances.
Executrix: Wife Sarah.
Witnesses: E. Price, Elizabeth Heumarsh and Charles Osborne.

LEWIS, RICHARD. Dolobran Mirod Parish, Montgomery County, [Wales]. Tailor.
4/16/1707. September 5, 1724. D. 399.
Executrix: Wife Mary.
Witnesses: James Davies, John Kelsall, these witnesses are in parts beyond the seas.
Original will missing.

OLDMAN, ELIZABETH. Philadelphia. Widow.
6/21/1724. September 10, 1724. D. 400.
Children: Joseph, Thomas, Ann, Sarah, Hester and Mary. John Hart mentioned.
Executors: Sons Thomas Oldman and Paul Preston.
Witnesses: Thomas Pryor and John Wood.

HUDDEN, JOHN. Philadelphia. Baker.
July 29, 1724. September 11, 1724. D. 400.
Sister Ann Webb of Milksham Parish, Wiltshire, Great Britain, and her children (no names given).
Executors: Alexander Legg, baker, Merick Davies, gentleman, for this side the seas. Thomas Bevan of Milksham Parish for Great Britain.
Witnesses: James Davis, Jane Clemens and Owen Owen.

OADE, JOSEPH. Philadelphia. Glass-seller.
August 12, 1724. September 16, 1724. D. 401.
Margaret Butler, testator's father in London, brother Thomas (ibidem) mentioned. Samuel Carpenter renounced leaving Joshua Maddox sole Executor.
Executors: Friends Joshua Maddox, merchant, and Samuel Carpenter, gentleman, (son of Joshua Carpenter late of Philadelphia, merchant, deceased.
Witnesses: Evan Owen, James Wasse and Edward Nichola.

EATON, JANE. Formerly the wife of George Eaton, yeoman, deceased. Dublin Township, Philadelphia County.
August 20, 1724. October 3, 1724. D. 402.
Ann wife of Charles Hufty, Jane daughter of Henry and Mary Stirk. Morris Gwin mentioned.
Executor: Kinsman, George son of John and Joan Eaton.
Witnesses: Hugh Curtes and Joshua Jones.

ALDEBURGH, RICHARD. Philadelphia. Gentleman.
November 1, 1723. October 9, 1724. D. 403.
Nieces Arathea and Alice Hitch. Friends Peter Evans, Josiah Rolfe, Benjamin Vining, Dr. Milner. Robert Tredway, Esquire, and Andrew Anduchene, Attornies in Jamaica, are requested to advise and assist the Executor in managing estate in Jamaica. The Executor is also directed to put a tombstone over testator's wife's grave in that province.
Executor: Nephew John Broadhurst.
Witnesses: John Eyer, William Chancellor, James Milner and Thomas Redman.

HAMER, MARGARET. Elethgoe, Philadelphia County.
August 19, 1724. October 10, 1724. D. 404.
Eldest son James and his two sons (names not given). Eldest daughter Margaret Bate and her three children (names not given). Daughters Sarah and Deborah. Mary Humphrey and her daughter (name not given) mentioned.
Executor: Son Adam.
Witnesses: Robert Thomas and Thomas Smallshaws.

KEÿSER, PETER. Germantown, Philadelphia County. Shoemaker.

August 10, 1724. October 16, 1724. D. 405.
Wife Margaret. Sons: Peter (land at Sippack), Dirck, mother-in-law Elizabeth.
Executors: Wife Margaret, her brother Andrew Souflis and son Dirck.

SHIPPEN, ESTHER. Philadelphia. Widow.
August 4, 1724. October 20, 1724. D. 407.
Son William. Sister Rachel, wife of Elisha Gatchell and her children. The children of sister Hannah, deceased, late wife of John Roads; also of sister Abigail, late wife of Samuel Powell; of brother Joseph Willcox, deceased; of daughter-in-law Susanna wife of Timothy Hanson. Edward, Joseph and William the sons of son-in-law Joseph Shippen of Philadelphia, merchant; Margaret daughter of son-in-law Edward Shippen, deceased. Mary daughter of John Annis late of London, mariner, deceased. Sarah Beaumont, daughter of testatrix's late husband Philip James, deceased, by a former wife and her children (no names given). Cousin Sarah Warren. Sister-in-law Ann, widow of brother Joseph Willcox, deceased. Hannah Hill and Elizabeth Griffith in trust. Charles Jones, Senior of the City of Bristol, soapboiler, testatrix's late husband Edward Shippen deceased, Rowland Ellis who owns land in Blockley Township, Philadelphia Liberties, George McAll mentioned.
Executors: Brother-in-law Samuel E. Powell of Philadelphia, carpenter, and friend Samuel Preston of Passyunk, Philadelphia County, merchant.
Witnesses: Charles Brockden, Charles Osborne and Sarah Warren.

GARRATT, WILLIAM. Late of Darby, Chester County, now of Philadelphia. Yeoman.
February 26, 1723. December 3, 1724. D. 409.
Children: William, Samuel, Sarah, wife of Randal Croxton, and her children (no names given), Alice Pennell, Hannah Tidmarsh and children of the two latter (no names given). Grand-children Hannah, Job and William Noble. Joseph Noble. William, Susanna and Hannah children of Thomas Garratt deceased. Kinswoman Sarah Dun. Executors receive land in Bucks County.
Executors: Son Samuel and sons-in-law Joseph Pennell and William Tidmarsh.
Witnesses: John Burge, Elizabeth Burge and Joseph Lawrence.

REDMAN, THOMAS. Philadelphia. Bricklayer.
February 11, 1723/4. December 28, 1724. Codicil - 4/10/1724. D. 411.
Children: John, Thomas, Joseph, Martha, Sarah and Rebecca. Kinsman Joseph Redman. William Monington, Thomas Tresse and brother Joseph. Mary Read mentioned.
Executrix: Wife Sarah.
Trustees: Henry Hodge and William Corker, Junior.
Witnesses: Samuel Harriott, William Chancellor, James Boyden, John Williamson, Isaac Cooper and James Steel.

BULLARD, HOPKIN.
November 6, 1722. January 6, 1724. D. 413.
Original will missing. Cousin Alice Thomas, Junior late of Maryann Parish, Great Britain, now of Philadelphia.
Executor: Brother Edward Bullard.
Witnesses: Charles Moore, Richard Kelley and William Davies.

SIMMONS, STEPHEN. Philadelphia. Mariner.
July 17, 1716. December 22, 1724. D. 413.
Children: Weldon, Stephen, Deborah and Mary. Joseph Richards mentioned.
Executrix: Wife Mary.
Trustee: Clement Plumstead of Philadelphia - for the children.
Witnesses: John Eyer, Joseph Antrobus and Thomas Stapleford.

PEART, THOMAS. Philadelphia. Smith.
June 16, 1724. January 6, 1724. D. 414.
Executors: Wife Mary and daughter Ann Loftus.
Witnesses: Timothy Stephenson, Joseph Breintnall and Charles Brockden.

FARMER, JOHN. Germantown, Philadelphia County. Wool-comber.
6/30/1724. January 11, 1724/5. D. 415.
Wife Mary of Saffron Walden in Essex, Great Britain. Only child Ann now or late of White Chappel near London in Middlesix, ibidem. She, together with Dirck Johnson, yeoman of Germantown, is named Executors, or if they are unwilling to act the names of Thomas White, Senior of Bristol Township, Philadelphia County, yeoman, and Peter

Wishart, Chandler of Philadelphia, are given instead. Dirck Johnson finally becomes Executor.
Witnesses: John Prigg, John Midwinter and Mary Prigg.

BIRD, GEORGE.
July 28, 1724. January 26, 1724. D. 416.
Original will missing.
Executrix: Wife Mary.
Witnesses: George Allen and John Cadwalader.

PETERS, THOMAS, SENIOR. Philadelphia. Cordwainer.
December 22, 1724. February 1, 1724/5. D. 417.
Wife Alice. Children: Thomas, Benjamin, Rees, Mary, William, Margaret, Elizabeth, child unborn.
Executors: Brother Rees Peters and eldest son Thomas.
Witnesses: Richard Preston, Rice Peters, Junior and James Burn.

GUSANBURY, ERICK. Lower Dublin Township, Philadelphia County. Yeoman.
May 28, 1719. February 9, 1724/5. D. 418.
Original will missing. Peter Johnson and Peter Jones testator's sister's sons. Mary and Bridget and Abigail Ward daughters of deceased brother Neels Gusanbury. Sister Breta Enoch. Nena wife of Garret Morton. Brother-in-law Neeals Liten. Robert Prismal and Neels Boon mentioned.
Executrix: Wife Hanshe.
Witnesses: James Fleming, Jedidah Adams and Nathaniel Walton, Junior.

JOLLEY, LEWIS. Philadelphia. Wheelwright.
February 17, 1724. March 10, 1724/5. D. 419.
Executrix: Wife Margaret.
Witnesses: Richard Redman, Mathien Garrigues, I. Classon and John Smith.

HAWKINS, WILLIAM. Philadelphia. Carpenter.
March 1, 1724/5. March 31, 1725. D. 420.
Executrix: Wife Jane.
Son James.

Overseers: Brother-in-law John Snowden of Philadelphia, tanner, and cousin Jacob Dubre near Philadelphia, yeoman.
Witnesses: David Shewring, Zachariah Hutchins and John Cadwalader.

DUNN, WILLIAM. Philadelphia. Yeoman.
1/5/1724. April 5, 1725. D. 422.
Father Thomas Dunn, brother Walter and his children Thomas and Mary. Sisters Elizabeth Leadbeater, Phoebe Norton, Lydia Matthews and her son Thomas. Friends Thomas Griffith of Philadelphia, cordwainer, Elizabeth his wife and Hannah Knowles her daughter.
Executrix: Wife Sarah.
Overseer: Friend Francis Knowles of Philadelphia, shopkeeper.
Witnesses: Thomas Chalkley, Richard Brockden and Mary Brockden.

HEARBIN, JACOB. Philadelphia. Locksmith.
February 4, 1724. May 8, 1725. D. 423.
Brothers: Abraham and Jonathan.
Executrix: Wife Margaret.
Witnesses: Anthony Duche, Mark Dalmas and Richard Brockden.

WARDER, WILLOUGHBY. Falls Township, Bucks County. Maultster.
2/24/1724. May 19, 1725. D. 424.
Son Willoughby, daughter Rachel wife of Samuel Baker and her children unborn. Wife Mary. Cousin John Warder of Philadelphia, hatter, and friend John Sotcher of Falls Township, yeoman, in trust.
Executor: Son Solomon.
Witnesses: Job Goodson, George Calvert and Charles Brockden.

DILLWORTH, WILLIAM. Philadelphia. Brewer.
April 17, 1725. June 9, 1725. D. 426.
Executors named renounced in favor of John Whitton.
Executors: Wife Elizabeth and mother Sarah Dillworth.
Witnesses: Charles Read and Daniel Jones.

CALVERT, GEORGE. Philadelphia. Shopkeeper.
5/13/1725. July 23, 1725. D. 426.
Daughters Mary and Elizabeth. Charles Brockden and John Warder to advise and assist.

Executrix: Wife Mary.
Witnesses: John Knight, Joseph Noble and Charles Brockden.

SPAKEMAN, RANDAL. Philadelphia. Tobacconist.
1/12. 1724/5. July 26, 1725. D. 427.
Grandsons: Nathaniel and Joseph Edgecomb and their father Nathaniel. Richard Townsend, the children of Joshua Johnson, tinman; the children of Peter Wisheart, tallow-chandler; Richard Hill of Philadelphia, merchant, for the poor of the Monthly Quaker Meeting in Philadelphia. John Knight and Joseph Noble mentioned. Charles Brockden of Philadelphia, gentleman, who is also to advise and assist the Executor.
Executor: Grandson Nathaniel Edgecomb.
Witnesses: Samuel Carpenter, Matthew Robinson and Charles Brockden.

FOSTER, ALLEN. Lower Dublin Township, Philadelphia County. Yeoman.
July 3, 1725. September 11, 1725. D. 428.
Wife Lydia. Sons Allen and Thomas. Daughters Sarah Mullin, Rebecca Bryon and Mary Fitchwater. Grandchildren Mary and Allen Bryon. Son-in-law Thomas Fitchwater.
Executor: Son Thomas.
Witnesses: John Hill, James Wotterman and John Simcock.

ALLEN, WILLIAM. Philadelphia. Merchant.
July 30, 1725. September 13, 1725. D. 429.
Sister Catherine Calby of Duganon Ireland. Children of Uncle William Craige, ibidem. Sons John and William in London. Son John also appointed Executor being deceased. Samuel Peres mentioned.
Executrix: Wife Mary.
Witnesses: Nathaniel Allen, Joseph Shippen, Junior and John Turner.

JONES, DAVID. Blockley, Philadelphia County. Yeoman.
5/16/1725. September 22, 1725. D. 430.
Children: James, John, Lewis, Isaac, Jacob, David, Susannah and Ellen.
Executors: Wife Katherine and son Lewis.

Witnesses: John Coffock, George Plim, Edward Williams and Robert Jones.

FISHER, JOHN. Philadelphia. Smith.
November 5, 1724. September 28, 1725. D. 431.
Sons John, James (land at Great Mantak Creek, Gloucester County, West New Jersey). Daughter Martha and her children Richard, John and Sarah. Granddaughter Hannah Taylor, grandson William Thomas. Son-in-law John Thomas and Sarah his wife. The former together with Charles Brockden of Philadelphia, gentleman, receive testator's island in the Delaware River and estate at Kingsess in trust, also a lot on Front St., Philadelphia. Joseph Shippen, Kirles mentioned.
Executrix: Wife Sarah.
Witnesses: Samuel Powell, Charles Brockden and Joseph Watson.

ZIMMERMANN, MARY MARGARET. Germantown, Philadelphia County.
5/29/1723. October 1, 1725. D. 433.
Sons Philip Christian, property in Germantown, Matthew, Jacob Christopher. Daughter Mary Margaret Biderman Christian and Hannah Biderman.
Administrator: Son Matthew.
Executor: None named.
Witnesses: Christopher Witt and Daniel Geissler.

WEAVER, HANS.
December 17, 1724. November 3, 1725. D. 434.
Children: Hans, Henry, Jacob and George. Son-in-law Lews.
Nuncupative will dated at Conestoga. Letters granted to son Hans.
Executrix: Wife Mary, who renounced.
Witnesses: Margaret Weaver, Hans Weaver, Johannes Bouünay, John Herr, Jerk Weber, Jacob Weber, Henrick Weaver, Benedig Landes and Wendel Bauman.

ROBERTS, JOHN. Gwynedd, Philadelphia County. Yeoman.
8/24/1725. November 10, 1725. D. 435.
Brother William Roberts. Cousins William, Daniel and James Williams; cousin Elizabeth daughter of George Lewis, Cadwalader

David, Jane Jones, cousin Samuel Thomas. Francis Griffith, Margaret wife of Richard William.
Executors: Wife Eleanor and brother Ellis Roberts (the latter became sole Executor, wife Eleanor being dead).
Witnesses: Peter Wells and Robert Parry.

ROBERTS, ELEANOR. Gwynedd, Philadelphia County. Widow.
9/2/1725. November 16, 1725. D. 436.
Sister Anne Roberts, cousin Katherine Roberts, brother Ellis Roberts. Nephews: William, Daniel and James Williams (their mother's name is not given and she is not a legatee). Sarah Pugh; Mary and Hannah Bennet. The wife of Humphrey Parker (name not given).
Executors: Rowland Roberts and nephew Daniel Williams.
Overseers: Evan Evans and John Jones.
Witnesses: Thomas Wiet and Francis Griffith.

BELL, CHARLES. Amity Township, Philadelphia County.
November 11, 1725. November 25, 1725. D. 437.
Father Henry Bell, daughter Rebecca. Henry Bell, Junior, mentioned.
Executors and Overseers: Wife Mary with friend Jonathan Robeson, ibidem, yeoman.
Witnesses: Israel Robeson, Mary Rumford and John Bell.

ROBERTS, OWEN. Merion, Pennsylvania.
March 30, 1706. December 29, 1725. D. 438.
Brother Edward Roberts; brother-in-law Evan Bewan and Robert Jones trustees and together with uncles John Roberts and Griffith John overseers of his children (names not mentioned).
Executrix: Wife Ann.
Witnesses: Griffith John, Evan Owen, John Roberts and Robert Jones.

JACKSON, RALPH. Philadelphia. Locksmith.
9/14/1718. January 5, 1725. D. 440.
Daughter Elizabeth and her husband Francis Harding. Poor of the Monthly Quaker Meeting in Philadelphia. Sisters Elizabeth Jackson, Mary Johnson. James Bringham mentioned.
Executrix: Wife Sarah.
Witnesses: Francis Knowles, David Evans and Em. Williams.

LANGWORTHY, JOHN. Radnor Township, Chester County. Yeoman.
January 17, 1725/6. January 26, 1725/6. D. 441.
Wife Genis. Daughter Sarah; children of daughter Mary. Son Benjamin. This will bears a codicil of equal date with the same witnesses.
Executors and Trustees: Friends Thomas Thomas and Caleb Evans of Radnor.
Witnesses: Richard Hughes, Philip Evans and John Evans.

BLYTH, JOHN. Philadelphia. Innholder.
January 3, 1725. February 2, 1725/6. D. 442.
Wife Sarah and her children Daniel and Sarah Tucket.
Executrix: Wife Sarah.
Witnesses: Peter Stretch, William Mason, Thomas Stretch and Nicholas Rogers.

HUGGEFORD, JOHN.
February 20, 1725/6. March 2, 1725/6. D. 443.
Father William Hugeford. Sister Elizabeth.
Executor: John Richeson.
Witnesses: Sarah De Haes, Robert Buckwell and Phillip Syng.

KERSEN, JOHN HENRY. Oley.
January 29, 1725/6. March 4, 1725. D. 444.
Son and two daughters. Sons John and Henry.
Administratrix: Wife Anna Margaret.
Witnesses: Stephen Messer Schmidt and Peter Form Wold.

WARNER, ISAAC. Philadelphia. Currier.
January 17, 1725. March 8, 1725. D. 445.
Sisters Anne Minchin and Mary Warner of Blockley Parish, Worcestershire, Great Britain. The former receives property in Blockley; the latter in Dracot.
Executrix: Cousin Mary Warner.
Witnesses: Elizabeth Walton, John Smith and Nicholas Rogers.

BICKLEY, ABRAHAM. Burlington, West New Jersey. Merchant.
October 13, 1725. March 28, 1726. D. 446.

Sons: William (property in Burlington now in tenure of Ann Stevenson, widow), Samuel, Abraham. Daughters: Elizabeth Polgreen; Hannah, Susannah and Mary Bickley (house in New York). Wife Dorothy. Sister Sarah Graves (debts due in Shrewsbury, Freehold and elsewhere in East Jersey). Patrick Baird, William Croswhit, Benjamin Pascall, Richard Clymer, George Cunningham, Matthias Aspden, Thomas Wetharell, Giles Cambridge, Thomas Chase, Abraham Griffith, Joseph Webb, Cornelius Cohoon, Randal Spakeman, heirs of son Abraham's grand-father Sam'l. Richardson; Joseph Jones, John Barns, Samuel Marmion, William Frampton, Philip Russel mentioned. Kinsman William Cook, his brother Thomas and sister Elizabeth; Matthew Birchfield. Kinswoman Mary Lambert. The Quaker poor in Philadelphia and in Burlington. Brother-in-law William Hudson.
Executors: Friends Henry Hodge, James Steel, George Fitzwater, John Jones, bolter and son Samuel.
Witnesses: Charles Read, John Hyatt and Peter Wishart.

HUDSON, SAMUEL. Philadelphia. Tanner.
February 11, 1724. March 30, 1726. D. 450.
Thomas Roberts, Andrew Hamilton, John Breintnall, Benjmain Bankson and Sarah Garrett mentioned. Wife Mary. Daughters: Elizabeth, Hannah and Mary.
Executors and Trustees: Father William Hudson, uncle Anthony Morris of Philadelphia, and brother Joseph Cowper, Junior of Gloucester County, West Jersey.
Witnesses: Richard Preston, John Breintnall and Joseph Breintnall.

CUNRADE, MATTHIAS. German Township, Philadelphia County. Husbandman.
8/29/1725. April 2, 1726. D. 454.
Children: Anthony, Margaret, Cornelius, Magdalen, William, John and Matthias.
Executrix: Wife (name not given).
Guardians and Overseers: Brothers John of Upper Dublin and Henry.
Witnesses: Rowland Ellis, Katherine Ellis and Rowland Ellis, Junior.

LOWDON, CONSTANCE. Philadelphia. Widow.
November 15, 1725. December 6, 1725. D. 455.

Daughter-in-law Susanna Gray of Great Britain and her daughters Elizabeth and Mary. Kinswoman Mary Mason. Friend Joshua Maddox of Philadelphia.
Executor: Grandson Robert Grace.
Witnesses: John Jones, Robert Bolton and Elizabeth Evans.

IRISH, JOSEPH. Late of St. George's Parish, Banils Marsh, Somerset County, Great Britain, now of Philadelphia. Mariner.
February 18, 1725/6. July 6, 1726. D. 456.
Executrix: Wife Anna.
Witnesses: John Hobart, John Williams and Thomas Ellis.

CORKER, WILLIAM. Philadelphia.
11/26/1721. July 7, 1726. D. 457.
Daughter Sarah Large and her three children (names not given).
Executor: Son William
Witnesses: William Chancellor, Thomas Redman and James Steel.

WATT, JOHN. Philadelphia. Merchant.
July 11, 1726. July 18, 1726. D. 458.
Brother David. Robert Elder, Sarah Bergis, aunt Martha Steel and her eldest son David. Reverend Mr. Andrews. Mrs. Lettice Dexter. Father whose name is not given.
Executor: Friend John Fulerton.
Witnesses: Evan Jones, Neill Gray and Samuel Ferguson.

DOWDNEY, NICHOLAS. Philadelphia.
July 21, 1726. August 15, 1726. D. 459.
Sons John, William and Thomas. Daughters Mary Dickson, Jane and Martha Dowdney.
Executrix: Wife Mary.
Witnesses: Jenkin Jones and John Holme.

THOMAS, WILLIAM. Radnor Township, Chester County. Yeoman.
September 8, 1724. August 17, 1726. D. 460.
Wife Margaret. Grandchildren Jasher, Abel and Evan. Sons John and William.
Executor: Son William.
Overseers: Richard Orme, John Morgan and Peter Jones.
Witnesses: Richard Orme, John Morgan and John Jerman.

LEECH, TOBY. Chestenham Township, Philadelphia County. Yeoman.
March 23, 1726. April 19, 1727. D. 462.
Sons Toby, Abraham, Isaac, Jacob. Wife Hannah. Richard Hill, Thomas Graves and Daniel Street mentioned. Daughters: Rebecca, Dorothy, Hester, Sarah, Hannah and Mary; John Junior son of brother John Leach, brother Isaac (lot in Philadelphia near John Oxley's lot). (This will is not signed).
Executors: Brothers Isaac and Jacob and friend Richard Martin, renounced June 7, 1727.

SHARP, THOMAS. Bristol, England. Mariner.
February 25, 1723. April 29, 1740. D. 465.
Proved at London.
Executor: Friend John Thomas of Bristol, baker.
Witnesses: Samuel Tyler, William Blackmore and William Scammell, Junior.

INDEX

-D-

-E-

-F-

-H-

-I-

-J-

-M-

-P-

-T-

Other books by F. Edward Wright:

Abstracts of Bucks County, Pennsylvania Wills, 1685-1785

Abstracts of Cumberland County, Pennsylvania Wills, 1750-1785

Abstracts of Cumberland County, Pennsylvania Wills, 1785-1825

Abstracts of Philadelphia County Wills, 1726-1747

Abstracts of Philadelphia County Wills, 1748-1763

Abstracts of Philadelphia County Wills, 1763-1784

Abstracts of Philadelphia County Wills, 1777-1790

Abstracts of Philadelphia County Wills, 1790-1802

Abstracts of Philadelphia County Wills, 1802-1809

Abstracts of Philadelphia County Wills, 1810-1815

Abstracts of Philadelphia County Wills, 1815-1819

Abstracts of Philadelphia County Wills, 1820-1825

Abstracts of Philadelphia County, Pennsylvania Wills, 1682-1726

Abstracts of South Central Pennsylvania Newspapers, Volume 1, 1785-1790

Abstracts of South Central Pennsylvania Newspapers, Volume 3, 1796-1800

Abstracts of the Newspapers of Georgetown and the Federal City, 1789-99

Abstracts of York County, Pennsylvania Wills, 1749-1819

Bucks County, Pennsylvania Church Records of the 17th and 18th Centuries
Volume 2: Quaker Records: Falls and Middletown Monthly Meetings
Anna Miller Watring and F. Edward Wright

Caroline County, Maryland Marriages, Births and Deaths, 1850-1880

Citizens of the Eastern Shore of Maryland, 1659-1750

Cumberland County, Pennsylvania Church Records of the 18th Century

Delaware Newspaper Abstracts, Volume 1: 1786-1795

Early Charles County, Maryland Settlers, 1658-1745
Marlene Strawser Bates and F. Edward Wright

Early Church Records of Alexandria City and Fairfax County, Virginia
F. Edward Wright and Wesley E. Pippenger

Early Church Records of New Castle County, Delaware, Volume 1, 1701-1800

Frederick County Militia in the War of 1812
Sallie A. Mallick and F. Edward Wright

Inhabitants of Baltimore County, 1692-1763

Land Records of Sussex County, Delaware, 1769-1782

Land Records of Sussex County, Delaware, 1782-1789
Elaine Hastings Mason and F. Edward Wright

Marriage Licenses of Washington, District of Columbia, 1811-1830

Marriages and Deaths from the Newspapers of Allegany and
Washington Counties, Maryland, 1820-1830

Marriages and Deaths from The York Recorder, 1821-1830

Marriages and Deaths in the Newspapers of Frederick and
Montgomery Counties, Maryland, 1820-1830

Marriages and Deaths in the Newspapers of Lancaster County, Pennsylvania, 1821-1830

Marriages and Deaths in the Newspapers of Lancaster County, Pennsylvania, 1831-1840

Marriages and Deaths of Cumberland County, [Pennsylvania], 1821-1830

Maryland Calendar of Wills Volume 9: 1744-1749

Maryland Calendar of Wills Volume 10: 1748-1753

Maryland Calendar of Wills Volume 11: 1753-1760

Maryland Calendar of Wills Volume 12: 1759-1764

Maryland Calendar of Wills Volume 13: 1764-1767

Maryland Calendar of Wills Volume 14: 1767-1772

Maryland Calendar of Wills Volume 15: 1772-1774

Maryland Calendar of Wills Volume 16: 1774-1777

Maryland Eastern Shore Newspaper Abstracts, Volume 1: 1790-1805

Maryland Eastern Shore Newspaper Abstracts, Volume 2: 1806-1812

Maryland Eastern Shore Newspaper Abstracts, Volume 3: 1813-1818

Maryland Eastern Shore Newspaper Abstracts, Volume 4: 1819-1824

Maryland Eastern Shore Newspaper Abstracts, Volume 5: Northern Counties, 1825-1829
F. Edward Wright and Irma Harper

Maryland Eastern Shore Newspaper Abstracts, Volume 6: Southern Counties, 1825-1829

Maryland Eastern Shore Newspaper Abstracts, Volume 7: Northern Counties, 1830-1834
Irma Harper and F. Edward Wright

Maryland Eastern Shore Newspaper Abstracts, Volume 8: Southern Counties, 1830-1834

Maryland Militia in the Revolutionary War
S. Eugene Clements and F. Edward Wright

Newspaper Abstracts of Allegany and Washington Counties, 1811-1815

Newspaper Abstracts of Cecil and Harford Counties, [Maryland], 1822-1830

Newspaper Abstracts of Frederick County, [Maryland], 1816-1819

Newspaper Abstracts of Frederick County, 1811-1815

Sketches of Maryland Eastern Shoremen

Tax List of Chester County, Pennsylvania 1768

Tax List of York County, Pennsylvania 1779

Washington County Church Records of the 18th Century, 1768-1800

Western Maryland Newspaper Abstracts, Volume 1: 1786-1798

Western Maryland Newspaper Abstracts, Volume 2: 1799-1805

Western Maryland Newspaper Abstracts, Volume 3: 1806-1810

Wills of Chester County, Pennsylvania, 1766-1778

www.ingramcontent.com/pod-product-compliance
Lightning Source LLC
LaVergne TN
LVHW011116300926
849160LV00008B/401